UNDERSTANDING MAR___ING

Alan West runs his own small business. He has worked in a managerial and consultancy role for major multinational companies including Unilever, Mars and Grand Metropolitan. He is also Visiting Fellow at Thames Polytechnic, London.

UNDERSTANDING MARKETING

ALAN WEST

Harper & Row, Publishers
London

Cambridge
Mexico City
New York
Philadelphia

San Francisco
São Paulo
Singapore
Sydney

First published 1987

Harper & Row Ltd
28 Tavistock Street
London WC2E 7PN

British Library Cataloguing in Publication Data
West, Alan
    Understanding marketing.
    1. Marketing
    I. Title
    658.8   HF5415

ISBN 0-06-318384-6

Typeset by Burns & Smith, Derby
Printed and bound by Redwood Burn Ltd, Trowbridge

To Anthony and Caroline.

CONTENTS

Part 5 ORGANIZATIONS

PREFACE AND ACKNOWLEDGEMENTS

This book is written with two intentions: first to provide an interesting and readable introduction to one of the most interesting and important areas of business, and one which has come to be seen as a vital part of business success; and second to provide a number of short up-to-date case studies which can either be read or used as classroom material.

The first reaction of the student to the traditional marketing text is that it is highly complex, and can only be understood by the marketing 'professional'. Marketing, in the view of the author, is both fun and interesting, involving as it does a need for broad awareness of all sorts of factors that may affect the future development of products and services. At an introductory level it should never be considered a dry, academic subject.

The reality of marketing is that it is about the real world; real companies taking real decisions that can lead either to fortune or disaster, and rarely producing the perfect classroom solution to a particular problem.

The emphasis of the book is therefore on real problems that firms have faced and how they either are attempting to or have overcome them. Most of the small case studies included explore specific problems that real companies have experienced, demonstrating marketing as a living and working discipline.

Specifically this book is designed for the BTEC student and the growing number of undergraduate and college students who are required to study marketing as a subsidiary subject. Increasingly these courses are demanding the uses of case study material as an integral part of the teaching programme, and the case studies are designed to provide material for hour-long discussions on a particular issue.

The author hopes that readers will read and enjoy what to him remains a continually changing and fascinating subject.

ACKNOWLEDGEMENTS

The case studies have drawn on material published in the following journals: *The Financial Times, The Economist, Marketing, Marketing Week, The Grocer, Campaign, Personal Computer World.*

In addition to these sources and company records, specific material for particular studies has been derived from the final-year projects of students at Thames Polytechnic, to whom I give thanks: Nicholas International – Elizabeth Gould; Sprint – D. Callow; HTI – G. Hooper; Milton Lloyd –T. Daniel; Yardley – Susan Jenkins; AMC – L. Sibley; ICL – N. Boarland; Yorkie – D. A. Mackintosh.

Additional assistance was provided by the staff at the City Business Library. I would like to thank Karen Peachey, Isabelle Szmigin and Susan Sutton for commenting on the development of the manuscript, and the last for inspiration of an equine nature.

THE COMPLEXITY OF MARKETING

Icebergs, we learn, conceal nine-tenths of their bulk beneath the surface of the sea; what we see above the waterline gives little indication of all that lies below. Marketing can mislead in a similar fashion. It is not just advertising, promotions, price cuts, packaging, public relations and surveys which make up the visible tip and which are most frequently considered to be the entirety of marketing. The fascination of marketing lies with the large hidden dimension: the definition of opportunity and the planning to achieve success.

SOME OF THE FACTORS INVOLVED IN MARKETING – AN ILLUSTRATION

The complexity of some of the factors involved can best be illustrated by visiting a local shop or supermarket. The issues raised will be examined in detail later, together with those dimensions of marketing that are not immediately apparent. However, our trip to the local shop will quickly make it clear that even some of the more obvious aspects of marketing are not as simple as they first appear.

Look at the product on the shop shelf. Usually you will find it attractive – a special colour may attract your eye, a particular shape will appeal, the name may be familiar, a number on it may seem lucky. These are the everyday facets of packaging a product to attract the consumer and that is one of the requirements of making the product achieve its sales level.

But what particular feature of the product would make you, as the consumer, buy an item? All sorts of influences are considered important: price, quality, knowledge of the manufacturing company and its products, previous experience of the product, promotions, culture, the customer's physical and psychological state. Each of these sets up potentials within the market which can either encourage or discourage purchase. Because of the wide range of factors no two companies will face identical problems even if they operate in the same part of the economy: the problems that an established company faces with an established brand will often be almost totally different from those experienced by the young company with a new product.

What made the store buy it? Now let us think of the factors involved in actually getting the product into the store. There will be a buyer for the store who will have a variety of motives for the decision he makes. He may be more interested in profit for his organization; or in the efficiency of his own part of the firm or his own status or popularity. The buyer will also have various objective criteria to take into consideration in deciding whether or not to stock a particular item. They will include price, available shelf space, competitive products.

The supplier company's sales staff will also have an integral part to play not only in persuading buyers to stock its products but also in ensuring that they remain on the shelves. To do this they will need to monitor the salesman's records, determine progress and direct his attention towards particular products and action concerning them as the need arises. Even so the product will only remain on the shelves if it is available to the store when it is needed. This means that the product must be moved efficiently via road, rail, water or air from the manufacturer to the store. This demands attention to the stocks of goods held by the manufacturer in warehouses throughout the country; and making sure by accurately forecasting demand that factories produce quantities that synchronize with requirements at every point in the system. The company must ensure that money is available to finance the production by achieving a satisfactory level of profit in the long term and must time its decisions to support its products at different stages and times to maximum effect.

Similar questions will be raised on a visit to a restaurant or a bank. Why is one crowded while another round the corner remains empty for most of the day? What factors have made one more successful than the other? The issues of marketing a service rather than a product may be slightly more complicated, but nevertheless the basic problems remain very much the same.

MARKETING AND DECISION-MAKING

Our discussion has clearly shown that the company's response to the market cannot be passive. It has to be continually responsive to a rapidly changing environment. The initial example was designed to introduce you to certain features of marketing, based on the familiar shopping environment. Although it has not yet attempted to deal with such issues as pricing and others related to the development of the product or service, it should be clear that marketing is involved in many decisions that eventually affect the customer purchasing the product.

Each decision will affect other areas of the company's activities and will determine the company's ability to sell its goods or services profitably. Developments in each area must, if possible, be foreseen and responded to – plans adjusted, products and profits monitored, sales and targets reviewed.

Marketing is therefore all about defining the market for a particular product or service; what the consumer may currently want or might want in the future, and what else is happening or might happen to affect this demand. The challenge of marketing is to define the needs of the market in relation to what the company can most profitably provide, and continue to make those decisions in a changing environment. In the case of a non-profit organization the criteria will be effectiveness – how can the organization most effectively meet the demands placed upon it.

That supplying a product or service and selling it profitably should be such an elaborate undertaking is undoubtedly due to the complexity of the environment in which the modern company operates. Companies have marketing departments because they need them; to survive and grow companies must take special measures to sustain demand for their products or services.

The task that they face is similar to the crofter producing a woollen sweater – to take a mass of raw wool, disentangle it, wash it, colour it and then try to ensure that the finished article is harmonious and effective for the specific requirement; purely functional for the local fisherman or purely decorative for the tourist.

Only a madman would today try to produce one product which could be sold to every member of the human race. Answers have to be found to the questions:
Who?
What?
When?
Where?
Why?
How shall we organize to sell?
Which competitors do we most need to take account of?

Finding the solutions is the unique contribution of marketing to a successful business operation. The questions arise because the scale and scope of human activity mean that situations are no longer clear cut as they were in the past. The speed of change demands more accurate definition of both problem and possible solution.

THE CHANGING WORLD

A planet with a population of 4.5 billion which will continue to increase well into the next century has almost universally committed itself to raising living standards and eradicating hunger, illiteracy, ill-health and unemployment among other things. Slowly and sometimes painfully the goals are being patchily achieved. People are generally better off, more educated, are employed in the cash economy, live longer and have more money to spend on goods and services.

Since there has also been a revolution in communications, more people and locations can have access to these goods and services and will know about them. Obviously these statements are truer of the developed world but should not be dismissed as looking at the Third World through rose-tinted spectacles. India for example, with 900 million people the majority of whom are poverty stricken, has one of the largest markets for gold jewellery in the world.

Indeed it might be claimed that one of the problems of modern technology is that it has been over-successful. Those concerned about the inequitable distribution of wealth around the world are frequently heard to say that there is enough produced today to give everyone a fair share. Citizens of the European Community will be familiar with wine lakes and butter mountains but the issue is even wider. With nearly half the world's population between them, China and India have not only succeeded in feeding their people but, in 1984, had surplus wheat to sell on the world market. In addition to wheat there are world surpluses of sugar, oil, coal and steel among others. There is over-capacity in such areas as oil-refining, car tyre production, construction, shipbuilding, domestic appliances.

The lesson for marketing is that where a product or service can be supplied profitably, there will be stiff competition because suppliers are plentiful. The position will be even more volatile where – as in the consumer goods area in the Western World – both money and products or services are abundant.

This point will be better understood if the reader considers the vast scale of goods produced and sold in the United States and the United Kingdom where companies in different sectors must cater for large markets and sophisticated consumers having very different needs.

In the USA every day:

10.9 million cows are milked;

176.8 million eggs are laid;

214,795 hogs are slaughtered;

$54,794 is spent to fight dandruff;

3 million people go to the movies;

88 million watch prime-time TV;

amateurs take 19.1 million snapshots;

people smoke 1.6 billion cigarettes;

tobacco chewers use up 1.3 million packets;

90 million cans of beer are drunk;

1.8 million Americans go to sleep in a motel.

In the UK:

Britain's 10 million children between the ages of 5 and 16 had around £10.09 million pocket money to spend each week during 1984.

The English are believed to eat enough Mars bars each year to circle the world. In 1984 they went through 4.45 billion bags of potato crisps and 1.35 billion packets of savoury snacks.

Such figures give an idea of the scale of consumption in two markets. They also give an insight into the enormous opportunities available to the successful company provided that it can find a clear way forward by identifying consumers for its own products. Here is an illustration of one company that has succeeded in using marketing to achieve this.

Compaq, the American computer company, raced from nowhere to become one of the world's 500 largest corporations in five years by accurately defining an opportunity within the personal computer market and successfully planning to take advantage of it.

Within markets there will be both similarities and variations in demand and expectations. For example, major companies may approach individual markets with a common view of the developmental process.

The multinational Unilever considers per capita Gross National Product (GNP) a key point in detergent consumption: a low GNP = bar soap; a middling one = detergent powder; and a higher one = fabric conditioner and a more sophisticated detergent.

The Unilever illustration points to an important consideration – that markets within economies that share certain characteristics like a high or low per capita income will often provide markets for similar products, services and technologies. This is also borne out by the fact that people with roughly the same income levels tend to share consumer aspirations although they may be living in countries with quite different social economic conditions. This is highlighted in an example from Africa.

'Wabenzi', a Swahili term, means 'Mercedes people'. It has been coined to describe the particular type of individuals – politicians, businessmen and the wealthy – for whom this particular motor car is a special symbol. A variation on the theme appears in West Africa where 'Mammas Benz' applies to the wealthy, frequently illiterate market-women who have developed a passion for powerful cars. The expressions are potentially applicable universally!

Within the pattern of perceptible though sometimes sketchy universal trends there are of course wide variations between countries, localities, people, needs: in income levels, living standards, educational attainment, technological sophistication, all of which will affect the nature of the market and access to it.

The company with more limited resources that wants to survive and grow will have to employ techniques to make it responsive to relatively smaller changes or opportunities in smaller areas of the market.

Bacardi is the world's main rum producer with about 35 per cent of the world market but there are still opportunities for the small company. Pusser's Rum, the main rum producer of the British Virgin Islands, persuaded the British Admiralty to divulge the secret for British Navy rum which had for 300 years constituted the daily rum allowance for British sailors. The small company has identified a small, but up-market American clientele who will find the British Admiralty link appealing. Its sales are about three million dollars a year.

Ever Ready, the UK battery manufacturer, introduced overseas a range of power packs called Black Power. It was highly successful in the Caribbean but not especially so elsewhere.

Health care spending in the USA was estimated to amount to $400 billion in 1984, the country's ageing population being largely responsible for the increase from $75 billion in 1970. This has led to the development of a huge market for home health care services currently estimated to be worth $9.6 billion a year, growing at between 20 and 30 per cent a year. This market has been identified by many companies as providing significant growth opportunities, initially in the United States but also eventually in Western Europe and Japan. Quality Care, the USA health care company acquired by Grand Metropolitan the multinational hotels, brewing and foods group in 1984, had 168 regional offices in 43 states across the USA and employed 1,000 permanent and 9,000 freelance staff.

As worldwide economic growth continues there is also a steadily expanding interdependence not only of national economies, but also those of the world. In the industrialized world people are almost wholly dependent on others to supply them with the goods and services they need.

In the modern world the smoothness of change in any area will depend on any number of related factors. The enormous strides made in improving conditions through the use of increasingly sophisticated machinery of one sort or another has been achieved at the cost of independence – the ability of any one country or group within a country to go its own way beyond the barest level of subsistence farming. Interdependence at every level – between countries and within them – correctly describes the current state of the planet. The following examples illustrate aspects of this.

> Oil price rises in the 1970s generated shock waves that hit governments and people all round the world. In some developing countries where the poor had begun to use kerosene for cooking and lighting they could no longer afford it. This in turn affected the manufacturers and suppliers of kerosene lamps and stoves, the world shipping market, tourism, air transport, the world car market, the home heating market and many others.

> Industrial disputes and strikes have been consistently blamed by one section of the British public and politicians for the consistently low performance of the UK economy. The 1984 miners' strike, the country's longest industrial battle, was largely responsible for the poor growth performance of the UK economy in that year. Strikes involving customs officers and ferry staff in Italy and the UK in 1984 and 1985 created problems not just for travellers but for transit lorries involved in taking goods across borders within the entire European Economic Community.

A further dimension to illustrate the degree of interdependence in today's world can be supplied by the multinationals whose importance to the world economy increases steadily.

> Multinationals are estimated to employ 45 million people – 40 million in the main industrialized countries, where they account for one-third of both manufacturing and service employment. In the UK, one in every two people in manufacturing works for a multinational company. Unilever, which had a turnover of £16.1 billion in 1984, employs more than 300,000 workers in 75 countries.

> General Motors, with sales in 1985 approaching $80 billion, is in terms of world business the equivalent of either Switzerland or Belgium, matching the GNP of both. General Motors is only one of fifty major corporations that dominate the multinational scene.

THE DEVELOPMENT OF THE MARKETING IDEA

In the twentieth century most new ideas about how business should be organized have come from North America and are a product of a different industrial history from that of Europe. American business managers were receptive to ideas that would improve profitability and business efficiency and were prepared to learn new skills. To support this, there emerged a large business education industry in the United States that reported on and codified the techniques that would lead to success.

Within the American market a series of stages has been identified in the development of successful business philosophies.

PRODUCTION

Initially many companies in developing fields of engineering, such as aircraft production and motor cars, found that by the standardization of components and wide-scale automation of the manufacturing process, they could out-compete the old craft industries of Europe which had far higher costs.

Concentration of effort on production developed such concepts as economies of scale, the importance of stock control and distribution.

Henry Ford epitomizes this period with the famous phrase concerning the model T Ford: 'You can have any colour as long as it's black'.

This has been commonly described as the 'build a better mousetrap' stage.

Boosey and Hawkes remains the sole European volume manufacturer of musical instruments. The introduction of production line techniques by both American and Japanese manufacturers has effectively undermined what was once entirely a European preserve.

SALES

The advent of the depression in the 1930s forced companies to become more competitive in the way that they promoted their goods. It was not enough merely to produce efficiently, the product had also to be aggressively promoted and 'sold'.

In the car market where some of the most aggressive sales techniques became developed this became known as 'moving metal'.

The sales strategy that many companies developed led to the growth of many promotional tools such as advertisements, sales promotions and competitions, which were relatively under-developed in the Europe of the time.

MARKETING

In the post-war period economic growth in the United States was exceptionally rapid with the GNP growing at an annual rate of over 6 per cent. Increasing affluence meant that consumers became more and more interested in diversity rather than similarity. The speed of change also substantially increased, with rapid replacement of consumer durables being the rule rather than the exception.

Ford, for example, lost market leadership in the United States to General Motors who introduced a mulitplicity of models providing increased consumer choice.

Growing markets were also attractive investment opportunities and many new companies became established to capitalize on growing demand. In consequence the market became more competitive, and companies had to understand more about which factors were most important in determining demand.

Neither concentration on sales nor on production was sufficient to ensure long-term survival.

Tupperware had concentrated exclusively on personal selling of its range of plastic containers via part-time housewife 'organizers'. Recently the company has had to change its approach to the consumer dramatically as sales and profitability have started to decline.

The marketing approach which concentrates on the problems of integrating the issues such as selling, pro luction, advertising, pricing, packaging, consumer preferences, and competitive action into a coherent short- and long-term strategy describes the underlying business philosophy of many of today's major US corporations.

Many companies, particularly those in the consumer markets, reorganized their management structures to recognize the complexities of the task involved, especially where there was an extensive product range. Job titles such as product or brand manager have been created for individuals who are responsible for the profitability of a specific product.

Procter and Gamble, the American detergent manufacturer, pioneered the product management concept. It believes in detailed market research, a high degree of production, sales, packaging, price and distribution planning followed by heavy advertising to achieve product sales. This approach has allowed it to remain one of the dominant forces in the detergent and toiletries market in the USA and in many other countries.

More recent developments

By the 1970s the marketing concept had become firmly established in the United States and to a lesser extent in Europe. The nature of the task was, however, changing. Economic growth had slowed, competition on a worldwide scale had become more severe, and the level of investment required to generate successful new products had mushroomed. Whereas in the 1950s the investment required for a nationwide launch of a new product in the United States was substantially less than $1 million, by the 1970s costs were often over $40 million.

These factors have led some firms to reassess the role of marketing to make it concentrate more on long-term issues – strategic marketing rather than total adherence to short-term tactical advantage.

These companies see the product manager as having responsibility for:
- product strategy
- capital expenditure
- sales forecasting
- advertising
- budgetary control
- quality control
- new product development.

In the majority of firms however the role of the product manager is more short-term with responsibility mainly for achieving budgetary targets (sales and profit) and being involved in short-term product planning.

The competitive environment has highlighted some of the shortcomings of the product manager system. Within a classical marketing department the marketing team can only institute change through senior management as they do not have direct authority over production, sales or finance departments (Figure 1.1).

Figure 1.1. Staff role of marketing management

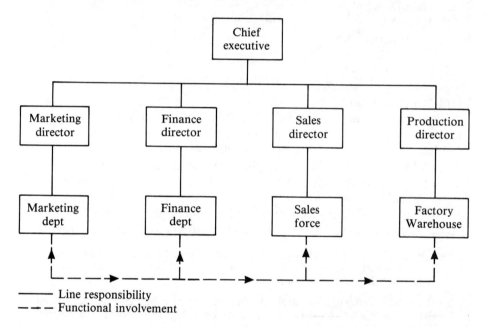

——— Line responsibility
— — — Functional involvement

In organizations where the senior management is not wholly supportive of marketing innovation, this has meant that the marketing department has become isolated and often ignored. In the face of declining profits in the 1970s many companies also reduced the numbers employed in the marketing department and directed those that remained towards gaining short-term sales rather than long-term strategic development.

SOCIAL

Both government and the consumer have made the task of marketing more complex, and some authors identify this as the social orientation phase into which marketing is now passing.

Government has had a significant effect both by formal and informal legislation. First, there is the list of legislation in the United Kingdom with which marketing departments must have at least a nodding acquaintance:

Advertisement (Hire Purchase) Act
Bills of Sale Acts
Carriage of Goods Act
Consumer Credit Acts
Consumer Protection Acts
Fair Trading Act
Food and Drug Acts
Hire Purchase Acts
Misrepresentation of Goods Act
Race Relations Acts
Resale Price Acts
Restrictive Practices Act
Sale of Goods Act
Trade Descriptions Act
Unfair Contract Terms Act
Unsolicited Goods and Services Act.

In addition there are many EEC rulings that affect British industry. Even the United States government has an effect on marketing policy with strict guidelines on technology transfer which mean that a British manufacturer is restricted on what can be done with a finished product if it has American components.

Along with these formal rules there are a number of informal controls that effectively channel action. The family planning industry, for example, is effectively limited to specialist magazines for promotional purposes.

Consumer attitudes and pressure groups have also become far more important.

John West, the Unilever subsidiary, has faced an uphill battle to re-establish the market for tinned salmon following the extensive newspaper coverage given to a single infected tin containing *botulinum*.

CAMRA, The Campaign for Real Ale, has had a major influence on the United Kingdom beer market. Its concern for 'traditional' beers has led to a substantial drop in demand for pressurized keg beers.

The detergent, Ariel Automatic, failed to make significant headway, in spite of very heavy expenditure, against the market leader, Persil Automatic, until changes in the formulation of Persil raised major press and TV comment on its effect on certain skin complaints.

Though it can be considered part of the 'consumerism' movement a broader issue that is increasingly discussed is how far it is acceptable to pursue the profit motive, and to maintain and create demand.

American surpluses are at the root of its keenly competitive environment and more than anywhere else in the world the American consumer is fully aware of the power to pick and choose between goods and services. One can say that the consumer orientation of American marketing demonstrates responsiveness to the power of the consumer; on the other hand one could strip down this statement of intent, and see beyond a strategy of marketing designed to stimulate and sustain demand for products and services to prevent a recurrence of the disaster of the Great Depression. This ethos of 'conspicuous consumption' has been subject to massive criticism by Americans themselves. The author remembers the scathing picture drawn by a critic describing her countrymen as stuffing themselves with food they didn't need thereby creating the most buoyant multi-million dollar market in the world for diet pills!

How far is it acceptable to develop consumer demand?

Before the oil boom Arabs in the Arabian Gulf were fairly poor, with limited diets and living accommodation. Oil money vastly extended the ownership of air conditioners, fridges, televisions, and cars. Accompanying this consumer durable boom was the dramatic growth in the sale of Western consumer goods such as hair conditioner, fabric conditioner, and powdered coffee.

Ghanaians regard imported Nescafé as far superior to the local excellent coffee bean.

Different educational and cultural backgrounds will also mean that what is acceptable in one country will be unacceptable in others. Issues such as whether schools, hospitals, prisons, local transport, power and water utilities should be run by profit-oriented companies will be hotly debated.

In the United States relinquishing the prison service to private companies has started to occur. In the United Kingdom the government has attempted to privatize hospital cleaning and laundry services.

We are now in a position to add demand to our initial idea of marketing. Company marketing can be seen to be designed to *create and sustain demand* for the organization's goods and services. Such a concept is often shrouded in verbiage to make the entire process more acceptable: 'fulfilling consumer needs' often replaces the creation and sustainment of demand as the main objective of marketing, and camouflages the essential commercial reality that marketing should face; that for all privately funded organizations profit is essential for continuing survival.

The statement of the close involvement of marketing with the generation of profit clearly defines the requirements of marketing within the narrow confines of the organization.

As firms grow larger and more international in nature, decisions that they take will have steadily greater effects on the economies in which they operate. The pursuit by these firms of profit beyond all else is seen as less and less acceptable, summarized by the comment of a British Prime Minister, Edward Heath, on the behaviour of one multinational: 'The unacceptable face of capitalism'.

These large firms are seen to have a social duty towards the societies in which they operate; to remain good employers and usefully contribute in other ways to the country – sponsoring artistic events, helping establish small businesses, fostering training and education, and preserving the environment. One can see many of these themes illustrated in corporate advertising campaigns.

Where then should the line be drawn between what is legitimate business and unnecessary exploitation?

Much of our judgement of the benefits or drawbacks of certain business practices will inevitably be based on hindsight. Two weeks before the Bhopal disaster Union Carbide was praised for its contribution to the Indian economy. Deregulation in the airline business has meant lower fares – might it mean that the rate of air accidents will become unacceptably high?

In conclusion, it is inevitable that consumer and governmental pressures on industry will increase and affect the role of business in society. Marketing departments will have to give more attention to wider issues of marketing planning than those relating purely to the aims and objectives of the company for which they work.

ASSIGNMENTS

1. Choose two retail outlets in the same type of trade. Note down the differences between the two. Prepare a report for a manager who is considering entering the retail market, describing the important issues that would need to be considered which explain the success of one outlet compared with another.
2. How far do you think that the commercialization of local council services should be expanded? Prepare a letter to your local councillor detailing your views.
3. Take two long-established UK companies. Use published material to analyse their trading histories and from that define in your view how important the use of marketing concepts has been in their development.

MÊLÉE FOODS – THE LIMITS OF MARKETING?

INTRODUCTION

The chairman of a regional development authority somewhere in England was surprised to learn, from a press release, of the pending closure, within the next six months, of the nearby Tasty Foods factory. The authority had a broad mandate within its area of operation which the chairman, George Farraday, used to its maximum effect. He set out to find out more about the Tasty operation.

The same scrap of paper was equally a cause of concern for Teddy Butler, the director of the local enterprise board. Placed in an area of high unemployment, the board was currently active in stimulating job-creating investment and in supporting local businesses. Butler was therefore particularly concerned to see what his organization could do to prevent the closure of the factory.

TASTY FOODS

Tasty Foods had been canning foods, including baby foods, and bottling sauces and pickles for almost half a century. Its products were well known and nationally liked. Improvements in production techniques had decreased the numbers employed without affecting productivity. Even so the plant still had a mainly female labour force of some 300. Good management and labour relations ensured that the enterprise was compact and efficient.

MÊLÉE FOODS

Tasty Foods had been taken over by a French multinational company, Mêlée Foods, at the end of the 1940s. Originally in confectionery, Mêlée had expanded into canned foods first in France and then overseas as the company's financial clout increased. Tasty's products fitted in well with those of its new parent and with its area of expertise.

The 1950s and 1960s were an era of growth and prosperity for Mêlée which proceeded to buy up other French and English canned food companies including some, like Tasty Foods, which were internationally well known.

Mêlée was a highly centralized company exercising a great deal of control over its subsidiary companies to ensure that profits were maximized to the advantage of the parent company. For example, an ethos of service to Mêlée was instilled into the managers of subsidiaries. To this end, training and orientation courses were specially designed for new recruits and in-post managers. Decisions on planning targets and investment levels were made centrally at annual Mêlée headquarters meetings, in Paris, which were attended by the board members of the subsidiaries involved. Progress during the year was similarly reviewed.

This process helped to cocoon the Mêlée Group from the worst effects of the recession at the end of the 1970s and its companies remained profitable. By then, however, new pressures distinct from the recession were becoming apparent in the market-place.

The growing strength of national retailing chains was particularly noticeable in the intensified UK competition between own-brand and branded canned foods. Mêlée was now facing a situation where there was little room for market expansion in traditional canned foods; where certain of its subsidiaries with similar products were already competing against each other; and where own-brand competition was growing.

THE REGIONAL DEVELOPMENT AUTHORITY'S REPORT

George Farraday, the chairman of the regional development authority, sought to arrange a meeting with the managing director of Tasty Foods to discuss the closure of the factory, but the latter declined the invitation.

Undeterred, Farraday appointed a team of consultants to prepare a report on Tasty Foods. They based their report on the company's annual financial statements but they were also able to secure details of investments in the company and the nature of its markets.

The consultants' report revealed that the company was basically profitable and that it could become more so given the opportunity. While its products' market share had not grown, neither had it declined substantially. Improvements in productivity had more than compensated. If the authority were interested in lending money to the company to buy its independence from Mêlée, the loan could be repaid within five years at current profit levels.

However, the report also said that Mêlée did not intend to sell the plant as a going venture but planned first to strip the factory of all its equipment which would either be relocated or sold off at auction.

ACTION BY THE LOCAL ENTERPRISE BOARD

The director of the local enterprise board, Teddy Butler, chose a more direct line of approach to the company. He spoke to the manager of the Tasty factory, Steven Lee, who was surprised at the decision to close the factory and concerned about the future of its employees. Lee agreed to see a consultant from the enterprise board with the aim of identifying alternatives.

The board's consultant, Christopher Elliott, spent some time at the factory familiarizing himself with the Tasty product range, sales and market share, identifying those products which were subject to the most severe competition, and making suggestions for possible new areas of expansion. His chief aim was to draw up a proposal which could be submitted to the local enterprise board for support. Before doing this, Elliott also researched recent changes in the canned food market in order to test the extent to which the company's experience conformed with them.

Elliott's main conclusion, according to his final report to Lee, was that Tasty should seriously consider launching a range of high-quality, luxury-type sauces

Table 1.1   Canned food products of Mêlée companies in UK market

Product	Company	Market share		Retailers' own brands	
		% 1975	% 1980	% 1975	% 1980
Canned soup	Penn	9	7	20	30
	Tasty	8	6	—	—
	Quick Food	14	14	—	—
Sauces*	Penn	10	9	15	29
	Tasty	5	5	—	—
	Quick Food	18	19	—	—
Sauces†	Penn	27	21	—	0.5
	Quick Food	22	27	—	—
Canned fruit*	Penn	11	9	13	19
	Quick Food	7	5	—	—
Canned fruit†	Penn	15	17	—	1
	Tasty	0	2	—	—
Pickle	Quick Food	8	6	15	15
	Tasty	11	10	—	—
Baby food	Penn	21	23	2	3
	Quick Food	27	25	—	—
	Tasty	11	13	—	—

Note: * Run of the mill
       † Exotic

and explore the potential for producing canned foods without additives for the health food market. Lee was in general agreement with Elliott but warned him that the report would have to be submitted to the managing director, and that final agreement to go ahead would have to come from Mêlée headquarters in Paris.

In his concluding report to the local enterprise board, Elliott stated that some time had elapsed before he was asked to attend a meeting with the Tasty managing director, accompanied by Lee. Elliott said that the tone of the meeting was generally unproductive. He could not elicit from the managing director's replies whether the proposal was acceptable or not. He was left with a general feeling that it was not and that the proposal had been turned down for political reasons at Mêlée headquarters because the proposed range would be competing with the products of other, more profitable, Mêlée subsidiaries (Table 1.1).

Comment

This case raises the issue of the effects large companies can have on local communities and how inflexible decisions at head office may often be. The question of political response is also relevant: what should the various authorities do?

PART 1

STRATEGIC FACTORS

2

STRATEGIC CONSTRAINTS

These are the voyages of the starship Enterprise. ... Its five-year mission ...
to boldly go where no man has gone before.

(Star Trek)

As Chapter 1 has stressed, markets have become more competitive and change
has become more rapid. A firm will only be able to make profits and survive by
being more effective than others in understanding where it should be going and
what it should be developing.

THE RELEVANCE OF STRATEGIC CONCEPTS

In order to be effective, the company will need to *plan* effectively, defining and
continually re-evaluating a number of key issues. These are:
1. the objectives or goals – or 'mission' in the language of *Star Trek* – which the
    firm is trying to achieve;
2. the strategy it favours to reach those objectives;
3. the tactics that will make this strategy viable.
    The 'mission' will be a long-term statement which is often based on a horizon
of ten years or more.
    The strategy will be more short-term, relating to shorter-term investment
decisions: where the company will invest and from where it will withdraw.
    The tactics will be important in the short term to define immediate responses to
the market and market forces.
    The development of strategic concepts allows the firm to: control the allocation
of its resources; and measure its progress by providing a benchmark or point of
reference to monitor its achievements.
    Let us take an example of a firm in the toiletries market.
    Its mission is 'to become the leading force in the premium female toiletries
market throughout the world'.

Its strategy is:

(a) 'to improve the return on capital employed by X per cent;
(b) to diversify product lines into growth areas such as aerosol sprays;
(c) to maintain a strong financial position by growing internally – achieving a level of sales growth of Y per cent per annum'.

Its tactics are: 'to concentrate on premium products and policies with high investment levels'.

THE CHARACTERISTICS OF A STRATEGIC PLAN

Obviously strategic planning, like all planning, needs to be strongly rooted in reality. In other words the plan must have certain characteristics:

1. The plan must be consistent. All elements of the plan should be following the same logical argument. It would be illogical for the company in our example, having stated that it was directing its strategic direction towards the expensive end of the market, to consider mass distribution tactics and pricing as a special focus of attention for the items of its range.

2. The plan must be attainable. A strategic plan must be realistic so that the strategy has a reasonable chance of success. That is the only way that the company can attempt to be certain that it is not attempting to move too quickly with too few resources – an example would be the ice cream manufacturer with a plan to diversify into nuclear power within five years.

3. The plan must be specific. The strategic plan must have particular targets built into it so that progress can be judged; it should avoid basing itself solely on general statements of intent.

4. The plan must be flexible. The plan should be able to cope with the rapidly changing environment within which the firm operates.

The long-term plan that conforms to these criteria will almost certainly contain a number of compromises between different goals because perceptions will vary about what is in the company's best interests and certain goals may be seen as conflicting with each other:

● profit versus market share
● immediate profit versus long-term profit
● growth versus stability
● profit versus social factors.

These compromises can be minimized by always relating the components of the plan back to the original goals or mission.

THE MARKETING MIX AND THE STRATEGIC PLAN

How can our hypothetical toiletries company develop a strategic plan?

First, it must be aware of the limitations that exist in the market in which it operates, and the skills it possesses in relation to that market.

Second, it needs to be aware of internal limitations that will also restrict its freedom of manoeuvre.

Third, our company will need to determine investment or disinvestment in certain areas of the business and, finally, decide the exact nature of the tactical interaction of all the main variables in the market-place. These variables are defined as the 'marketing mix'.

Classically these variables have been known as the 'four Ps'.
1. Price: how the product is priced.
2. Place: how the product is distributed.
3. Promotion: how the product is promoted.
4. Product: the nature of the product.

Recently the steady increase in the importance of both competition and growth in the service sector has suggested that further criteria should be added to the original four Ps.
5. Parity: how the company stands in relation to the competition.
6. Physical: the environment of the transaction – particularly important for the service sector.
7. People: the way the employees of the organization operate – again crucial in the service context.
8. Process: the way in which the customer is served, also important in the service context.

These factors will also interact and require the same degree of care in development as the overall strategy. Take, for example, two marketing mixes, one relating to an 'exclusive' product the other to a 'mass market' product.

These are the features of the exclusive product.
High quality product.
Low volume production.
Limited distribution.
Restricted promotion.
High price.
Quality packaging.

Here is the profile of the mass market product.
Medium quality product.
High volume production.
Mass distribution.
Wide-scale and heavy promotion.
Moderate price.
Functional packaging.

STRATEGIC PLANNING TASKS

Although most companies review all strategies together, it is worth considering the exercise as a linear one to clarify the issues involved (Figure 2.1). The sequence of tasks can be remembered by the mnemonic EDAD which if you get it wrong will make your company DEAD – its anagram.

Figure 2.1. The development of marketing strategy

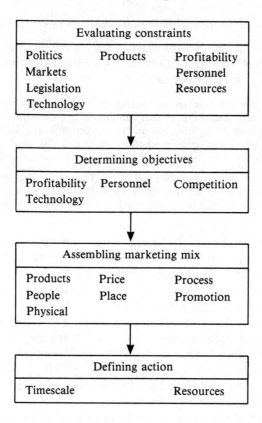

Task one: evaluating constraints.
Task two: defining goals.
Task three: analysing strategy.
Task four: defining the marketing mix to achieve strategy.

Before a firm can consider how to develop a market strategy it must evaluate the main problem *constraints* facing it both externally and internally, as otherwise the strategy will fail to be either objective or attainable.

A useful analogy is to consider a man in the middle of the desert with no visible sign of human habitation having to decide which way he should go. If he looks at the immediate surroundings he cannot decide, but a short distance away to the east is a line of vertical cliffs, to the south is a violent dust storm, to the west is a deep canyon, and to the north is open country. The constraints on direction would suggest that he either waits for the dust storm to settle to go south, climbs up the hills on the east or down the canyon to the west – provided of course that he is an experienced climber – or walks north.

The firm, similarly, has to consider a large range of external and internal constraints on strategy before deciding on viable objectives.

EXTERNAL FACTORS

The market in which the firm operates

Crucial to the evaluation of a strategy is a clear concept of what market the organization is involved with. Too narrow a definition can make the company fail to overcome the right problems.

> The Swiss watch industry survived by realizing that in addition to producing watches it was effectively manufacturing jewellery and clothing accessories. The first idea led it successfully to combat Japanese products by superior styling, and the second has allowed it to re-enter the mass market by producing different coloured plastic watches or 'swatches'.

> The British motorcycle industry (Norton, BSA, Triumph) on the other hand failed to realize that the mass market was for cheap and easy transport, and the advent of low priced, four-stroke, easily started machines from Japan destroyed its existing market.

Like the Swiss watch manufacturers, other companies can reappraise their activities and the opportunities in the market in order to confirm or alter their position in it. Thus, an oil company could see itself as being in either the energy sector or in mineral extraction. A producer of baked beans may see itself as being basically a tinned snack meal manufacturer.

Heinz, for example, has found that when the price of baked beans increases its sales decline to be replaced by increased sales of tinned spaghetti. A definition of the baked bean as a tinned snack food would therefore appear to be realistic. Too broad a definition would obviously also have its pitfalls, producing unworkable generalizations. For example, the baked bean could be placed – using American jargon – in the 'oral satisfaction' market.

Whatever the oil company or the baked beans producer decides as being its main market or area of operation, it will have to be clear about which market it is pursuing. The oil company may be sufficiently prosperous to handle both energy and mineral extraction markets but each will make different demands on the company.

A useful technique is to consider what market the product might enter if it became either substantially more expensive or considerably cheaper. An air charter firm might find that it was in the luxury travel business as well as the freight and cheap travel market – it could redefine its role as providing rapid transport rather than purely air charter.

Defining the nature of the market in which the company operates will help to identify areas of strength and weakness and allow it to determine in the short term the potential avenues for development.

> Until the early 1970s the Burton Group perceived its role as manufacturer and retailer of mass market clothes. Profits stagnated until redefinition as a fashion retailer led to dramatic changes in the structure of the group, with Top Shop, Dorothy Perkins, Principles, and the Burton shops themselves all serving different areas of the market.

The economy

The economy overall will greatly influence what is achievable, and certain companies use economic indicators to determine strategic development.

The example of the use of such a system by Unilever to evaluate likely changes in detergent consumption was mentioned in Chapter 1. Coca-Cola also derives elements of strategy from changes in economic performance, determining likely levels of consumption. Frequently the presence or absence of certain international companies can serve as an indicator of what is happening overall. Thus, the sudden fierce competition between Coca-Cola and Pepsi in the Indian market may be said to be a pointer to economic developments favouring an expansion of the soft drinks market.

Politics and legislation

Increasingly, political and legal systems can have significant effects on marketing policies and strategies. Tobacco companies, for example, have suffered from legislation designed to limit tobacco smoking in the Western World. In the United Kingdom, and in the majority of other countries in Western Europe, the numbers employed in the tobacco industry have dramatically declined due to government attitudes towards the duty levels on cigarettes. This has meant that the companies need to look elsewhere for sales and profit growth.

British American Tobacco has over the last ten years developed interests in perfumes (Yardley – since disposed of), stores (International – since disposed of), insurance (Eagle Star and Hambro Life), and paper (Wiggins Teape).

Legislation can also significantly change the pattern of an industry and how it evaluates return on investment. Within the drug industry the testing procedures have become steadily more stringent since 1945. Two to three years would then have been the norm, but by the 1980s this had often lengthened to over fifteen years. The level of risk associated with investment in a new drug has dramatically increased in consequence. The response of the drug companies has been to reduce the level of investment in new areas of development that require a lengthy testing procedure and concentrate on minor changes to existing products.

Governments can have immediate effects on an industry by altering the level of support it receives. The rise in milk production over consumption in the EEC led to the introduction of quotas. Though these only involved a reduction in production of 7 per cent, they created a drop in the sale of milking machinery of around 50 per cent in the first year, and continuing problems for those firms that managed to survive in the industry.

By altering safety codes a government can effectively control market development. Japan has long been notorious in such areas; continually changing safety regulations have made it extremely difficult and often impossible for long-term penetration of the Japanese market for foreign companies.

Voluntary international codes of conduct can also have a considerable influence. One such is currently operating in the powdered baby food, sometimes called infant formula, market. Due to pressures from international agencies a code of conduct has been established which restricts the use of free samples, and other promotional activities.

> Following the adoption in the 1980s of the International Code of Baby Food Marketing under the auspices of the World Health Organization many Third World countries have adopted legislation making it difficult for manufacturers of powdered milk to advertise – they are often required to state that 'breast is best'; and often banning the distribution of free samples unless under medical supervision.

These examples of political and legislative effects are all indirect. There are also instances of direct effects on specific companies. Anti-trust legislation in the United States largely prevents companies growing too strong in a certain direction, and has for example split up AT&T because of its monopoly within the telephone market. Less effective controls exist within other countries though they will still have their effects.

> The UK detergent market is largely dominated by Unilever and Procter and Gamble, and this was investigated by the Monopolies and Mergers Commission in the 1960s. One of the consequences of this investigation was the agreement by these two large organizations to produce 'value for money' brands, Daz and Surf.

Direct legislation can also affect the internal policies of the firm with regard to minimum levels of wages, the number of people that must be employed, and their ethnic composition. In Italy for example, draconian trade union legislation applies to firms with more than thirty-five employees. In consequence many firms will try to maintain their numbers below this figure. In India, where similar legislation attempts to improve the working conditions of women in low-paid jobs, employers will sack employees before they can fulfil the minimum employment period required to qualify for the benefits.

Speed of change and the impact of technology

The speed of change in the environment will have a major impact on the way the company's strategy needs to be directed.

This is most severe when a company diversifies into new areas – the way the market responds to successful techniques developed in other industries may be very different.

> Argyll Foods, the retailing group comprising Liptons and Presto, is encountering similar problems with the development of the products of Barton Distilleries, a range of little-known Scotch whiskies. These do not respond at the same speed as retail outlets to the impact of pricing and promotion.

Competition and market share

The company's position and strengths in relation to the competition and its market share will also have a very important influence on company strategy.

In many markets what the competition is doing may be the most important single fact in determining strategy especially for the company with limited resources. Some companies will therefore adopt what could be termed a *competitor orientation* deriving their strategy primarily from the competition rather than a *customer orientation* strategy.

Established markets such as tinned soup will show clear market leader(s) – Heinz; market challenger(s) – Campbell; market specialist(s) – Baxters; and commodity producers – own-label products.

Market leaders. The history of marketing success and failure shows us that it is very difficult to dislodge a market leader once one has become established in a particular market sector.

> Guinness remains dominant as a stout, Uncle Ben's Rice, Mars, Kit-Kat, Kelloggs Corn Flakes, Bacardi, Silko thread, Hilton, Kodak, Levi-Strauss, Coca-Cola, Martell, Gucci, Mercedes, Chanel, Badedas, Olivetti, IBM, Xerox are all examples of such a dominance continuing over a long period in their particular market sectors. Examples of products losing to competition are more limited – L'Oreal to Elida Gibbs in the shampoo market, Ford to General Motors in cars, Wimpy to McDonald in the fast food sector.

The conclusion that can be drawn from such a list is that the market leader, in military terminology, can take advantage of the high ground to dominate the market and prevent rivals from becoming established. There are a number of ways in which this high ground can be maintained.

1. Product development. A high level of new product development will discourage the competition from being able to find a competitive advantage.
2. Manufacturing efficiency. The leading company can take advantage of its high volume to produce high quality product and a wide product range at a price which will further complicate matters for the competitive entrant.
3. Strong continuing promotional activity. Heavy advertising, a strong sales force, active promotional spending will all make the market more risky for a competitor to enter.
4. Rapid tactical activity. The market leader is able to control markets on a short-term basis by influencing distributors, suppliers, and consumers. Test markets of new products are particularly good examples of such activity. It is in the interests of the dominant firm to ensure that the results of the test market discourage a competitive firm from entering the market. The market leader will therefore discount the price to the consumer, provide additional discounts to the retailer or wholesaler to take large quantities of his stock rather than the competitor, indulge in denigrating the competing product via the sales force, and increase the advertising weight in that particular area.

   The market leader is able to take such action because its position is so much more profitable than the new entrant – a short-term dip in profitability for the market leader will be nothing in comparison with the far more substantial losses inflicted on the competitor with a weaker market position.

Market challengers. The position of the second company or major competitor in the market can be summarized by the well-known dictum of Avis, 'We're number two and we try harder'.

1. Direct attack. The competitor can attempt to outspend the market leader in promotional expenditure. Procter and Gamble often follows this approach in

those market sectors where it is not well established, spending over £6 million per year on Ariel Automatic against the established Persil Automatic with a £2 million expenditure on television.

2. Price reduction. Offering a similar product to the market leader at a discount can enable a market challenger to gain significant brand share, provided that the market leader does not respond. The computer market is a good example of such an approach. Apricot, the main British personal computer manufacturer, underprices IBM, the industry leader, by around 25 per cent for a comparable system. This has ensured that it has gained increasing acceptance with individual purchasers though it faces continuing problems in the corporate sector.

3. Product differentiation. Gaps may exist within the market either at the top or at the bottom, and the market challenger can gain dominance at either end.

Japanese four-wheeled vehicles, for example, introduced a range of products less sophisticated than the European equivalents and rapidly gained market dominance in many world markets.

JCB, the producer of earth-moving equipment, similarly manufactured more basic products than those that had previously been on offer.

BMW and Porsche have successfully followed the alternative strategy, that of introducing prestige products. In both cases they have managed to dominate the competition – Rover and Triumph.

4. Product innovation. Finding a totally new market sector by large-scale investment in research and development can be a highly successful strategy for a market challenger.

Polaroid is a classic example of such a company; it did not compete directly with Kodak but instead concentrated its efforts on a new camera – one providing instant photographs.

McCain's introduced a new frozen oven-ready chip; other examples are electronic watches by Casio, home computers by Sinclair.

5. Distribution innovation. Changing distribution policy can often allow a market challenger to gain a dominant position. Photographic firms such as Tru-Print in the UK have become well established by initially concentrating on direct door-to-door sales.

6. People, process or physical. Improving the physical environment and the service process can also be important in the development of share by the market challenger. The untidy, badly organized Lyons tea shops gave way to the more modern Wimpy bars, which in turn have succumbed to the cleanliness and speed of McDonalds.

Market specialist. The market specialist will identify a small gap in the market which it can effectively service, and which is sufficiently profitable to ensure long-term survival. This specialization can be by location, customer type or nature of service. A local industrial cleaning company centred on Cambridge has proved so successful by providing a range of services to the local community that the national firms have been excluded.

Morgan cars of Wales has continued to produce small quantities of its old-style sports car for a specialist market. The firm has not attempted to expand from its area of traditional expertise.

Commodity suppliers. Many firms concentrate on manufacturing efficiency, and operate in fairly unsophisticated markets providing a cost-effective, efficient service. Manufacturers that supply own-label products are an important element of this group.

Nottingham Manufacturing is an example of a company which has substantially improved both sales and profitability over a twenty-year period. It has been the main supplier to Marks and Spencer.

With the increasing concentration of purchasing power both within retailing chains – over 60 per cent of grocery and electrical business is now accounted for by five or six chains in the UK, with a similar picture elsewhere – and 50 per cent of the total work-force in manufacturing industry employed by multinationals, the development of this type of strategy will become more and more relevant.

Market size and growth

The size of the market will also be an important element in the firm's strategy. Many large firms will not be able to handle small market sectors effectively and will concentrate on developing mass market products and services.

Unilever bought one of the premium perfume firms in England, Atkinsons, which had provided the miniatures for Queen Mary's doll's house at Windsor Castle. Consistent with its policy of producing mass market products it developed a range of cheap cosmetics based on the Atkinson name selling through the discount store of that period, Woolworths. The result was that the Atkinson name became downgraded and when the range was withdrawn there was no possibility of re-establishing the premium image.

The rate of growth in the market may also have important strategic implications. As market share increases percentage growth will inevitably slow; it will be far easier to grow from 1 to 2 per cent in the market than from 20 to 40 per cent, and companies looking for continued development will need to look elsewhere.

Studies show that concentration on growth markets may be a two-edged sword. Growth encourages the development of rapid competitor entry into a market, often producing considerable over-supply.

In the nylon industry the attractive initial growth encouraged large numbers of firms to build plant and enter the market. Inevitably there was fierce competition as a result of over-supply.

Similarly, growth in sherry markets in the 1960s encouraged a great expansion in vineyards in Jerez in Spain. By the time that these were producing it was clear that demand was no longer growing. The resulting glut has forced down prices and often quality – which will further complicate the future.

The compact disc market may also face similar over-production as more and more companies establish manufacturing plants.

Nature of the buyer

In many markets the way in which the product reaches the end user will have important influences on the development of a viable strategy.

Within the United Kingdom grocery market the major retailing chains such as Sainsbury's, Tesco, Asda, Dee, and Argyll Foods control well over half the total sales to the consumer. The reaction of a small group of individuals will in consequence have a potentially deciding influence on the likely success or failure of any product.

Similar problems have been found by many firms trying to expand in the Japanese market; the close relationship between the major industrial groups often precludes the foreign firm gaining access. The trade balance between Japan and America in silicon chip manufacture has steadily worsened as a result of such exclusion.

Nature of the supplier

The relationship between the component manufacturer and the dominant companies within the market can effectively control market development. Take for example a supplier of components for video machines. Though theoretically independent, the supplier depending on a few major companies is unlikely to be willing to start supplying a small independent competitor, which in consequence is effectively isolated from the market.

Logistics (geography, communication)

Expansion either within a country or overseas will create considerable control problems for the organization. Overseas subsidiaries can lead to disaster.

Apricot, the main independent British business computer manufacturer, experienced severe problems when trying to expand in the United States partially because communication between the parent company and the US subsidiary created severe difficulties.

Distribution

Distribution constraints may severely restrict the freedom of manoeuvre in many markets.

The Japanese consumer market is heavily dependent on wholesalers for its distribution rather than the use of the direct sales force as in the United Kingdom. Distribution problems posed by this system have had a role in preventing the food multinational Nestlé from firmly establishing its chocolate products in Japan.

Twydale, a major British turkey supplier, has the sale of its chilled prepared turkey products limited to those retailers that can maintain a chilled distribution system from warehouse to retail outlet to ensure that no quality problems occur. This restricts Twydale to supplying the major retailing groups such as Tesco, Asda and Marks and Spencer.

The threat of new market entrants or substitutes

Changes in technology within one market sector may create instant competition in an unrelated sector.

The development of the low-cost integrated circuit put the clockwork watch industry under intense competition. Electronic manufacturers such as Texas Instruments and Casio were quick to see the potential and rapidly became established as major forces in the watch industry.

INTERNAL FACTORS

Constraints and opportunities within the company are as important as the external influences on the development of a market strategy.

Sales or volume objectives

The organization may set an objective for growth in sales volume. This is often found in small businesses operating on the assumption that if they can grow sufficiently rapidly the problems that they currently face will be overcome.

Increasing sales will, however, mean that they will need more capital to finance stocks and credit for customers, which often means that profitable companies go bankrupt because they no longer have sufficient cash to pay outstanding bills. Sales levels can also be achieved by heavy discounting with each unit selling at a loss. It is more useful for the company to set targets such as profit objectives.

Profit objectives (or return on capital employed)

Crucial to the development of any business activity will be the level of profitability achieved measured by the return on capital employed. This is often central to many organizations' strategic planning when each activity is evaluated on this basis. Many retailing organizations concentrate exclusively on analysing business opportunities in this fashion.

Asda, one of the most successful British retailers with over 100 superstores, considers that the minimum 25 per cent return is the acceptable level of return on its operations.

Mars, the confectionery and petfood manufacturer, has faced problems in diversification because of its requirement of high levels of return on capital employed in any business venture. Diversifications into toys (Uncle Remus) and catering (Vendepac) have failed to meet the profit requirements and have been disposed of. Though the company has a range of emerging new business areas: research (Mars Group Services), instant beverages (Klix), and electronic systems (MMS), none has yet reached the level of return achieved from Mars confectionery or Pedigree Petfood.

Risk factors

Another internal objective that will concern the company is the level of risk that is acceptable for each area of activity, measured against the amount of return that can be expected – a high risk yielding a high level of return.

Companies should consider the level of risk that each activity faces to determine the overall level that is being considered. An individual may place some of his savings in a house, some on deposit in the bank, own an insurance policy, and only then invest in more risky stocks and shares. Companies can follow similar approaches to strategic risk management, which will often depend on the company's financial strength.

> Xerox, the photocopier manufacturer, will be prepared for example to maintain an office in Moscow which, though extremely expensive and not productive in the short term, *might* be highly effective in eventually opening the Soviet market, with the substantial profitability this would produce.

New developments can however substantially increase the likely level of risk.

> The Warner Corporation's expansion into video games with its Atari subsidiary from its base in films and entertainment led to an enormous initial increase in profits. This was however followed by a near collapse of the entire group as the video games market fell apart.

Research and development levels

Research and development of new products require a long timespan and therefore consistency in this area is crucial. It will take five years to produce a new car, perhaps ten years for a new aeroplane, two years for a new brand of breakfast cereal.

Commitment to either a high or low continuing level of research and development is a viable strategy in differing industries, but short-term variations will be inefficient. High levels of research and development obviously conflict with short-term profitability goals; a company like ICI may dramatically improve profitability by reducing the level of investment in research and development.

Capital investment levels

Businesses need clear objectives about the level of capital investment in the activities in which they are involved.

The level of capital investment and investment in research and development will interact with the nature of the market in which the firm is operating. One key factor appears to be the degree to which differences, apparent or real, can be established between the company's product and its competitors'. This can be termed the potential competitive advantage. Figure 2.2 shows the four types of investment strategy.

1. Fragmented. An example of the fragmented market is the premium wine trade and the perfume business; low levels of capital investment with relative ease of achieving competitive advantage.
2. Specialized. Much larger investment required but also yielding a high degree of competitive advantage. A classical example would be IBM in the

mainframe computer business; a high level of capital and research and development costs yielding a substantial competitive advantage.

3. Volume. High investment required in complex manufacturing plants yet not yielding a substantial competitive advantage; the large petrochemical companies would be examples of such companies.

4. Commodity. Low investment and low achievable product advantage: industrial detergents and most package holidays are good examples.

Figure 2.2. Effect on strategy of level of capital investment

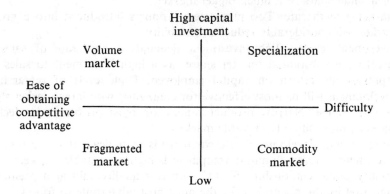

Many markets have very high *barriers to entry* – relating to the degree of investment that is needed to enter the market effectively.

The volume car market poses massive barriers to entry. Any new manufacturer would have to propose spending hundreds of millions of pounds developing products, building plants, training labour, establishing dealership, and promoting products.

In the early days of Silicon Valley, the centre of integrated circuit manufacture in the United States, barriers to entry were low. Engineers could and did set up in garages and produce highly successful equipment with very low budgets – the Apple Corporation is one such example. As the manufacturing process has become more complex, the barriers to entry have steadily risen.

Human strengths and weaknesses and the firm's personnel objectives

Any organization will have to take into account the strengths and weaknesses of the individuals that it employs as either an opportunity or a problem for the future.

Personnel objectives like the maintenance of employment, and the level of benefits paid to staff will all have strategic consequences.

The John Lewis Partnership, the retail chain, is so named because its permanent employees are partners in the enterprise. This structure means that any planned strategic alteration can only be achieved with the agreement of the majority of the partnership. Such consultation would mean that though the change in direction might perhaps be slower than that of a competitor the full-scale agreement of the work-force would ensure that the change was carried through more effectively.

THE PIMS STUDIES

A complex study carried out in the United States on the profit impact of marketing strategies has identified certain key factors as an aid to strategic development.

1. Market share. Profitability measured by return on capital employed increases with market share. Companies with large market shares will be more profitable than those with small. This may suggest that a company will be better advised to develop market dominance in a small market rather than try for a small share of a much bigger market.
2. Market growth rate. Too many new products introduced into a growing market will considerably reduce profitability.
3. Investment levels. High investment demands a high rate of sales and therefore a substantial market share, as a high investment to sales ratio depresses the return on capital employed. High levels of research and development will be most effective for companies with large market shares.
4. Product range. Narrow product ranges are most profitable in declining markets; most suitable in stable markets.
5. Research and development. Research tends to indicate that the return on investment in research and development is highest in stable markets.
6. Quality/price relationship. Slightly superior quality sold at a premium is suggested by the research to be the most profitable route to follow.

The findings of the PIMS studies need to be treated with caution. The work is highly statistical in nature, extremely complex, and limited to a small number of industries. However they appear to offer some guidelines for policy development.

Summary

Every organization needs to know where it is going, and this demands the development of a strategic or long-term marketing plan. Such a plan demands the consideration of a number of interrelated factors to produce a coherent, feasible and achievable result. The strategy can be based on competitive position, policy towards the consumer, financial objectives or a mixture of all three.

A SUCCESSFUL MARKET STRATEGY – AN ILLUSTRATION

Hanson Trust is an example of a highly successful British company which has followed a consistent strategy in developing its business. In the nine years from 1979 to 1984 earnings per share had risen sixteen times, and profits overall from $20 million to $300 million.

Its success has stemmed from a coherent strategy it has continued to follow from the initial days as a fertilizer manufacturer.

- The company has concentrated on two markets: the UK and USA.
- It has bought companies that require low investment in research and development.

- It has bought companies in stable markets with large or fairly large market shares.
- It has bought companies with low capital investment requirements.
- It has concentrated on improving the return on capital employed in all businesses, achieving a target rate of over 20 per cent.
- It operates a policy of profit sharing for management in all successful ventures.
- It has concentrated on low risk businesses – vending, agricultural supplies, building materials, clothing retailing, textiles, batteries, industrial raw materials and food processing.

The spread of profits is broadly as follows (estimates from the annual report):
building materials – 20 per cent;
batteries – 12.5 per cent;
retailing – 10 per cent;
engineering – 13 per cent;
textiles – 8 per cent;
furniture – 9 per cent;
services – 9 per cent;
food – 8 per cent;
construction – 11 per cent.

The strategy can be clearly seen in the bid made for the Imperial Group and SCM in 1985. Both derived the majority of their sales from basic industries: the Imperial Group from tobacco, beer, hotels and food, SCM from industrial raw materials.

A NATIONAL MARKET STRATEGY

Post-war Japan is an example of a country that has followed a consistent plan for the application of government resources to industrial development.

By the use of grants it initially encouraged the development of labour intensive textile, steel and shipbuilding industries. Before these industries faced severe competition from lower labour cost areas such as Korea and the Republic of China it shifted its support into car, motorcycle, optical and watchmaking industries. As these markets too became difficult, the emphasis switched into television and video products followed by the silicon chip and biotechnology.

Similar planned developments have acquired world leadership for Japan in many industrial sectors, such as machine tools and printing technology. Such a structured approach by the trade and industry department, MITI, has seen the per capita income of Japan rise to equal (shortly to surpass) that of the United States and West Germany.

More recently, with the rise in the value of the yen against other currencies and an increasing level of protectionism against Japanese manufactured goods, MITI has been encouraging Japanese companies to invest abroad. Examples include Toyota, Nissan, Hitachi, and Mitsubishi setting up foreign plants.

This policy is now also being pursued in other areas in which the Japanese economy has been historically weak. In pharmaceuticals, the market price within Japan is being maintained at a level higher than competitor countries such as the United Kingdom. This is to allow Japanese drug companies a high level of return on investment at home to enable them to invest in continued high levels of research and development in order to compete on the world scene.

ASSIGNMENTS

1. Choose a large publicly quoted industrial company. Using the last five years' balance sheets and other published material write a memorandum to the managing director of a competitive firm commenting on the strategy that the firm you have chosen appears to have followed.
2. What are the most important constraints facing your school or college? How do these affect the strategy that it might develop? Outline the issues involved in a memorandum to the principal of the college.
3. You are employed in government. Write a memorandum outlining the strategic constraints affecting British Leyland and how these might influence future investment policy.
4. How should the law on monopolies and mergers be phrased? Write a letter to your local MP taking account of his or her political persuasion.

GENERAL MOTORS – AN UNFINISHED STORY

General Motors (GM), originally the second mass manufacturer in the American car market, came to dominate the development of the motor car and motor car marketing in pre- and post-war America, and to a lesser extent throughout the world.

The company's initial success had been largely due to the effort that it put in effectively to segment the market for producing cars to meet the special needs of consumers of different ages in different income groups (Table 2.1).

Table 2.1   Market segments for GM car production

Product range	Socio-economic group	Age
Cadillac	A	45 +
Oldsmobile	A/B	45 +
Buick	A/B	25 +
Pontiac	B/C	35 +
Chevrolet	C/D	Any

The success of these cars reflects the company's skill in making a reality of the motto: 'a car for every purse and purpose' – the slogan of Alfred Sloan who spearheaded the initial strategy.

After the Second World War the group expanded overseas with large European operations (Vauxhall, Opel, Simca and Bedford) into Australasia and South America. These overseas operations remained largely unprofitable – GM Europe made its first operating profit, $6.2 million, in 1982. By the 1970s the company employed 800,000 people worldwide.

By the early 1970s, while the group was achieving sales of $20 billion and profits of $3 billion, the industry environment was rapidly changing.

First, the major rise in oil costs following the Arab–Israeli war made fuel consumption a major consideration for the first time and reduced the average annual mileage travelled. Second, the ensuing recession made American consumers more cost conscious. Third, the changing structure of the US society – by the mid 1970s only 16 per cent of households fell into the classical picture of two parents with two or three children – meant that the large family car was less and less relevant to consumer requirements. Increasing affluence and sophistication within the A/B socio-economic groups encouraged movement away from traditional products. Finally, the deregulation of the airlines meant that for longer distances Americans were deserting the roads for the air.

The recession also deeply affected the speed at which companies replaced their trucks, with the industry replacement average increasing by 1.8 years between 1972 and 1978.

THE GROWING COMPETITION

From the early 1970s Japanese manufacturers, Nissan, Toyota and Mitsubishi, began to eat into the market shares of the three American manufacturers, General Motors, Ford and Chrysler, with their ranges of small, compact cars priced well below the limited equivalent competition. In the 1970s it was costing General Motors £2,500 more to build a similar car to the Japanese competition.

European competition, notably BMW, Mercedes, Volkswagen and its Audi subsidiary began to make inroads into the sales of middle-range American cars; for example, by 1985 Volkswagen was exporting 103,000 cars to the United States in addition to the 74,000 manufactured locally. The Japanese local manufacture also expanded market share. Hyundai of Korea also entered the market in the early 1980s.

The overall result was that, by the 1980s, imports were achieving around 30 per cent market share and were considered likely to continue to grow between 36 and 40 per cent by the end of the decade.

The industry had made many predictions about the changing nature of the motor car industry:

- changes in engine design – rotary engines, lean-burn, catalytic converters;
- contents of body shell and chassis – aluminium, glass fibre, plastic composites, carbon fibre;
- impact of electronics – electronic ignition, power control.

Few of these forecasts had become reality. By contrast, changes in manufacturing policy such as robotics and computer-aided design had a far more significant impact. General Motors however believed that electronics would become more and more important. At its research centre in Europe work started on electronic integration: electronic fuel injection, electronic ignition, electronic control of suspension, electronic gear selection, automatic engine tuning, and exhaust gases monitored and controlled to minimize pollution.

THE GM STRATEGY

While sales continued to grow margins were increasingly restricted and, in 1980, the company made a loss for the first time in 60 years (Table 2.2).

Table 2.2.   GM results 1973–84

Year	Sales ($ billion)	Profit ($ billion)	Margin (%)
1973	40	3	7
1974	35	1.5	3
1975	40	1.8	4
1976	55	3.5	6
1977	60	4	7
1978	60	4	7
1979	66	3	5
1980	50	(0.7)	
1981	60	0.5	1
1982	60	1	1.5
1983	70	4	5
1984	80	5	6

Although the world vehicle market continued to experience difficulties throughout the 1970s and early 1980s, other sectors such as electronics, defence, computer hardware and software had shown continuing growth. For example, the turnover of IBM in 1970 was only $7.5 billion; by 1984 it was $46 billion.

General Motors has responded to problems that it faces in a number of ways.
1. Reorganizing its volume car production into two new divisions – one for large and one for small cars each entirely responsible for manufacturing and marketing.
2. Reducing the product range by developing new international models. The Astra, Nova and Cavalier reflect a growing international bias towards a world car, produced both in America and Europe. Further investment of around nine billion dollars a year is being made in integrating new truck development and in the redesign of the mid-car range.
3. Forming a new company, the Saturn Corporation, to develop a new range of small cars for the world market incorporating the latest manufacturing technology, the costs involved being of the order of five billion dollars.
4. Buying, in 1984, Electronic Data Systems (EDS) for $2.55 billion to integrate all General Motors' management information and production control within one system.

5. Buying, in 1985, the Hughes Aircraft Corporation for five billion dollars. The Corporation was one of the leading American electronic aerospace companies with broadly based sales of radar, communications satellites, weapons systems and major elements of the space shuttle.

A CONTRASTING STRATEGY

As a contrasting strategy it is interesting to compare the progress of Chrysler, the smallest of the three major American car manufacturers. Chrysler suffered much more severe losses in the early 1980s than GM (Table 2.3).

Table 2.3. Chrysler results 1980–85

Year	Sales ($ billion)	Profit ($ billion)	Margin (%)
1980	10	(1.8)	
1981	10	(.5)	
1982	11	.2	1
1983	12	.8	6
1984	15	1.5	10
1985	18	2.3	13

Since the early 1980s Chrysler has seen its market share rise from 10 to 14 per cent; it has had considerable market success with its range of small vans; sports cars for the affluent under-35s have also increased profitability. Chrysler has largely disposed of its loss-making European production interests – it sold Peugeot – and has entered into co-operative ventures with Mitsubishi and Samsung in Korea.

Comment

This case serves to illustrate a number of points in strategic development. First is the problem of timescale especially where large investments are concerned. Second, the importance of environmental factors in deciding strategy. Third, the difficulty of setting goals for a market leader in a rapidly changing industry.

THE LAUNCH OF THE IBM PC

BACKGROUND

The growth of the personal computer (PC) or microcomputer market dates from the introduction of the Commodore PET in 1977, closely followed by the Apple II.

Second generation computers based on 8-bit technology – that is, the amount of information that the central processing system can handle – had by the end of 1982 been superseded by 16-bit machines such as the ACT Sirius. The standard product was one which offered one 5″ disk drive, with 64k memory storage, retailing for between £1,500 and £2,500.

Much of the growth of microcomputer sales had been due to the vast development of off-the-shelf software or computer programs that could be used with it. Unwieldy operating systems were steadily giving way to more 'user friendly' software.

Another major growth area was the development of peripheral devices with which the computer could interact, particularly the wide range of printers.

Purchasers of microcomputers were usually not the buying company's computer 'professionals'. They were managers who did not have a great deal of time to devote to learning the intricacies of the computer; they wanted a product that would work and produce results in their area of activity.

It had become apparent in the early 1980s that the microcomputer sector would be responsible for an increasing share of the total computer market (Table 2.4).

Table 2.4. World computer market 1976–88

Type	Sales ($ billion)						
	1976	1978	1980	1982	1984	1986	1988
Mainframe	6	8	8	12	12	15	18
Minicomputer	1	2	8	17	25	27	30
PC	—	1	1	5	18	26	36

For many years it had been more cost-effective for companies to buy the largest computer consistent with processing needs. With the advent of the microcomputer it became more cost-effective to buy microcomputers and link them via a network so that information could be transferred and individually processed.

The sale of network systems was expected to grow dramatically through the late 1980s and early 1990s, and eventually account for 40 per cent of microcomputer sales.

IBM

IBM, International Business Machines, had grown to dominate the world computer industry in the manufacturing and supply of mainframe computers and the operating software to run them. By 1984 its worldwide revenues were $46 billion, its profits $6.6 billion. The company controlled 75 per cent of the world mainframe market, but was less dominant in the minicomputer area with between 20 and 25 per cent of the medium and small minicomputer world market.

In 1980, 30 per cent of its revenues came from the rental of computer equipment, 10 per cent from the sale of software and associated services, and 60 per cent from machine sales. By 1985 the rental proportion had dropped to 11 per cent; services had grown to 23 per cent reflecting the increasing emphasis being placed on software development. IBM forecast that software would make up an increasing proportion of sales, rising to perhaps 60 per cent in the 1990s.

The IBM long-term strategy has been quite simply stated: to become the largest company in the world.

This strategy, when translated into operational terms means that IBM:
(a) will need to grow in all areas of the computer industry;
(b) will need to master new areas such as telecommunications, factory automation and network systems;
(c) must continue to show product leadership in all major areas of operation;
(d) must sustain profitability.

With hindsight, expansion into the microcomputer area can therefore be seen as an essential development for IBM.

COMPETITION IN THE MICROCOMPUTER MARKET

There were three main types of company active in the market:
1. A number of minicomputer manufacturers moved into the microcomputer market from their existing base including DEC, ICL, Hewlett Packard and Honeywell.
2. Electronic component manufacturers and producers of office equipment such as Commodore, Olivetti and Triumph Adler.
3. New companies such as Apple and Acorn.

THE PC

The IBM PC was designed to meet the basic market criteria for a personal computer:
- it had 64k memory, with extra memory available as an option
- it had a single disk drive, with an extra available as an option
- it used a standard industry microprocessor
- it was priced in the £1,500 to £2,500 bracket
- it was backed by a large advertising and promotional campaign: in 1983 IBM spent £3 million.

However there were a number of shortcomings:
1. the microprocessor was already slower than many in the market, and could not handle multi-tasking;
2. the machine was bulky and poorly designed;
3. it would not produce a colour display without expensive additions;
4. it limited the number of peripheral units that could be added to the system;
5. it was more expensive than the bulk of the competition;
6. the competition were also increasing their advertising expenditure considerably: in 1983 ICL spent £2.84 million, ACT £1 million and Commodore £0.9 million.

As a product in isolation therefore the IBM PC was limited and might have been expected to follow IBM's entry into the home computer market with the PC jnr: withdrawn from the world market after eighteen months.

WHERE WAS THE PRODUCT PLUS?

First, the microcomputer market was becoming *software* driven; purchasers were less interested in the hardware and more interested in the software applications which could be run on the particular system.

IBM published the internal architecture of the machine (the full operating layout) and:

(a)   contracted outside software houses to write programs for the machine;
(b)   developed and approved software produced by non-IBM authors;
(c)   developed software internally: by 1985 over 20,000 of IBM's 400,000 employees were involved in software development.

As a result, a vast range of application software became available for the machine; for new authors the first step was to produce for IBM, and only then to modify for other machines. Similar considerations lead to a substantial range of peripheral devices rapidly becoming available for the PC.

As a by-product it also meant the development of a new market sector – IBM-compatible machines such as Olivetti and Compaq.

Second, IBM set up a separate distribution network for the PC, and developed strict criteria for its outlets:

- they must have their own (not subcontracted) service team
- they must have experienced sales and marketing personnel
- they must have financial stability.

By 1983 there were over 150 as well as a number of IBM retail outlets.

This was essential in providing inexperienced customers with the back-up that was required for effective utilization of a new item of office equipment.

Third, the company ensured the degree of transferability of data within the IBM personal computer 'family': buyers would not be left with data that could not be moved to other machines. This proved another major element in the success of the PC.

SUCCESS?

By 1984, the IBM share of the world personal computer market had risen to 30 per cent, with a revenue of $5.5 billion.

Nevertheless, the company was still failing to develop effectively from this base. The PCAT and PCXT were both suffering from technical problems. In addition, IBM had not made any significant progress in the development of effective network systems.

Comment

IBM has the overall goal of becoming the largest company in the world by the year 2000. What constraints are likely to prevent this and how should IBM respond?

3

COPING WITH CHANGE

The first two chapters have stressed the complexity of the modern environment. The challenge for marketing within any one company is to break down and dissect the overall, intricate picture into manageable sections and there look for similarities and variations, trends and discrepancies to help it deal effectively with its own particular patch.

The process is very complex, demanding continual readjustment to market conditions. Unfortunately there is no single philosopher's stone to guarantee continued success. This year's highly successful company will often become next year's dramatic failure. For example, of the thirty-two companies identified in a popular management book in 1982 as the most effective companies in the USA, no less than fourteen had run into difficulties by 1985. Initial success is no guarantee of continued excellence; companies can only thrive by perpetual vigilance and readjustment of medium- and short-term strategies.

To illustrate the continuing importance of aligning the general characteristics of a particular market with the specific needs of a company operating in that market in a complex, rapidly changing world, we shall now look at a number of companies which experienced difficulties. The companies were all aware of the need for change – there were indicators like declining sales, alterations in the age structure of the markets, in consumer habits, and so on.

The examples given in this chapter of both large and small companies illustrate some of the continuing problems that face marketing management. In some management coped with change and developed new and successful strategies; in others they failed.

ACORN COMPUTERS

Early in 1985, after six years of meteoric growth, the UK company Acorn Computers was faced with a situation where it could not pay its bills. In 1983 the company had been valued at £135 million; the 1985 refinancing package agreed with Olivetti valued it at just below £21 million. Acorn reported an £11 million loss in the six months to December 1984 caused by stock write-downs and withdrawal from the US and West German markets.

THE BACKGROUND

The success of the company had depended heavily on the contract, won some years earlier, to supply the BBC micro: a computer on which all BBC progammes on computing and education were to be based.

The BBC has a long-standing reputation for excellence and innovaton in the development of educational material in the UK. Winning the contract to produce this computer gave Acorn ready access to a secure market. Moreover, the BBC micro proved itself worthy of the Corporation's confidence. By all accounts it was a very good product, being a comparatively powerful computer which surpassed its competitors, gaining laurels in the *Which* consumer magazine.

Even though the BBC micro was more expensive than the competition, the visibility that the computer gained through the BBC meant that it quickly came to dominate the UK educational market. The problem of price was helped by the government providing financial assistance to schools wanting to install computers.

By the end of 1984 the UK computer market had begun to show signs of saturation and volatility, and sales slumped over the Christmas period. This slump was accompanied by increasingly heavy discounting as the majority of manufacturers (with the exception of Acorn) fought to maintain market share.

For Acorn the period of the BBC contract was drawing to a close as was government funding of computers for schools. Since the government did not pursue a 'buy British' policy, competition with other manufacturers offering cheaper, and sometimes more powerful, computers had begun to increase.

Marketing had contributed nothing to the initial success of Acorn Computers. The company, however, quickly reached a stage when it became necessary to try to establish itself in markets independently of the BBC. It had been a small, fast-growing company with a staff of 470 mainly in the Cambridge area and senior managers had been anxious to make Acorn a firmly based, medium-sized company. A programme of expansion was launched.

ACORN'S STRENGTHS

1. In the year to July 1984 the company had made pre-tax profits of £10.3 million on sales of £93.1 million.
2. It had an extremely talented research and development team and its technical expertise was excellent. The BBC had won universal acclaim as a quality product.
3. It had a very strong position in the top part of the the UK home computer market – the BBC having the largest share of machines in homes above the £300 price bracket.

4. Acorn had a dominant position in the UK education and training market with over 75 per cent of the market.
5. Its computers were also well represented in government and industry research and development labs.

ACORN'S WEAKNESSES

1. Single ageing product.
2. Single highly competitive market.

ACORN'S SOLUTION

1. To develop a product for the cheaper end of the market which would run the majority of the BBC programs and would provide volume sales, the Electron.
2. To expand overseas especially in the United States.
3. To develop a computer that could compete at the bottom end of the business market.

The programme of expansion was stretching the company's financial and management resources. Acorn's problems arose because of the attempt to expand into the American market and the relative failure of the Electron in the fiercely competitive UK market. The company was also on the verge of entering the business computer market with its range of ABC machines. The UK business personal computer market is dominated by IBM and Applied Computer Techniques.

Some £7 million of the losses represented a substantial write-down of stocks and cancelled orders. This was caused when the Electron, designed as a low-cost home computer, had disappointing pre-Christmas sales. In January 1985 the company cut the cost of the Electron from £200 to £130 in a bid to stimulate sales, generate cash and reduce stocks. Stocks of the Electron were estimated to be worth about £20 million. The company also had to write down stocks of other computers made for overseas markets from which it had withdrawn.

A further £8 million represented the cost of closing Acorn's operations in the USA and West Germany and the trading losses in those two countries.

Acorn's ambitious plans to capture 10 per cent of the US educational market ran into three main problems. The more stringent technical requirements added to the cost and delayed the launch. Loss-leading by the established American companies such as Apple and IBM made the market exceptionally difficult. The USA's education authorities operated a 'buy American' policy. Securing distributors to cover the entire USA proved well nigh impossible.

ACORN REORGANIZED

The company was reorganized following the rescue by Olivetti.
1. The business sector would develop products to be sold by other companies under their own names only. This effectively acknowledged that Acorn did

not have the marketing or commercial muscle to compete with companies like IBM. Olivetti however could well sell Acorn-developed products.

2. A consumer division would aim predominantly at the top end of the home computer market where the BBC had been successful. It would avoid the lower end, dominated by games, where competition is very fierce.

3. The education and training division would aim to safeguard and expand Acorn's already strong position in this market with new machines.

4. A scientific and industrial section would try to meet the specialist needs of research and development departments.

GRAYS OF CAMBRIDGE

Grays of Cambridge (International) is a small, family owned business which has for the past 130 years manufactured bats, sticks and rackets for the world of sport. The company attempted to meet the requirements of the sports player from school to champion. It also acted as a distributor for sporting equipment manufactured by others. During the period with which we are concerned, three of the Grays family were on the company's six-member board.

THE BACKGROUND

Despite the fashion for leisure-time sport, few of the activities pursued need the traditional, hand-made, wooden products of the UK sports equipment industry. There has been a move away from a craft-based, wooden racket industry to a more industrialized process which has increased competition.

After rapid growth in the late 1970s, the overall UK market for sports equipment began to stagnate from 1980 onwards. It was worth £319 million in 1983 – a decline in real terms on the £310 million in 1980.

After a reasonably profitable 1982, when pre-tax profits were £192,000 on sales of £5.2 million, Grays plunged into a loss of £454,000 on sales of £4.9 million in 1983. The company was obliged to sell *Wisden's Cricketers' Almanack*, the bible of the sport, for £400,000 to McCorquodale, the printing and packaging group with expanding publishing interests.

PROBLEMS

Squash, cricket and hockey equipment accounted for between 60 and 70 per cent of the company's business. It also had interests in snooker, bowls and fishing tackle.

Squash is a relatively expensive sport, with most clubs charging an annual membership fee of £100 in addition to £1.50 a player for a 45-minute session. As a result of the high cost of the sport many people have given it up or are saving money on equipment.

Cheap imported rackets, mainly from Taiwan, undercut the UK manufacturers' prices. Many have responded by acting as distributors for imported equipment but this activity has lower margins while the strength of the US dollar increased the bought-in cost.

The impact of technology is also apparent at the upper end of the market. Dunlop gave up manufacturing wooden rackets and, during 1984, proceeded to dispose of its stocks at very low prices. Grays had considered the possibility of setting up its own carbon fibre production line but scrapped the idea because of the high cost. Many players, however, disliked the new carbon fibre rackets which break more easily as well as being less flexible.

Low-cost imports were also making considerable inroads into two other important areas of Grays' business: snooker which was steadily growing in popularity, and the fishing tackle market where imported products were undercutting European products by up to 40 per cent.

ACTION

Following the sale of *Wisden* the company made 74 of its work-force of 190 redundant – most of these were employed in the manufacture of rackets. A former senior partner with the management consultant Urwick Orr was recruited as chief executive and chairman of the board.

In 1984 Grays completed its move out of the fishing tackle business. It had acted as an agent for a number of outside manufacturers but found that this did not fit in with the mainstream products. Nevertheless the company continues to act as distributors for products which extend its own range. For example, it sells the Grays Merco squash ball, which is made by an Australian company.

A further series of measures was taken to rationalize the company's approach to the products sold.
1. Some Grays' equipment had been sold under the names of subsidiary companies which were hardly known outside the trade. The company took steps to ensure that eventually everything will be sold under the better known Grays name.
2. The product range was streamlined to reduce duplication. In one of the areas which has continued to prosper, a Pakistan-made hockey stick was introduced.
3. Investment in developing new products was increased to meet the changing market conditions and to improve the product range in growing market sectors.

AIRFIX

A SUCCESSFUL COMPANY

Airfix, best known for its large range of plastic model kits, began trading in the mid-1950s over a printing shop in Wandsworth. By utilizing the new plastic technology then available, the company created a new toy product which gained instant acceptance and popularity.

Initially selling a range of small kits through a limited range of outlets, turnover rapidly increased accompanied by impressive profitability: though the costs of producing the steel mould were relatively high, the raw material and manufacturing costs per kit were very low in relation to the final selling price. Once the mould had been paid for, the marginal profitability on each kit was extremely high.

Following this early success, Airfix continued to expand the range of its moulds, reacting to the fashion demands of the consumer – new kits for the model-making fanatic who naturally did not want to build the same model again. Distribution also expanded and Airfix developed a larger sales force.

COPING WITH SUCCESS

The issue then facing the company was how to capitalize on this success. The firm proceeded in a number of directions.

1. Overseas expansion. Overseas distributors were appointed for the kit range, with France, West Germany and Australia proving especially profitable.
2. Sales integration. This policy was followed through in West Germany and America where the group eventually bought out its distributors, Plasty and Ava, thereby integrating the supply and sales operations in these two countries.
3. Range extension. A steadily larger range of kits was produced in a greater and greater variety of subjects – wildlife, historical figures, space, and civil aircraft.
4. Integrative production development. The firm looked for items that could use the same plastics technology, producing a range of pre-school plastic figures, the Weebles.
5. Integrative market development. The firm moved into other toy areas. It launched a range of electric trains (GMR); introduced a range of 'action' figures (Eagles); space figures (Micronauts); developed a range of battery driven toys (Super Toys); board games; toy guns; arts and crafts (New Artist); and junior sports equipment (Sportstime). Airfix also acquired a firm producing snap-together kits (Scalecraft), a firm producing car racing kits, an interest in a firm producing dolls in Singapore, and the metal construction toy firm Meccano which also produced Dinky toys.
6. Opportunity development. Management felt that there could be a market for high quality plastic homeware and set up a new division called Airfix Plastics. This produced homeware (Crayonne) and foam plastic products (Declon). Another possible market gap in packaging was identified from which emerged Airfix Packaging Development (APD). Together these led to the establishment of a design company (Benchmark). Similar considerations led to the setting up of a shoe company (Airfix Footwear) and a firm importing quality leather from Italy (Tal Impex) and finally computers (FileTab Support Services). Group profits reached a peak of just under £5 million before tax in the year 1976/77.

In early 1981, Airfix called in the receiver, and later in that year the remaining part of the company was sold to General Mills for an undisclosed sum, believed to be in the region of £3.5 million.

WHAT WENT WRONG?

The group failed to solve many of the problems caused by each of the development routes that they had chosen.

1. Overseas expansion. Distributors were largely left to fend for themselves – the Australian operation was not visited for fifteen years even though sales were running at £500,000 per annum. When problems caused by competition occurred there was no way of counteracting them.

2. Sales integration. The acquisition of overseas distributors created a whole series of additional product ranges, and required the financing of large sales forces in a period of deep recession in the late 1970s.

3. Range extension. The increase in range meant that more and more capital was being tied up in moulds. It also meant that higher and higher inventories were becoming established – at the time of collapse, certain lines had over twenty-two years' stock. Design teams were also lagging behind market demands. Though the Spitfire had been ideal in the late 1950s, by the late 1970s demand had changed to jets. One of the final aircraft kits that the company produced was a large Focke-Wulf with a mould costing over £100,000, and with an estimated repayment period of over twenty years. Concentration of resources in these areas had also meant that the production efficiency of the factory steadily declined, as investment was not being made in this area – costs of production relative to the competition steadily increased.

4. Integration production development. This produced many of the same problems of high inventories, and high investment levels in moulds.

5. Integrative market development. This required a vast redirection of resources. Estimates of market potential proved to be wrong in major areas such as GMR and Micronauts leading to chronic overstocking (at the collapse there were 20,000 standard British Rail diesels in stock, and over £2 million stock of Micronauts at list price). Costs of tooling for the Super Toy range proved astronomical and ran into major quality control problems.

   Meccano and Dinky proved a similar major headache to the Airfix group. Antiquated production methods and bad labour relations were compounded by a continuing change in consumer taste towards plastic block toys such as Lego and low-cost die-cast toy competition from the Far East. Inventories again showed the same sorry picture with 750,000 units of one item of plastic plate (about ten years' stock) at the time of closure.

   Other developments were less expensive but did little to enhance Airfix's reputation with the toy retailers.

6. Opportunity development. Market and management difficulties bedevilled the company in this area also. The market for plastic homeware was very different from toys. This operation did not move into some form of profit until the late 1970s. Airfix Footwear depended on one major customer –

Marks and Spencer – and when the contract terminated minor losses turned into major ones. Neither packaging nor design greatly benefited the group – the use of in-house design generally increased design costs.

Comment

These case studies underline the problems facing all companies and organizations – that of handling change effectively. Some degree of failure is inevitable; due to the complexities of the business environment many decisions will be incorrect.

VOLKSWAGEN

The European car manufacturing industry is bedevilled by problems of excess capacity, intense competition, negligible profits and low growth in demand in the home markets. Demand is estimated to be growing at 1.5 per cent a year compared with 3 per cent in the 1970s. Labour costs consume an estimated 25 per cent of the European industry's revenue and it has been calculated that there would have to be a reduction of 500,000 in the European vehicle industry work-force before it can hope to compete with Japanese manufacturers' lower cost levels.

It is clear that Europe's volume car producers have been slow to adjust to changing market conditions. This is reflected in certain attitudes. European governments had tended to take the view that a national motor industry was a 'good thing', being essential to a modern economy, and a substantial part of the industry is state owned. This form of nationalism even within an increasingly integrated European common market has created a situation in which EEC car manufacturers continue to view other member countries as legitimate 'export' markets thereby intensifying competition between themselves and allowing Japanese and American manufacturers to strengthen their hold.

By contrast, Ford, General Motors and Chrysler, the three major American volume car producers, having reduced costs in their domestic markets have set about strengthening their links with Japanese manufacturers: Ford with Mazda; General Motors with Toyota, Isuzu and Suzuki; Chrysler with Mitsubishi. The Japanese manufacturers, who already sell about one million cars a year in Europe – giving them about 10 per cent of the market – have sorted out production in North America and are seeking to extend their investment in assembly plants in Europe.

THE VOLKSWAGEN STRATEGY

In 1976 Volkswagen, the West German company, faced a severe problem of declining demand both at home and abroad. Its main model, the famous Beetle, was increasingly out-competed by the more stylish introductions of other companies, often at a lower price. With market share being eroded and the company sliding into loss, it was forced to re-evaluate its product and production policy to meet the increasing worldwide competition in the car market. The company decided to invest large sums in the development of totally new ranges of small cars, which became the Golf and Polo. The Golf, though initially criticized, has since become Europe's best selling car, with strong market shares even in nationalistic markets such as France and Italy. Volkswagen has since proceeded to show that it is one of the few European car manufacturers to act on the knowledge that market changes demand an alteration in competitive strategy in an area where Japanese and American companies have already laid down some of the rules (Table 3.1).

Table 3.1.   New car market share in Western Europe 1985

Company	1985(%)	1984(%)
Volkswagen-Audi	12.9	12
Fiat	12.2	12.7
Ford	11.9	12.8
Peugeot-Citroen-Talbot	11.6	11.5
GM, Opel-Vauxhall	11.4	11.1
Renault	10.7	10.9

In the motor car industry American and Japanese companies have in effect exploited their multinational status to a much greater extent than in the past and the Volkswagen strategy is based upon a similar approach. Collaboration across countries is much easier within the single entity supplied by the multinational, giving benefits in relatively more simple decision making, in product development, and maximizing the benefits of economies of scale. Components for example can be exported to Europe from the rest of the world but still on an in-house basis.

To provide greater flexibility and room for manoeuvre in the competitive European market, Volkswagen has for some time recognized the importance of its operations in Brazil and the USA, and its links with Nissan in Japan which is building about 25,000 of the VW Santana under licence, mainly for sale in Japan.

For many years Volkswagen has used Latin America as a source of components – engines similar to those produced at Saltzgitter have been made over the past twenty years by the Brazilian VW company; and by a Mexican subsidiary for ten. The company has therefore acquired experience in the exchange of components as well as becoming involved in the export of cars from Brazil to Mexico, and is also one of the top two exporters of cars from Brazil to the Middle East. The Latin American operation, with much lower production costs than West Germany's, allows Volkswagen to compete more effectively with the Japanese in a number of markets, and there are plans to extend the strategy further with the agreement to produce the Santana in China.

Volkswagen has also been expanding its production base in Europe. In 1980 Fiat of Italy ended its thirty-year links with Seat, the Spanish state-owned group. VW began by providing technical expertise and help in enabling the Spanish company to set up its own European distribution system. In return, Seat offers

VW cars through its own distribution network in Spain, thereby helping to push up the VW's market share from 0.5 per cent in 1982 to around 5 per cent. Seat is also manufacturing VW Polos, Santana and Passat models under licence. In 1986 Volkswagen announced the agreement of the Spanish government for its eventual purchase of the Seat operation.

The company's operations in the USA have not been without difficulties but Volkswagen is determined to maintain a manufacturing presence there in order to keep its future options open. Thus, a substantial fall in the value of the dollar would make West German cars too expensive and increased protectionism would affect car imports from Europe. The company's plant in Westmoreland, Pennsylvania, began to assemble versions of the Golf in 1978 in an effort to help boost VW's share of the American car market to 5 per cent by 1985. Instead, sales of products plummeted from 177,000 to 74,000 in 1984. The company subsequently sold off to Chrysler a second assembly plant built in the hope of a VW sales boom in the USA. Sales of imported VW cars, however, increased in 1984 from 77,000 to 103,000 and those of the up-market Audis went from 48,000 to 71,000.

As part of its long-term strategy, Volkswagen has separated the Audi operations giving the Audi management the job of developing an up-market sporty image, this being one of the market niches which motor car companies like Mercedes, BMW and Volvo have found profitable. The benefits of this strategy can be seen in the highly profitable US market where Audi outsold BMW for the first time in 1984, and are rapidly overhauling Mercedes, leaving only Volvo ahead of them. Audi already sells four times more cars in the US than Jaguar.

SALES IN 1985

World car sales reached 31.89 million in 1985 of which six markets – the USA, West Germany, Japan, the UK, France, Italy – accounted for more than 68 per cent of the total (Table 3.2).

Table 3.2.   Volkswagen in six countries 1985 (combined Audi/VW)

Country	Total market	VW sales	VW (%)
USA	11,042,658	214,566	1.94
West Germany	2,379,261	679,987	28.60
Japan	3,104,146	18,378	0.59
UK	1,832,408	103,877	5.67
Italy	1,748,303	142,236	8.5
France	1,766,661	111,508	6.3

DEFINING STRATEGY

Once the limitations of strategy have been determined the company is able to create a series of broad objectives or goals.

SETTING OBJECTIVES

Broad objectives are usually statements dealing with a number of areas.
1. Market position – ABC Ltd sees its future in the vehicle component manufacture market.
2. Competitive position – ABC Ltd will be number 3 in the industry for the foreseeable future.
3. Profitability objectives – ABC Ltd has a target of reaching a 25 per cent return on capital employed.
4. Research and development objectives – ABC Ltd is aiming to continue to invest 5 per cent of turnover in the development of profitable new products.
5. Personnel objectives – ABC Ltd aims to maintain full employment.

Once these objectives have been formulated the company is faced with the more detailed task of evaluating its current position and determining where future direction is required to meet the long-term goals.

EXAMINING THE OPTIONS

Different areas within the organization will often demand different forms of action. These are the four main investment options.
1. Growth – the continued investment into areas of the business.
2. Maintenance – holding on to a current business position.
3. Disinvestment – withdrawing from a business operation.
4. Denuding – removing assets from one part of the business to support another.

In order to make the assessment of business opportunities easier, many major companies divide the operating units either into *profit centres* or *strategic business units* (SBUs) so that the specific needs of each unit can be accurately determined.

The division of an organization into these units can however be artificial, creating anomalies in planning especially where common overheads are shared. This is an issue discussed at greater length in Chapter 9.

INTEGRATION AND STRATEGIC PLANNING

A crucial goal of the strategic plan is to integrate both the overall goals of the company and the detailed issues that will need to be addressed in the marketing mix.

Any strategic change must take account of certain issues.

1. Production – for example, the degree of integration of the manufacturing process, the sophistication of technology required, and so on.
2. Research and development – the level of research and development that will be required for a particular developmental path.
3. Personnel numbers and training.
4. Finance – the costs of carrying out a particular strategy are often ignored: yet it is a major factor in new product failure discussed in Chapter 8.
5. Marketing mix issues – price, credit, distribution, promotion – will all need to be considered.
6. Other environmental issues – political and legislative factors – will also need to be considered.

Many of these issues are obviously included among those considered in the examination of external and internal limitations on strategy, but it is essential that the company continues to be aware of the implications of its changing role in particular business areas.

General Motors has since 1983 been disinvesting from its UK Bedford plant at Luton. The political problems that this may cause would have to be considered as part of the overall strategy.

STRATEGIC PLANNING TECHNIQUES

A number of analytical techniques are available for the company to define more accurately the problems and opportunities that confront it.

These techniques can be either applied on a product by a product basis, by profit centre, or to the company overall. They include:

- SWOT analysis
- PLC analysis
- product viability
- portfolio analysis
- ROCE/Risk analysis.

SWOT ANALYSIS

The SWOT analysis (short for Strengths, Weaknesses, Opportunities and Threats) provides a logical framework for an overview of major factors that affect the operating unit.

As a rule of thumb strengths and weaknesses apply to the internal structure of the company, opportunities and threats to the external environment.

Taking a hypothetical perfume company as an example, let us analyse its situation using SWOT analysis.

1. Strengths:
   - old-established and fairly large perfume company
   - subsidiary of major company
   - reputation for reliable and good quality products
   - own specialized sales force effectively controlling distribution
   - high promotional expenditure
   - good trade relations.
2. Weaknesses:
   - weak in certain product areas such as the skin care market
   - a staid consumer image
   - poor product development and lack of new product successes.
3. Opportunities:
   - men's market
   - children's market
   - skin care market
   - changing pattern of consumer demand for more floral fragrance.
4. Threats:
   - competitors' new product development
   - price cutting
   - recession
   - poor internal communication between sales and marketing departments.

Although the SWOT analysis is valuable it does little to quantify the nature of product change and how rapidly it is occurring. The first attempt to so do was the development of the product life cycle concept. When the activities of the vast majority of companies are examined over time it can be seen that original business areas no longer yield the same proportion of profit. Here are some examples that make this plain.

IBM orginally made all its money from typewriters and adding machines: by 1980 the vast majority of its income was coming from mainframe computers.

Unilever originally made most of its money from soap and some from margarine; by the 1980s soap had been replaced by food products as the main income generator.

ICI has moved from the production of bulk chemicals and industrial raw materials such as synthetic fibres into areas including pharmaceuticals and specialist plastics.

Bass originally made the bulk of its profits from beer. Recently wine, lager, and food have become more and more important income sources.

Firms that have failed to learn the lessons of reassessing their products and adjusting to change over time either have been taken over or have steadily faded from the industrial scene. There are many illustrations of this.

British Leyland failed to take account of the increasingly sophisticated, competitive products available in the car market.

Gestetner, once a dominant force in office copying, failed to appreciate the impact of photocopying.

Massey Ferguson failed to understand the changing nature of the farm equipment market.

For many years Woolworths did not realize that the concept of the variety store was out of date for the high street.

PRODUCT LIFE CYCLE

Even when one considers those companies successfully surviving in one field, such as mineral exploration or oil-refining, closer inspection will reveal that they are often involved in activities significantly different from those of ten years ago.

This picture of continual change in products is further developed by surveys showing that the majority of firms depend on recently introduced products for a substantial part of their profitability (Figure 4.1).

Figure 4.1. *Importance of new products to both consumer and industrial companies – typical turnover patterns*

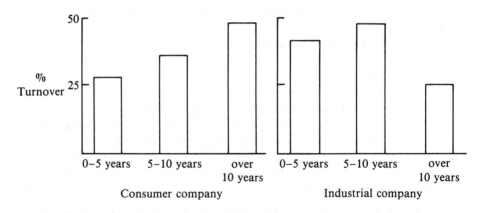

In more affluent markets like Japan this trend is accelerating with a higher and higher proportion of turnover coming from new products.

The apparent growth and decay of products exemplified in company experience led to the development of the theory known as the product life cycle or PLC. This states that products go through a period of introduction growth and maturity followed by a period of decline (Figure 4.2).

The limitations of PLC can be seen in the substantial list of items that are still there on the grocery shelves after fifty or more years – Kit-Kat, Smarties, Black

Magic, Aero, and Mars are all examples from the highly competitive confectionery market.

Figure 4.2.   The classic product life cycle

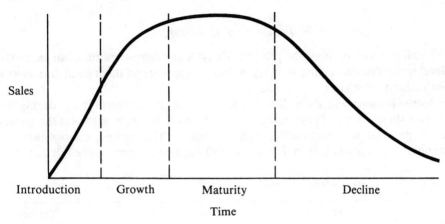

Critics claim that similar products will show entirely different growth patterns which means that the product life cycle concept is useless as a method of *prediction*. The test of a scientific hypothesis is that the outcome of a given set of experimental conditions is always repeatable; no such claim has ever been made of the product life cycle theory. Distinctions should also be made between product fields – chocolate bars – and brands, like Cadbury's Dairy Milk, which may show different patterns. Concentration on the product life cycle as a method of strategic analysis can also lead to a fatalistic acceptance of defeat. The reasoning would be that since the product is old it must be on the verge of retirement. This attitude may in turn lead to the elimination of support for a product at the time that it is required, thereby accelerating the decline of the product.

Some writers have also blamed the PLC idea for the high level of new product failure that has occurred in consumer goods since the 1960s, as it has led to an

Figure 4.3.   Other possible life cycle patterns

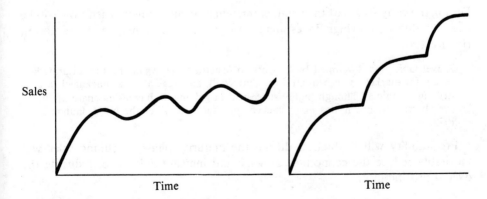

over-concentration on new product development rather than continuing detailed
support of the current range. This is especially true when the product can either
recycle (show continuing growth after a period of decline) or show growth in a
step-by-step fashion (Figure 4.3).

Products and resources

With all its shortcomings, the product life cycle can remain useful as an aid to the
development of marketing strategy by providing a broad theoretical framework
for planning purposes.

As the product will show different levels of return to the company during the
various stages of the life cycle, the way in which the company allocates the money
at its disposal will necessarily need to change. The various factors that are
involved are summarized in Table 4.1, and each component is then discussed.

Table 4.1. Components in the product life cycle

	Introduction	Growth	Maturity	Decline
Sales	Low	Increasing	Slower	Dropping
Profits	Minus	Maximum	Dropping	Low
Buyers	Innovators	Early adopters	Majority	Laggards
Competition	Few	Increasing	Many	Fewer
Price	Low	Higher	Highest	Reduced
Product	Basic	Improved	Extended	Reduced
Ad. spend (%)	High	Lower	Lowest	Low
Promotion	Brand awareness	Preference	Loyalty	Various
Distribution	Limited	Expanded	Maximum	Reducing

Sales

During the introduction phase sales will inevitably be most limited, peaking in the
maturity phase.

Profits

During the early stages of the product introduction and growth, cash flow will be
negative due to the high investment costs in new machinery and promotion
(Figure 4.4).

> St Ivel Gold was developed by Unigate to penetrate the expanding low saturated
> yellow fat market, with a mixture of buttermilk and vegetable fat packaged in a
> striking container. Though highly successful in gaining an increasing share of the
> overall market, profit was not achieved for four years after the initial launch in
> 1979.

Profitability will be highest during the maturity phase; declining sales will
inevitably reduce the economies of scale and increase unit price, reducing the
overall profitability.

Figure 4.4. Investment and the PLC

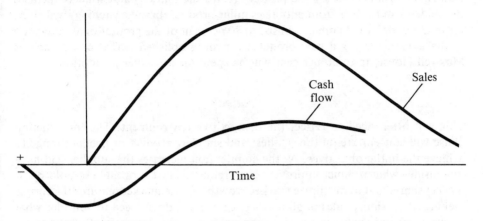

Buyers

Several authors consider that the buying population can be divided into those that are highly experimental (innovators); those who are more cautious but still regard themselves as opinion leaders (early adopters); and the remainder. In common with many models of consumer behaviour this idea cannot be quantified or applied in any systematic form. It does suggest that early advertising might be more effective if it concentrated on the novelty, encouraging the innovators to try it; there does not however appear to be any evidence to support this view.

Competition

Depending on the technical complexity of the product and whether a patent can be obtained, the manufacturer will have a varying length of time before competition appears. If the market is growing rapidly many other manufacturers will be tempted in and competition will become steadily more severe. As the market decreases in importance, those suppliers with small market shares and unprofitable brands are likely to withdraw from the market.

> The pot noodle market was developed and initially dominated by Golden Wonder. As sales grew to £70 million, many other food manufacturers entered with a dazzling range of varieties. The rapid market growth was followed by an equally sharp decline. As the overall market slumped to £30 million many of the initial competitive firms decided to withdraw their products.

Price

Manufacturers will tend to use low prices initially to encourage trial, and spend heavily on advertising and free samples. As the product becomes established prices will rise, promotion will decline as a percentage – though for some consumer products it will be important to maintain sales in established markets by the use of promotional methods such as coupons or discounts.

As a product becomes established, the balance between what is spent to persuade consumers to try the product (enter the market) and what is spent to persuade them to shift from another similar product (brand switching) will alter. General Foods, for example, will spend 80 per cent of the promotional budget on media advertising for a new product; for an established coffee brand such as Maxwell House up to 50 per cent will be spent on consumer promotion.

Product

This will often need to reflect the competitive environment. The introduction phase will concentrate on the smallest and simplest product or product range to achieve the initial objectives. As the competition increases the supplier will have to consider what product improvements are necessary to continue to hold on to market share, and to maximize market growth. As the market matures the firm is seeking to maximize sales in all market segments and will need to consider what range extensions could meet a wider consumer demand. Increasing the number of variants will mean higher inventories, and higher per unit production costs. In consequence, as the market declines there will be a tendency to reduce the number of variants on offer to try to improve unit profitability.

> Sony with its Walkman range has responded to increasing competition by introducing variants such as Jogger Walkman as the market for personal stereo sets began to mature.

Advertising as a percentage of expenditure

This will be highest during the introduction phase when volumes are low and expenditures are high. The percentage will steadily decrease as volumes grow during the maturity phase, and start to rise again as the market sales volume reduces.

Promotional techniques

During the introduction phase the company will be trying to achieve trial. Emphasis will need to be placed on increasing the awareness of the product. As competition increases, the demands of building brand loyalty will become more and more acute.

Distribution

Gaining distribution will be crucial during the early stages of a product's introduction. Once it becomes established more and more intermediaries will tend to stock it to ensure that the service they offer end users is not bettered by any other organization. As the sales volume drops this pressure will be removed and the company will have to spend increasingly on maintaining the distribution of the product.

The actual type of curve seen is crucial for decision-making in many industries.

For example, the product curve typically found in the clothing, entertainment, publishing, perfumery, toy and allied industries shows a different pattern from the classic product life cycle curve (Figure 4.5).

Figure 4.5. A 'fashion' or 'fad' sales curve

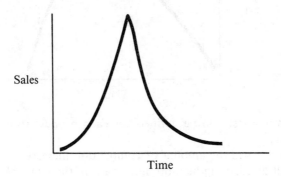

This is the 'fashion' curve and different strategies will need to be applied. For example, as the return on investment will need to be more rapid, initial pricing will be high. A substantial initial investment in advertising will be required to gain a rapid return on the investment.

> The Sinclair ZX-1 with 1k of memory was introduced in the early 1980s with a mail order price of over £100. By 1985 the Sinclair 125 with 48k was being sold at discount for well under £80.

In cases like the Sinclair example, the product must be made available in a single complete form. Because of the short time involved, there will be little point in wide-scale product differentiation.

The issues of investment levels, pricing and speed of growth, will demand that company management consider the implications at each stage of the product's evolution. Will investment in advertising at a certain stage speed up the growth of the product? How should the product be altered or extended as the market develops? The decision will depend on the overall company strategy and the industry in which it operates. Each solution will demand that resources be allocated in a particular direction, and not in others.

PRODUCT VIABILITY

In defining future trends within the product range it is more useful for the company to consider factors that might reduce the sale of the product in the short, medium and long term.

Take the sales of Carlsberg beer in Nigeria (Figure 4.6).

Any manager would be foolish in deciding that the product showed a typical product life cycle: the reason for the decline is much simpler. Shortage of foreign exchange in Nigeria meant that imported products were no longer freely available.

Figure 4.6.   Carlsberg in Nigeria – a PLC fallacy

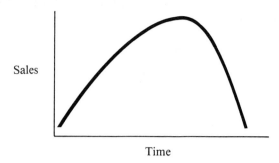

Factors such as these can be defined for each product to consider issues of product viability.
1. Competition – will the amount of competition increase?
2. Price – will discounting be more important in the market?
3. Economic – will demand be maintained?
4. Packaging – will the packaging be increasingly outdated?
5. Technology – will the product lose its technical edge?

This approach can be allied to the forecasting techniques discussed in Chapter 7 to produce a grid system as in Table 4.2.

Table 4.2.   Viability framework

Factor	Short term	Medium term	Long term
Economic		/	///
Technology	/	///	///
Price	//	/	
Competition	/	//	//
Packaging	///	///	///

/   = slight competitive problem
/// = severe competitive problem

The use of a viability framework concentrates the attention on future rather than past events. It suggests that management should attempt to anticipate rather than merely react to changes in the environment.

Candle manufacturers, for example, have faced a considerable decline in sales due to the introduction of electric light. Continual product modifications into ornamental, gift and other areas have enabled many to continue to survive.

PORTFOLIO ANALYSIS

Another strategic planning approach is to separate products into groups, and define the attention each should receive. At an elementary level such portfolio analysis might be rather like Table 4.3.

Table 4.3. Portfolio analysis

Product	Revenue	Position	Prospects
A	£5.0 million	Leader for 3 years	Good but better with support
B	£6.5 million	Number 3 – losing share	Moderate – can hold position
C	£2.5 million	Poor – 8 years' nil growth	Decline will continue

This method of dividing products can be continued until a substantial list is developed and calls for further classification. One system of classification may appear like this:

- today's breadwinners
- tomorrow's breadwinners
- yesterday's breadwinners
- failures
- repair jobs
- management madnesses.

Division in this fashion creates problems in the objective identification of individual products' strengths and weaknesses, as such an approach depends on a subjective evaluation of performance. The first approach to an objective assessment of SBU performance was developed by the Boston Consulting Group. The BCG matrix considers two criteria – the current relative market share, and the growth rate of the particular product. It separates products into four areas.

1. 'Stars' – high growth rates and high relative market shares.
2. 'Question marks' – high growth rates but low relative market shares.
3. 'Cash cows' – high market shares but low growth rates.
4. 'Dogs' – low growth rates and low market shares (Figure 4.7).

Figure 4.7. Boston Consulting Group market share analysis

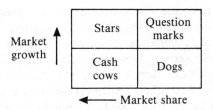

Cash cows can be identified as those providing large positive cash flows. Long-established cash cows also benefit from low production costs, reaping the advantages of the experience or learning curve mentioned in Chapter 9.

Stars are those products that will become the cash cows of later years, but are currently unlikely to be generating a high level of revenue due to the high level of investment required to expand the product. Organizations should attempt to maintain the progress of stars within the market as return on capital employed tends to increase both with the level of brand share, and with the level of investment.

Question marks are those products that are also not generating profit and, because of their poor market position, are unlikely ever to be profitable. These are often second or third brands introduced into the market. They pose a serious problem with respect to the allocation of resources.

Lastly, dogs are old-established products that are not developing in any positive fashion. They are likely to be generating low level profit, but may consume valuable management time. Should they comprise substantial volume, reasonable growth opportunities, reasonable market share and a *clearly* identifiable problem, alterations in the marketing mix will prove rewarding, otherwise the organization will need to consider the implications of phasing the product out of the portfolio.

Let us consider how a portfolio analysis might be applied to a frozen food firm.

- Cash cows   Fish fingers
                     Beefburgers
                     Peas
                     Beans
                     Ice cream
                     Sponge cake
- Dogs   Sweet corn
                     Frozen chips
                     Cauliflower
                     Fish in sauce
                     Steaklets
                     Ready meals
                     Cheesecake
- Stars   Mini-roasts
                     Speciality ice cream
- Question marks   Ethnic food

The firm will have to decide how to allocate the resources necessary to maintain or further develop products within different categories. It may, for example, decide that it is crucial to underline the quality of the beans and peas to prevent own-brand competition turning these products from cash cows to dogs. Using this form of analysis, the firm can consider the economic aspects of its development policy, and the likely return on different options.

The BCG portfolio has been criticized on a number of grounds. First, it totally ignores the problem of new product development. Second, markets with high growth rates are far less common in the recession driven 1980s than in the 1960s. Third, equating high market share with large positive cash flows may not be entirely accurate.

Further grid approaches have been evolved based on other criteria. One developed by the General Electric Corporation in the United States compares market strength with market attractiveness on a product or product group basis (Table 4.4).

Table 4.4. The GEC approach

Industry attractiveness	Business position
Market size	Size
Growth	Growth
Diversity	Market share
Competitive intensity	Position
Industry profitability	Profit margin
Technical content	Price position
Likely inflation	Quality
Social/Environment	Technical edge
Legal/Human	Market knowledge
	Image

The criterion used is return on capital employed, unlike the market growth/market share model which is based on cash flow. Different business units will fall into different areas (Figure 4.8).

Figure 4.8. GEC portfolio

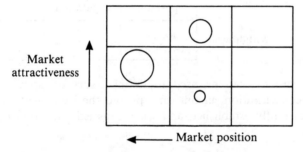

The model suggests that if the business unit falls into squares 1–3 the company should invest in it and build further on the position. Should the business unit fall into squares 4–6 the aim should be to hold position and improve cost-effectiveness. Should the business unit fall into squares 7–9 the policy decision should be either to harvest or divest. The GEC matrix's strength is that it is able to define more accurately the strategies that should be followed in each segment (Figure 4.9).

Figure 4.9. GEC portfolio and strategic options

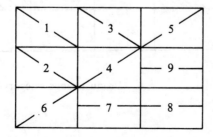

The GEC analysis still fails to cope effectively with new product introductions and this has led to the development of further matrices which attempt to define ideal positions for company profit, growth in relation to competitive position, and stage of the product life cycle (Figure 4.10).

Figure 4.10. Strategic options and market position

Market stage	Market share:	High	Average	Low
	Introduction	Maximize share	Selective action	Differentiate
	Growth	Maintain share	Selective action	Concentrate on segments
	Maturity	Maintain share	Niche	Phased withdrawal
	Decline	Hold position	Phased withdrawal	
	Withdrawal	Reduce overheads		

Other grid systems can be used to define issues of price, product type, geographical concentration, income groups and the like, identifying where the company is currently established and what gaps exist for future development (Figure 4.11).

Figure 4.11. Typical customer/product grid analysis

Family income category
1
2
3
4
1
2
3
4
5
Product range category

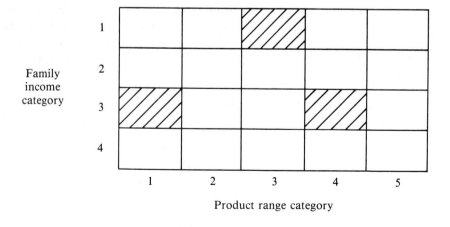

Information to provide these analyses will often be difficult and expensive to obtain, and only valuable to the larger company within a major market. All strategic models have a number of shortcomings – there is no single solution to any particular problem. The use of such models by both large and small firms does however, even at a rough and ready level, provide the firm with a method of defining its current products in relation to the marketing strategy.

RETURN ON CAPITAL EMPLOYED/RISK

A major shortcoming of the strategic models already discussed is that they fail to consider the need for evaluating the risk element in the investment process. Companies need to develop some method of measuring the likely risk of a particular project against the level of likely return.

Most companies use return on capital employed (ROCE) as one of the methods by which projects can be compared. The planned return on capital employed for each project is measured against the probability that this will be achieved. Combining the two will give a measure of the risk/return ratio to the company.

For example, a company might be making 20 per cent return on capital in its current operation, and consider that it would have a 95 per cent chance of continuing to achieve this level of return. In contrast, a totally new area of business might yield prospective returns of 25 and 32 per cent, but in each case with a corresponding lower probability of success (Table 4.5).

Table 4.5.   ROCE/risk compared

Business area	ROCE	Probability	Return
1	20%	90%	18%
2	25%	80%	20%
3	32%	60%	19%

The probabilistic return, that is the likely rate of return multiplied by the probability of achieving it, will be greatest in business area 2. This presents the best option for the company, on the assumptions on which the probability is assessed.

Any marketing plan will need therefore to consider closely the level of risk associated with new developments and weight the product decisions accordingly.

In general terms, as the company moves away from its main area of expertise, the greater the risk and the need for higher levels of return. This is commented on again in Chapter 8.

The Imperial Group, with major interests in tobacco (Players), food (Ross) and brewing (Courage), saw an opportunity to expand into catering in the United States, which appeared to meet all its strategic goals. Purchasing the Howard Johnson chain for $610 million was, however, a major mistake; the subsidiary continued to lose money and had to be sold in 1985 for around $350 million.

Summary

Strategy involves investment decisions; where the company should move money to meet its long-term goals and objectives. The company must be aware of the implications of the strategic decisions that it takes, and the techniques which it can use to define the direction in which it should go.

ASSIGNMENTS

1. Your company is thinking about entering the sports good market. Write a memo on the problems of the PLC with reference to the trends shown by skateboards, roller-skates and windsurfing boards.
2. You are working with a nuts and bolts manufacturer with over 500 products. Outline how portfolio analysis could help your company in defining the direction it should follow and the problems that might be encountered.
3. Choose a store on the high street and prepare a SWOT analysis for a possible competitor.
4. You are working in government and are asked to apply strategic models to the main sectors of the British economy to help the direction of government investment in industry. Prepare a report on this approach.

NICHOLAS INTERNATIONAL

Nicholas International, an Australian based company employed 2,750 people by 1982. Though operating in 63 countries, the United Kingdom market represented 35 per cent of the A$158 million turnover.

In the UK the company had interests in three areas:
1. home medicines   36 per cent of turnover;
2. toiletries   45 per cent of turnover;
3. prescription medicines 18 per cent of turnover.

NICHOLAS' MEDICINES AND TOILETRIES

Since most of Nicholas International's turnover and profit came from home medicines and toiletries, the case study will concentrate on issues in these areas in outlining how strategic analytical techniques can be used by a company to define the best direction for development. These are the products, by brand and market sector.

1. Home medicines

Rennie	oral antacid
Aspro regular	oral analgesic
Aspro clear	oral analgesic
Feminax	oral analgesic
Kwells	oral antiemetic

Interdens sticks	dental sticks
Interdens brushes	toothbrushes

2. Toiletries

Radox salts	bath salts
Radox herbal bath	bath foam
Radox showerfresh	shower additives
Matey	children's bath additives

Home medicines

Rennie. Rennie was launched in the UK over 50 years ago, and holds 40 per cent of the UK market for antacid products, valued at around £18 million (1981 retail prices).

The market has remained static over the last five years with the four subsectors of the market: tablets, liquids, powder, and effervescent, showing little change. The main competition was Settlers which had 12 per cent of the market by 1981.

Aspro regular. This brand was launched 60 years ago as the first branded analgesic to be sold outside the chemist. Though the overall market for analgesics was showing slight growth the insoluble aspirin segment was steadily declining in importance (Table 4.6).

Table 4.6. The analgesic market 1980–85

Market segment	Market share	
	1980	1985
Insoluble aspirin	38%	27%
Soluble aspirin	22%	29%
Paracetamol	38%	40%
Others	2%	4%

Though total volume sales for insoluble aspirin had declined around 20 per cent between 1976 and 1980, sales of Aspro regular had declined much more severely than those of the competition: by 1980 Anadin and Phensic had a 3 per cent market share of the total analgesic market or 11.5 per cent of the insoluble aspirin segment.

Aspro clear. Aspro clear, launched in 1976, had made impressive progress in a growing sector of the market, though still far behind the market leader Disprin. The latter accounted for 18 per cent of all analgesic sales in 1980, compared with the 4 per cent for Aspro clear.

Feminax. Feminax, launched in the 1970s, holds a dominant position in the dysmenorrhea or period pain segment of the analgesic market with an 80 per cent share, growing at 21 per cent per annum though it still remains small in total volume in comparison with the other analgesic sectors.

Kwells. The market for antiemetic drugs has been slowly declining at around 3 per cent per annum over the last ten years. The design of Channel ferries has improved and people are more accustomed to travel. In addition, ventilation in car, coach, and train has also improved.

Kwells, with a 40 per cent market share, suffers from this decline like other similar products in ther market.

Interdens sticks. Interdens sticks are wood products coated with antiseptic to improve gum circulation and remove plaque. Though the market is very small, it appears to be growing rapidly at around 15 per cent per annum with large-scale support from the emphasis placed on the product by the dental profession. Though Interdens sticks were market leaders with 40 per cent of the market, both Boots and Gillette had introduced competitive products.

Interdens brushes. Manufactured by a third party, brush sales have never made much impact on a large but slowly growing market dominated by such brands as Wisdom and Addis. The Interdens brand share is around 2 per cent.

Toiletries

Radox salts. The overall market for bath salts in the UK has been declining steadily by 8 per cent per annum. Radox, one of the earliest products, appeared in the UK market during the 1930s and still has a 40 per cent market share of this declining sector.

Radox herbal bath. The bubble bath market, by contrast, grew in volume terms by 30 per cent between 1976 and 1981. The competition in the market has led to a considerble proliferation of own brands, particularly Boots and the supermarket chains. As a result, although in 1971 the Radox herbal bath was one of the earliest products in the market, its share has been steadily eroded: from the bottom by the own brands and from the top by brands such as Badedas and range extensions of perfumes.

Radox showerfresh. Showerfresh was launched in 1975 as a shower gel product. The market growth in this sector has been considerably held back by the effects of the recession. Although the product holds 70 per cent of the total market it still remains a very small sector, representing less than 3 per cent of the bubble bath market in volume terms.

Matey. The launch of Matey in 1974 practically created the children's bubble bath market. Volume continues to climb at around 10 per cent per annum and now has reached 10 per cent of the adult volume at around three million litres. The market share for Matey has continued to be held at around 40 per cent.

Comment

This case explores the strategic issues that Nicholas faces, and how the various strategic models can be used to clarify the planning required.

HALL THERMOTANK INTERNATIONAL LTD

BACKGROUND

In the late 1970s HTI, a part of the industrial holding company APV, employed 1,200 people at its Dartford site in the production of specialist and custom-built refrigeration equipment for two markets: brewing and ships. Another 250 staff were employed overseas in various locations.

For the industry the technology employed was fairly sophisticated with increasing use of electronic controls. Central to the product range was a variety of compressors which provided the pumping for all systems.

The two markets, traditionally fairly stable, had both been experiencing difficulties.

By the late 1970s the brewing industry was experiencing a flattening of demand partly as a result of the recession but also in response to a slow consumer switch to wine. Beer consumption, which had risen annually by around 3 per cent between 1973 and 1978, showed no growth in 1979 and fell by 4 per cent in both 1980 and 1981. In 1984 consumption had fallen below the 1973 figure of 62,600,000 hl.

Overseas debt problems in the main African markets such as Nigeria were causing delay in the placing of new orders and concern about payment.

As a result of the worldwide glut of ships, the steadily increasing size of those that were constructed caused by the movement towards containerization and bulk tankers, and the declining competitiveness of British shipyards, the amount of marine work had dropped steadily since the early 1970s. The prospect of reduced naval construction would probably further reduce the prospects for the marine division of HTI.

Historically the industry had shown both poor profit margins on sales and bad return on capital employed. Whereas the average profit margin of the industry had remained at 6 per cent from 1975 to 1981, HTI had dropped from 4 to 1 per cent, with a similar poor showing against the 8 per cent average return on capital employed (down from 13 to 2 per cent).

Energy control was increasingly identified by companies as having an important influence on profitability. Over 5,000 companies now have full-time energy managers and energy demand in industry had declined 10 per cent between 1980 and 1983, in agriculture by 19 per cent, and in public buildings by 7 per cent.

Company objectives

These were perceived to be the development of profitable alternative activities in the refrigeration or air-conditioning market within which the company was identified as having sufficient skills to build up a strong market presence.

THE MARKET SECTORS

Four fairly clearly defined market sectors existed in the late 1970s with one future prospective area.

1. The refrigeration market (Table 4.7).
2. The air-conditioning market (Table 4.8).
3. Space-heating market (Table 4.9).
4. Ventilating market (Table 4.9).
5. Heat recovery (Table 4.10).

The refrigeration market

Table 4.7. The refrigeration market

Year	1975	1976	1977	1978	1979	1980	1985 (projection)
£ million	211	225	236	217	208	169	187

The market was largely dominated by the demands of the big food retailers, which had increasing buying power. The market had shown a steady growth in the percentage of imports, and was highly competitive both in relation to the sale of standard units and to the provision of maintenance contracts, which required a substantial availability of local engineers to provide the necessary level of service.

The air-conditioning market

Table 4.8. The air-conditioning market (£ million)

	1975	1977	1979
Industrial	36	35	33
Commercial	93	80	86
Domestic	1	1	2

There had been a steady increase in the sale of room or packaged units compared with large central plants. Rising energy prices were acting as a major restriction to future growth, as was the shortage of skilled maintenance engineers to service the equipment.

Heating and ventilating market

Table 4.9. The heating and ventilating market

Year	1975	1976	1977	1978	1979	1980	1985 (projection)
Heating (£ million)	283	265	284	321	352	298	331
Ventilation (£ million)	119	123	136	147	131	132	161

The contracting industry is dominated by a few firms that can sell complete systems such as Haden Young and the How Group and the subsidiaries of UK companies whose interests lie outside the heating and ventilating market such as GKN. The industry is highly fragmented in the component area which includes compressors and ducting with several hundred small contractors. Profit margins were traditionally often under 2 per cent.

Government cut-backs would also mean that major construction projects would be reduced in the 1980s.

Heat recovery

Table 4.10. The heat recovery market (£ million)

Year	1975	1977	1979
	2	4	6

With over 3,000,000 units installed in the United States, at 30,000 the installations within the EEC remain a small figure in proportion. The heat pump is perceived to offer energy control in a number of areas: pre-heating with full air recirculation, warm air heating, cooling resulting from heat gains from people, controlled rate of fresh air change. Central to any system would be the use of a variable speed compressor, microprocessor controlled to ensure minimum energy input and maximum output.

In addition to the commercial development, the replacement of domestic boilers with air to water heat pumps may be an important part of the potential for heat pump development.

PART 2

DEFINING MARKETING OPPORTUNITIES

SEGMENTATION: IMPLEMENTING THE STRATEGY

Occam's Razor: Abstractions must not be multiplied beyond necessity.

THE IMPORTANCE OF SEGMENTATION

In a coral reef the high level of environmental stability supports an enormous species diversity; in order to compete and survive each individual species must become more and more specialized and occupy a niche or area of the environment that no other species is as well equipped to exploit.

In the increasingly competitive, industrialized business world, similar processes mean that more emphasis has to be placed on the splitting up or segmenting of overall markets into areas of specialization that the firm can occupy more effectively than the competition. Accurately defining the market and market demand is therefore crucial in order to improve the firm's competitive advantage.

Manufacturers and suppliers of services must be able to define:
(a)   the exact part of the market from which demand is likely to come;
(b)   the way in which individuals in that market sector are likely to react;
(c)   the combination of factors, the marketing mix, that are most likely to appeal to them.

In common with the inhabitants of the coral reef, the manufacturer or service provider has to decide whether it will totally specialize – a market niche strategy; occupy a number of areas within the market – a multiple niche strategy; or produce mass market products (Figure 5.1).

The decision that the company takes will depend on the market conditions under which it is operating, where it stands in relation to the competition, and the stage of the growth or decline of the market.

Police forces were the first to recognize the essential differences between

Figure 5.1. Different forms of segmentation

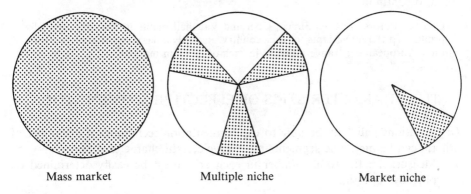

Mass market   Multiple niche   Market niche

individuals by introducing fingerprints as an international means of identification; retinal patterns within the eye also appear to show personal variations. At the other extreme all humanity needs a certain quantity of water every day to survive. Between the totally individualistic and the totally general lie an enormous number of demand patterns. By defining these demand patterns the company can determine *what product* is demanded by *what people*, and *why it will be bought.*

Naturally there will always be a conflict between the demands of manufacture which will be to turn out the same product in as high a volume as possible, and the demands of the individual consumer which may be as varied as their fingerprints. Achieving a balance between these two conflicting demands will be very important. It will ensure that the company can:

(a) achieve sufficient economies of scale to produce a profitable product;
(b) prevent any competitor entering the market with a product that is more satisfactory to a large number of its current consumers.

Increasing affluence in the majority of Western markets has meant that the divisions within the market generally continue to proliferate. Take for example flour. In a developing country flour will be a basic commodity produced from one standard grain; in the wealthy West we are offered plain flour, self raising flour, wholemeal flour, cornflour, stone ground flour and so on.

In many sectors, however, the increasing costs of manufacturing investment are tending to decrease the willingness of companies to offer a wide number of variants for each particular market; instead there are pressures for standardization even on a worldwide basis: a process known as *globalization.* Though each market sector may be different and have different demands, it may be that these individual preferences will be forgone if the product is sufficiently attractive in broad terms and very competitively priced. There will be a pay-off between specific individualistic consumer preferences and the price advantages of high volume production.

The process of globalization is already far advanced in aircraft, computers, drugs, cars, trucks, and construction equipment; far less developed in food and clothing. How far this globalization process will continue is unknown but as the world economy becomes increasingly interdependent the tendency will be for the trend to continue.

General Motors, with its Simca, Opel and Vauxhall plants in Europe, originally produced different variants for each country. Recently it has concentrated its efforts on a 'European car' range identical in each of its main markets.

THE CHARACTERISTICS OF EFFECTIVE SEGMENTATION

Organizations will only be able to use segmentation techniques if a number of criteria can be met. The segments must have certain characteristics.
1. Measurable: the total number in each area must be easily determined on objective criteria.

The Barclays 'Gold Card' is designed for the individual earning more than £20,000 a year – there is no distinction of age or sex; the segment of high income earners can be measured from Inland Revenue reports.

2. Accessible: the potential customers in each segment must be easy to reach.

Drinks vending companies such as Autobar use trade directories to provide lists of all firms in specified areas on the assumption that all firms having more than six employees are probably in the market for a vending machine of some description.

3. Substantial: the segment should be the largest homogeneous element that can be defined in the market. The larger the market segment the greater the market opportunities – provided that no other constraint exists.

Persil Automatic has attempted to provide the broadest possible appeal to washing machine owners by obtaining endorsements from all leading manufacturers of washing machines.

4. Sustainable: the segment will continue to exist for a period of time.

Disposable nappies, one of the most successful grocery product introductions in the 1970s is an example of the identification and development of demand in a long-term market sector.

APPROACHES TO SEGMENTATION

Most segmentation exercises tend to concentrate on the more clearly defined economic and demographic factors such as age, income, sex, family status, education, occupation, location. Recently there has been a steady growth in the importance given to behavioural – or psychographic – characteristics in differentiating the market and defining the most likely target group on which to concentrate.

DEMOGRAPHIC FACTORS

Age

People in different age groups will want different accommodation, clothing, food, entertainment and leisure-time activities.

Derwent Foods, a small independent manufacturer based in the Midlands, started to produce a range of adult snacks in 1982 under the Phileas Fogg brand name: tortilla and corn chips, garlic spiced fried bread, and Shanghai nuts. Turnover by 1985 had reached £4 million. The product was designed to appeal to the older snack eater wanting a different, more sophisticated flavour.

Florida grew enormously in prosperity on the back of the post-war retirement boom in the United States.

Sex

It seems rather obvious to say that men and women have differing product requirements but this can exercise subtle influences in the market-place. For example, it is mainly women who buy aftershave lotions for their men as presents.

Palitoy, part of General Mills, identified the fact that boys would be prepared to play with dolls *provided* that the doll was suitably presented in male rather than female roles. Out of this came the highly successful 'Action Man' series with deep-sea diver, army, helicopter pilot, and skiing costumes and equipment.

Occupation

Certain jobs will have clearly defined occupational product requirements: consider for example the needs of the business traveller, or of the farmer.

Forbes, the American business magazine, clearly identified a major part of the information requirements of the American executive market; the company's turnover now exceeds $500 million.

Family size

Changing family size patterns can cause substantial variations in demand both for goods and services.

Barratt, the leading UK housebuilder, pioneered the development of bachelor flats to meet the growing demand from single householders. This area has been one of its profitable developments.

Education

Higher education may have implications for demand patterns.

Several insurance companies concentrate their effort on the graduate market as having a potentially greater interest in savings policies than the rest of the population.

Religion

Though religion is often related to culture, there are specific market influences created by religious differences.

Walls produced a special beef sausage for the Middle Eastern markets with no pork additives.

Location

Not only will overall location often be important – for example, skis sell best in countries close to snow-covered mountains and not in the tropics – but there may be variations between town and country, north and south.

A firm producing plastic garden composters found the market better in towns than outside – rural gardens had more space in which to pile grass and leaf cuttings and had no need to buy plastic containers to keep the process neat.

Climate

Climatic conditions will inevitably affect the demand for certain products: air-conditioning equipment, for example, has never become strongly established in temperate Western Europe.

Demand for indoor board games appears to be at least in part determined by climatic conditions. Sales per capita are much lower in Australia than Scandinavia reflecting the outdoor life of one area and the long, dark winters of the other.

Physical type

Different physiques demand differing treatment.

Recently there has been a substantial increase in the market for ethnic hair care products, and the market is now estimated to be worth £18 million. Particular products such as hair relaxers and hot oil products sell only in this market.

ECONOMIC

Earlier chapters have stressed the importance that per capita income levels have on the purchase of most products. Rising incomes or significant changes in level of product prices will have a rapid effect on the level of demand.

Sinclair Research was successful in introducing low-cost computing with the ZX 81, opening up an entire new market, and by 1985 achieving a turnover of £100 million.

Rising butter prices since the 1960s have steadily reduced demand.

Due to the importance of economic factors in determining demand there has been the development of methods by which consumers can be grouped according to purchasing power.

The most widely used is the socio-economic division into groups A, B, C1, C2, D, and E. The division is achieved by a combination of income, education and social status.

Table 5.1 gives a summary of the type of distinctions involved, and Tables 5.2 and 5.3 give population distribution and the JICNARS definitions.

Table 5.1. Examples of socio-economic groups

Group	Income	Education	Job	Type of demand
A	Highest	University	Administrator	Specialist shop/top range car
B	High	College	Manager	Marks and Spencer/2-litre car
C1	Medium	A-Level	Supervisor	Sainsbury's/family car
C2	Med/low	CSE	Manual/skilled	Asda/family car
D	Low	On job	Unskilled	Kwik Save/second-hand car
E	Lowest	Various	None/pension	Local store/no car

Table 5.2. Distribution of the population by social grade

Social Grade	All adults Over 15		Men		Women		Housewives* (Female)	
	'000	%	'000	%	'000	%	'000	%
A	1,349	3.1	678	3.2	670	2.9	584	3.0
B	6,123	13.9	3,087	14.6	3,036	13.2	2,570	13.3
C1	9,772	22.2	4,516	21.4	5,255	22.9	4,330	22.4
C2	12,540	28.4	6,642	31.4	5,898	25.7	4,868	25.1
D	7,919	18.0	3,879	18.3	4,039	17.6	3,324	17.2
E	6,398	14.5	2,338	11.1	4,060	17.7	3,693	19.1
Total	44,100	100.0	21,141	100.0	22,960	100.0	19,369	100.0

*The social grade of a housewife is based on the occupation of the head of the household.
Source JICNARS National Readership Survey, Jan–Dec 1984.

*Table 5.3. JICNARS social grade definitions**

Social Grade	Social status	Occupation
A	Upper middle class	Higher managerial, administrative or professional
B	Middle class	Intermediate managerial, administrative or professional
C1	Lower middle class	Supervisory or clerical, and junior managerial, administrative or professional
C2	Skilled working class	Skilled manual workers
D	Working class	Semi and unskilled manual workers
E	Those at lowest level of subsistence	State pensioners or widows (no other earner), casual or lowest-grade workers

* These are the standard social grade classifications using definitions agreed between Research Services Ltd and JICNARS. They are described in a JICNARS publication, *Social Grading on the National Readership Survey.*
Source JICNARS National Readership Survey, Jan–Dec 1984.

Socio-economic group is also a major influence guiding advertising agencies in defining the target audience for specific campaigns.

With the increasing sophistication of the postal services, the use of housing types to define the potential within the market has been expanded separating districts into housing types such as: detached (old), detached (new), semi-detached, terraced, old terraced, service flats, non-service flats and so on (Table 5.4).

Table 5.4.   ACORN profile of Great Britain

ACORN stands for 'A Classification of Residential Neighbourhoods'. The system was developed by CACI. The table below shows ACORN'S 38 neighbourhood types, the 11 groups they form, and their share of the GB population of 53,556,911. ACORN is based on the government's Census of Great Britain last conducted in 1981. The figures therefore refer to 1981. CACI are currently compiling updated information relating to the populations of the ACORN neighbourhoods. This will be used to amend the classification during 1985/86.

ACORN types		% population	ACORN groups	
A	1 Agricultural villages	2.6		
A	2 Areas of farms and smallholdings	0.8	3.4 Agricultural areas	A
B	3 Cheap modern private housing	4.1		
B	4 Recent private housing, young families	3.1		
B	5 Modern private housing, older children	5.8	16.2 Modern family housing, higher incomes	B
B	6 New detached houses, young families	2.6		
B	7 Military bases	0.5		
C	8 Mixed owner-occ'd & council estates	3.5		
C	9 Small town centres & flats above shops	4.0		
C	10 Villages with non-farm employment	4.6	17.6 Older housing of intermediate status	C
C	11 Older private housing, skilled workers	5.5		
D	12 Unimproved terraces with old people	2.5		
D	13 Pre-1914 terraces, low income families	1.4	4.3 Poor quality older terraced housing	D
D	14 Tenement flats lacking amenities	0.4		
E	15 Council estates, well-off older workers	3.6	13.0 Better-off council estates	E
E	16 Recent council estates	2.6		

ACORN types	% population	ACORN groups
E 17 Council estates, well-off young workers	4.9	
E 18 Small council houses, often Scottish	2.0	13.0 Better-off council estates E
F 19 Low rise estates in industrial towns	4.7	
F 20 Inter-war council estates, older people	3.1	9.4 Less well-off council estates F
F 21 Council housing for the elderly	1.5	
G 22 New council estates in inner cities	2.0	
G 23 Overspill estates, high unemployment	3.2	
G 24 Council estates with overcrowding	1.6	7.6 Poorest council estates G
G 25 Council estates with worst poverty	0.7	
H 26 Multi-occupied terraces, poor Asians	0.4	
H 27 Owner-occupied terraces with Asians	1.1	
H 28 Multi-let housing with Afro-Caribbeans	0.7	3.9 Multi-racial areas H
H 29 Better-off multi-ethnic areas	1.7	
I 30 High status areas, few children	2.1	
I 31 Multi-let big old houses and flats	1.5	4.2 High status non-family areas I
I 32 Furnished flats, mostly single people	0.6	
J 33 Inter-war semis, white collar workers	5.7	
J 34 Spacious inter-war semis, big gardens	5.0	
J 35 Villages with wealthy older commuters	2.9	15.9 Affluent suburban housing J
J 36 Detached houses, exclusive suburbs	2.3	
K 37 Private houses, well-off elderly	2.2	
K 38 Private flats with single pensioners	1.6	3.8 Better-off retirement areas K
U 39 Unclassified	0.7	0.7 Unclassified U
	100.0	

Source   CACI *Market Analysis Division's User Guide,* published 1983.

Great Universal Stores (GUS) uses a sophisticated method of analysing likely potential and risk when deciding whether to send out a mail order catalogue to a postal enquiry. This includes an evaluation of the likely buying power of the area from which the enquiry originated.

Increasingly, marketing departments are also deriving a relationship between the stage of family life and the likely products that are purchased (Table 5.5).

Table 5.5. Stage of life/likely purchases

Stage	Finances	Purchases
Single	Good	Cars/holidays/clothes/entertainment
Newly weds	Strained	House equipment/entertainment
Young children	Very strained	Basics/baby food/nappies
Elder children	Strained	Bulk shopping/some holidays
College children	Better	Furniture/drink/holidays
Children working	Good	Luxuries/travel/entertainment
Retired	Strained	Little

PSYCHOLOGICAL

As societies grow more affluent there is a tendency for consumers to move beyond considering products purely on physical attributes. It has been observed that they are less concerned with 'will it be nutritious?', or 'will it keep me warm?', but more preoccupied with factors like 'will it keep me healthy?', and 'will it make me look fashionable?'

The example of flour in developed markets mentioned earlier in the chapter exemplifies the first case: consumers have moved beyond the pure food value in their demands and are now considering health, or ease of cooking. The second case is similarly illustrated by the purely functional aspect of clothing becoming secondary to fashion, particularly in areas such as sportswear.

One can summarize this trend by stating that consumers become more interested in 'intangible' factors as affluence increases. Firms interested in maintaining a competitive advantage will need to understand the implications of these changes in specific product fields (Figure 5.2).

Figure 5.2. Changing segmentation demands

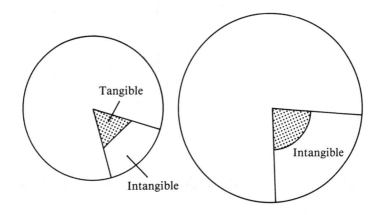

The importance of intangible factors has led to a large body of work that has attempted to explain and predict how individuals will react, to aid organizations in defining product change. There have been numerous attempts since the pioneer work of Freud to develop models of individual behaviour that can accurately predict reaction in particular circumstances. None has yet passed the acid test of being usable as a practical aid to decision-making, remaining at best an indication of what may be occurring.

The complexity of the decision-making process can be underlined by breaking down the consumer buying process into its various stages. It is apparent that individual attitudes can, and do, vary from stage to stage and from product to product.

Demand definition ⟶ Information search ⟶ Evaluation behaviour ⟶ Purchase decision ⟶ Post purchase feelings

This model suggests that individuals first decide on a particular area (cars, television sets, restaurants), look for information concerning the possible alternatives available in the market, decide by the use of specific criteria what is most suitable, and then review the purchase afterwards. This will affect repeat purchase decisions.

At each stage individual reactions will affect the buying process. Faced with such variety, it is often surprising that any product is sold to any consumer! Such a model underlines the problems that consumer behaviour theory has in defining how any individual will respond to a given product. As the product/market sector interaction becomes more difficult to define from first principles (the interference of intangible factors being of greater and greater importance) the necessity of research specifically directed at the product and the market will become greater.

The failure of the Sinclair C5 is an example of intangible factors having a crucial influence on success or failure. The main criticism of the product was its poor safety – its vulnerability to weather, wind and other road users. Specific research would hopefully have identified this major problem and reduced some of the £10 million plus that the project lost.

Even though it is difficult to generalize on aspects of consumer behaviour, certain important elements have been isolated which should be considered for each product in each sector.

Culture

The degree to which cultural rather than economic and demographic factors are important in shaping demand has long been a source of much discussion. The most popular TV programme in Italy in 1984 was *Dallas* – but both India and Japan retain a large, thriving and individualistic, film industry. Cultural variations will differ from product sector to product sector, but in many industries will still remain an important aspect of segmentation strategy.

Indonesia has an extremely large herbal remedy industry, with a turnover in excess of $400 million. Remedies include Simona face cream 'protecting from every atmospheric influence', and Obat Kuping 'for those wishing to diminish badly smelling ears'.

'Mushy' peas, produced by boiling processed peas for a lengthy period, have for long been a favourite part of the diet in the North of England. Batchelors introduced a new product, tinned mushy peas, which has been extremely successful.

Contact with Denmark has created a far larger market for unsalted butter in the north-east of the country than in any other region.

Life styles

Changing attitudes towards employment, such as the increasing number of women at work, will also influence market demand.

As family structure becomes increasingly fragmented, segmentations of this nature are becoming more and more important.

Along with other frozen food manufacturers Birds Eye has clearly identified the single household as a major growth area for convenience food. Its 'Menu Masters' range targeted at the young, single householder has become brand leader in this growing market segment.

Social influences

The effects of neighbours, friends and family can be very important in the spread of new ideas. The concept of innovators and early adopters has already been mentioned in the context of the product life cycle and, though on an individual level it cannot be used as a predictive method, social influences are a factor that all segmentation exercises will need to consider.

Social factors can be of great importance in sporting goods for example. The endorsement of a particular brand by a leading player can cause an immediate and dramatic increase in sales.

DIFFICULTIES IN ACHIEVING ACCURATE SEGMENTATION

COMPLEXITY

No segmentation exercise will ever be easy or complete. The more measures the company uses to divide the market, the more accurate its understanding of the relationship between customer and product.

It is, however, often easy for a company to miss an evolving market segment as the next example illlustrates.

Smash Hits, a music periodical, was successfully launched in the mid-1970s at a time when all established magazines were losing circulation. It was aimed at the nine to sixteen-year-old group, especially at the younger girls who were the main purchasers of single records; up to this point the industry had considered that the most suitable target group would be the boy of sixteen or over.

Options, a major magazine launch by IPC, was theoretically targeted at the twenty to forty-year-old, middle or upper middle class married woman. In reality the magazine was read more by younger, single women lower down the social scale.

SPECIFICITY

There will often be a large number of ways of relating the product to the market.

The types of market that a product appeals to will vary with product range. For example, a large packet of detergent such as the 6 kg or E20 pack can be seen as addressing the large family; the E2 will be more suitable for the bachelor or retired households. Similarly, cross-head screws of a certain type may be purchased by industry as well as the consumer sector. Specificity of use is one of the main problems of segmenting the industrial market which is discussed in Chapter 16. A company with a broad product range might see a pattern emerging which can be illustrated as in Table 5.6.

Table 5.6.   Product range and demand

| Product type | Most likely demand group | | | | |
	1	2	3	4	5
1		/	//	///	/
2			///	/	
3	///		/		//

The different product types or sizes will appeal to different segments.

EMPHASIS

A manufacturer may carry out a segmentation exercise which yields five or six ways in which a particular product can be segmented. This can often create the problem of deciding on which sector the company should concentrate.

Purchasers of Porsche motor cars tend to be over thirty-five, are generally in business in a senior managerial position, have good incomes, tend to have no children or a small family, consider themselves 'sophisticated' and 'modern'.

PRACTICALITIES OF SEGMENTATION

All companies will be forced to restrict themselves to a limited number of ways of identifying potential markets, though continually experimenting with other approaches that may be more successful.

Procter and Gamble was one of the first companies fully to develop the marketing concept. Though it segments the market it does so on a practical basis, researching each individual product thoroughly and evaluating it on its own merits. From such analyses the largest rather than the smallest possible segment is defined. Head and Shoulders shampoo of the same packaging and formulation is sold in all the countries of Continental Europe: in many it is the leading shampoo.

Summary

Market segmentation is one key to competitive advantage by enabling the company to provide specific products to particular parts of the market. Nevertheless, specificity is not the sole recipe for success as is demonstrated by the increasing number of multinational companies selling a standardized product.

There are a large number of methods available by which markets can be segmented, some of which are more immediately applicable than others but all of which increase the understanding of the product/market interaction.

ASSIGNMENTS

1. You are asked by a manufacturer of record players to prepare a report on how they might segment the market for a range of medium priced compact disc players.
2. As a marketing consultant you are asked by a major electrical appliance manufacturer to write a report on how changing social trends will affect the market segmentation for refrigerators.
3. You are asked by a manufacturer of sweets to write a report about the segmentation issues involved in the introduction of a range of chocolate liqueurs.

YARDLEY GOLD

THE COMPANY

Yardley is an old, British company which had become part of British American Tobacco and was part of their cosmetics division which accounted for 3 per cent of turnover. In 1984 Yardley was sold to Beechams.

The mainstay of the company had been Yardley Lavender, an old established women's fragrance. Recently there had been a number of new women's fragrances launched but increasing attention was being given to the men's toiletry division.

Since the 1950s the male fragrance product range had consisted of three products.

1. Yardley Original, launched in 1955, had in later years declined in sales and was, by 1982, restricted to the export market.
2. Yardley Black Label had been launched in 1970 as a top range, sophisticated male fragrance but had achieved only a small market share.
3. Sven, launched in 1976 and discontinued in 1982, had been aimed at the man who wanted to capture 'the Scandinavian life'.

If Yardley was going to explore possibilities in the men's perfume market, it was therefore essential to develop new products for the market. Prior to the launch of Yardley Gold, the company examined various trends in the market.

THE MEN'S FRAGRANCE MARKET

Before the advent of Yardley Gold the market for men's perfumes and skin care in the UK had not yet seen the considerable growth experienced in countries such as Italy and France. This was a reflection of the infrequent use of male toiletries shown in Table 5.7.

Table 5.7.   UK use of men's toiletries

	Aftershave %	Talcum %
Used on most days	36	33
Weekly	32	23
Never/don't know	32	44

In real terms (after inflation) the market had been declining (Table 5.8).

Table 5.8.   The UK market for men's toiletries 1978–83

Year	1978	1979	1980	1981	1982	1983
Sales (£ million)	85	92	108	115	121	130

Aftershave was by far the most important component of the market with 70 per cent of the total; talcum powder accounted for 10 per cent and deodorant for 18 per cent. Minor product areas included shampoo, bath additives, soap and hair spray.

Though there were a large number of brands in the market, five products held 52 per cent of total sales of aftershave (Table 5.9).

Table 5.9.   Leading brands of men's toiletries

Brand	Market share %
Aramis	18
Brut 33	18
Avon	8
Old Spice	11
Denim	7

Distribution was mainly through: Boots, accounting for 30 per cent of total market sales; other chemists, 17 per cent; and department stores, 25 per cent.

The gift element was very strong – over 50 per cent of the products were bought by women for men; and highly seasonal – 40 per cent of total volume was sold between November and December.

Fragrance trends

Trends in the market suggested a movement from the product that had originally developed the market – Old Spice – in favour of new types of fragrance.

1. Late 1950s –Old Spice. Masculine fragrance – medicinal image, similar to the concept used to develop the sales of Lifebuoy soap: 'stay fresh all day with Lifebuoy'.
2. Early 1960s – Brut Original. Aftershave to attract women for use on special occasions.
3. Early 1970s – Brut 33. Aftershave acceptable for everyday use, aimed at the 'sporting man'.
4. Early 1980s – Brut becoming dated; heavy musk perfume regarded as too 'blatant', growth of more sophisticated perfumes such as Aramis.

DIVIDING THE MARKET

Age of user (Table 5.10)

Table 5.10. Users of men's toiletry brands by age

	Brut 33 %	Aramis %	Old Spice %
Up to 17	6	—	4
Up to 20	15	6	6
Up to 24	28	8	10
Up to 34	15	35	18
Up to 44	12	30	22
Up to 64	12	17	25
64 plus	9	4	15

The market clearly showed a preponderance of the younger consumer using Brut and the older Old Spice, with Aramis primarily used by the over thirty-fives market.

Socio-economic group (Table 5.11)

Table 5.11. Users of men's toiletry brands by socio-economic group

Group	Brut 33 %	Aramis %	Old Spice %
AB	14	42	12
C1	24	34	21
C2	39	18	48
DE	24	6	27

Both Brut and Old Spice were purchased most heavily by the lower socio-economic groups, with Old Spice particularly heavily weighted towards that end of the market.

Division on price

The market showed considerable variation on price dividing into four sectors:

1. Expensive: £7 for 100 ml (Aramis);
2. Premium: £4 (Noir);
3. Mass market: £2.50 (Brut and Old Spice);
4. Own label: £1.50 (Boots).

Aramis had spearheaded the acceptance of more highly priced male fragrances and it appeared that the market for such products would continue to expand at the expense of the mass market products.

YARDLEY GOLD – PRODUCT POSITIONING

The main target market for Yardley Gold was men aged between thirty and forty, social classes C1 and C2, priced above Brut and Old Spice at £3 per 100 ml. The fragrance chosen was 'oriental and spicy', the packaging supporting a sporting theme at the time of launch, 1984 – an Olympic year.

Yardley perceived the consumer as:

- married with young family
- currently a squash player who had played football when younger
- leading an active social life centred on clubs
- reading the *Daily Telegraph* and magazines such as *What Car*
- taking package holidays with his family.

The Yardley Gold range of aftershave, shower talcum, splash-on, and deodorant spray was launched with a £500,000 advertising campaign using sport as a theme, aggressive point of sale and introductory price offers during Olympic year 1984. By early 1985, Yardley had captured around 1.5 per cent of the male fragrance market, valuing the brand at around £2 million.

Comment

The Yardley case illustrates some of the market segmentation criteria considered by a company in a sector where intangible product factors are very important.

AMC LTD

A small Midlands-based company, AMC (UK) Fasteners Ltd began trading in 1977 as a distributor of industrial fasteners.

The fastener market is made up of seven segments: screws; bolts; nuts; cotters and cotter pins; rivets; washers; and nails, tacks and staples.

AMC is involved in only three of the seven segments: it distributes and manufactures nuts, and distributes washers and rivets. Nuts, however, account for approximately 95 per cent of AMC's turnover, 35 per cent of them manufactured by the company itself. It is possible to subdivide these segments further but here we shall be concerned only with those segments in which AMC is operating (Figure 5.3).

Figure 5.3.   Product segmentation in AMC's market

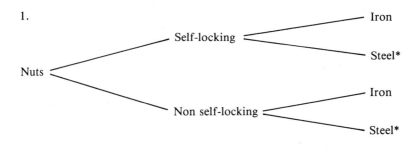

1.

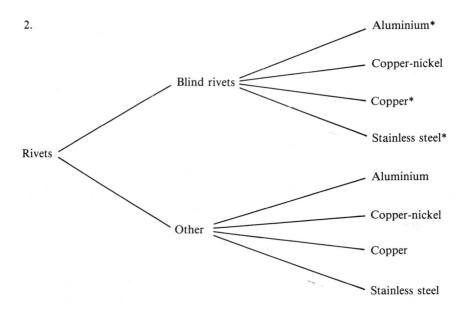

2.

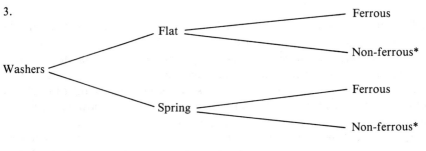

3.

*products distributed by AMC

AMC AS A DISTRIBUTOR

AMC is dependent on suppliers for 65 per cent of its products including all of its blind rivets and washers. Its suppliers are in the UK, mainland China and the Far East including Malaysia and Korea, Rumania, West Germany and Norway. Its main customers are bolt manufacturers in the UK, where AMC follows a policy of distributing nationally, Sweden, Norway, Denmark, Holland, Eire and West Germany (Figure 5.4). In addition the company also supplies forging tools to its West German supplier. Its business can be split up as shown in Table 5.12.

Figure 5.4.   AMC's role as a distributor

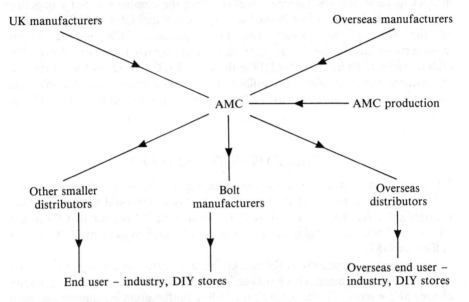

Table 5.12.   AMC's product split

Product	%
Nuts	95
Rivets	4
Washers	0.5
Forging tools	0.5

AMC IN THE MARKET

AMC has about 5.5 per cent of the nut market with its cold-forging plant manufacturing about 35 per cent of total sales. The specialization in nuts allows the company to offer its customers, through either its own production facilities or its suppliers, a comprehensive range of all forms of standard, non-preferred and special steel nuts with thread diameters from 4.8 mm to 88.9 mm. The manufacturing operation allows AMC to supply special nuts to meet the customer's own specifications.

The company was one of the first to start stocking and supplying the fairly innovative blind rivets – one of the new product developments in the industry over the past few years. In this segment it again offers a comprehensive range.

Dealing with a large number of suppliers and being supported by its own manufacturing activity gives AMC a fair degree of independence and flexibility particularly as regards pricing. It prices products not on the basis of cost but according to how high a price the market will stand – although this effectively means that the gross profit margins on each product will vary throughout the year.

These facets of AMC and its insistence on high quality together provide a distinct niche in the UK fastener market where the company is not competing directly with the major firms in the industry – GKN and Glynwed. Operating in all the bolt, screw, washer and nut segments, GKN is the largest manufacturer/distributor in the market with an annual turnover of over £50 million compared with AMC's £1.18 million in 1983. Glynwed, with a turnover in the fastener market of about £40 million, is the largest distributor. It operates in all segments of the market buying from many suppliers both in the UK and overseas.

PROBLEMS IN THE MARKET

There has been an overall contraction of 28 per cent in the UK fastener market since 1979, and in 1981 and 1983 AMC made losses. The total market for nuts, washers and rivets has decreased by £20 million from £97 million in 1979 to £71 million in 1983. AMC sales have dropped from £1.5 million in 1978 to £1.1 million in 1983.

The biggest contractions in the market have occurred in the high-tensile and mild steel bolt categories. This has been largely responsible for the decline in sales of nuts and washers (Table 5.13) as the bolt manufacturers are among the main purchasers. AMC found that instead of buying for and keeping stock, many of its customers were only buying to order because of the poor economic climate. Table 5.14 shows AMC's position in the UK fastener market, and Table 5.15 AMC's sales by segment.

Table 5.13. UK nuts, rivets and washers market 1979–83 (£000)

Segment	1979	1980	1981	1982	1983
Nuts	38,446	28,681	24,412	22,009	20,465
Rivets	38,654	38,216	33,661	35,171	38,745
Washers	20,154	13,966	12,656	12,337	12,088

Table 5.14.   AMC in the UK fastener market

	1979	1980	1981	1982	1983
Total fastener market (£000)	345,555	282,300	248,426	236,269	247,840
Nuts, washers and rivets	97,254	80,863	70,729	69,517	71,298
AMC sales	1,523	1,345	1,370	1,325	1,182
AMC market share (%)					
Total market	0.44	0.48	0.55	0.56	0.48
Nuts, washers and rivets	1.57	1.66	1.94	1.91	1.66

Table 5.15.   AMC sales by segment (£000)

Segment	1979	1980	1981	1982	1983
Nuts	1,447	1,278	1,302	1,259	1,123
Rivets	61	54	55	53	47
Washers	8	7	7	7	6

The number of firms in the UK fastener market has virtually halved since 1979 when there were 720 firms involved. Currently there are an estimated 370 companies in the market. Table 5.16 gives the figures for the nut, rivet and washer segments.

Table 5.16.   Firms in the nut, rivet and washer segments 1979–83

Segment	1979	1980	1981	1982	1983
Nuts	81	67	59	49	41
Rivets	32	27	29	28	27
Washers	36	30	26	22	18

(Most firms operate in more than one segment)

THE AMC SOLUTION

AMC has taken the view that the nut segment of its business will not expand in the foreseeable future and that the company must increase its market share by increasing sales and concentrating on particular segments. Since 1981 the company has trebled the number of its customers, due partly to promotional activities. Following upon the losses made in 1981 and 1983 the company tried to reduce expenses in order to achieve a lower breakeven point.

Comment

AMC operates in a competitive declining market, both manufacturing on its own account and acting as a distributor for other firms. The complexity of the market suggests that efficient segmentation is a vital technique for survival.

6

MARKETING INFORMATION

Don't confuse me with facts.

(Anon)

Knowledge itself is power.

(Francis Bacon)

THE NEED FOR INFORMATION

In order to plan for the future, the company must first find the available opportunities and must continually monitor its progress in taking advantage of these opportunities. Good military intelligence allows the general to anticipate rather than solely react to what the opposition is doing – which is very similar to the problems faced by the marketing department.

Information is crucial to the process of strategic planning. Obviously, different companies will need varying types of information but the company that has a greater understanding of the particular market sector than its competitor will have a significant competitive advantage. It will benefit from both the speed of reaction to changing conditions and the ability to define opportunities more accurately than its competitor. Such advantages will only materialize if the company is able to interpret accurately, and use effectively, the information that is available.

THE SIX Os OF MARKETING

The company that has a greater understanding of the issues raised in Chapter 1 will tend to be more successful than the company with limited or non-existent information about these matters. Since these issues are very important within the marketing information context, we shall repeat them here:

- who are the potential consumers (Occupants)?
- what do they currently buy (Objects)?
- why do they currently buy what they buy (Objectives)?
- do consumers influence each other in the purchase decision and, if so, how (Organization)?
- when do they buy (Occasions)?
- where do they buy (Operations)?

The words in brackets refer to the mnemonic by which these factors are remembered – the six 'Os' of marketing.

THE ROLE OF MARKETING INFORMATION

Accurate marketing information will enable the company to:
1. recognize developing trends more quickly than the competition;
2. evaluate marketing action and planning more thoroughly;
3. allow a large and diverse firm to integrate information for central planning purposes – essential for strategy development.

Great Universal Stores, GUS, the leading mail order company in the United Kingdom, has always faced a problem of determining which customers were likely to be better credit risks than others. Over the years the company developed a sophisticated credit control system which minimized the level of risk. This enabled GUS continually to maintain a lower level of bad debt than its competitors. So successful is this credit control information system, that GUS has developed a profitable subsidiary to develop the sale of expertise in this area.

Du Pont, the largest American chemical company, used its extensive information on customer deliveries and demands to redefine its distribution system with savings of hundreds of millions of dollars.

The examples of Great Universal Stores and Du Pont underline the point that the creation and maintenance of a management information system – or MIS – which supplies the company with information about external and internal change will be vital to enable the organization to respond accurately to changing conditions and to develop effective strategies.

DEFINING INFORMATION NEEDS

Most organizations do not have sufficient data on which to take action; some suffer at the other extreme in having too much. Central to any information system is that it provides data which is:
- simple
- accurate
- useful.

Each company will need to be very specific about defining its information needs, developing sources from which the information can be derived, and creating a system whereby this data can be organized into providing comparative analyses which can be used to decide what action would be most effective.

The stages involved in the development of an information system will be the same for whatever action that the firm proposes.

1.   It will need to define the problem in specific terms.
2.   The company has to decide on the amount and type of information required to solve the problem.
3.   A systematic method for collecting and analysing will have to be established and maintained.
4.   Alternative possible paths of action will have to be decided upon and criteria established (action standards) by which their success or failure will be judged.
5.   The data should then be used with the action standards to determine the best possible course of action. This action will then affect the future information that the company receives. In other words, a decision loop will be created (Figure 6.1).

Figure 6.1.   Decision loop and control system

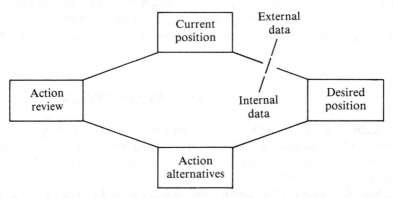

A structured approach creates a procedure which attempts to remove the large element of subjectivity that tends to become established in information requirements – managers often only accepting information that fits in with preconceived ideas.

For example, a company might find that sales to one customer type are falling well below expectations. It might be thought in the company that the most likely explanation is poor pricing, but collecting a range of data would allow the organization to evaluate other possible reasons such as poor competitive position, or poor distribution.

Designing information systems will, however, require that management considers the level of investment related to the likely reduction in risk. Each decision that management takes will involve a level of risk; in general terms the more important the decision, the lower the level of acceptable risk that the decision will be wrong, and the greater the need to ensure that all possible information has been collected to minimize the likelihood of the decision being based on incorrect or erroneous assumptions.

One might, for example, consider the planning of next year's household budget. Current information suggests that the rent will increase by 10 per cent, though it is possible that it will go up by a still acceptable 15 per cent. However, should the probability of the rent increasing by more than 15 per cent be substantially increased, it would be worth the tenant spending time finding out the exact nature of the increase and likely costs of alternative accommodation.

For complex decisions involving a high level of risk – for example, the construction of the Channel tunnel at a cost of £2,500 million over a ten-year period – considerable time and money should be invested to ensure that all the factors affecting the decision have been collected and analysed. In other instances, the speed at which the decision must be arrived at and the level of risk associated with it means that the information system should be of a more basic type. In other words, the nature of the information system will be closely tied to the organizational strategy and the accuracy with which it needs to understand either the general or specific business environment in which it is operating.

The steadily decreasing cost of data storage has meant that companies are more able to analyse effectively the internal information they have at their disposal: a computer costing £750,000 ten years ago which filled two rooms can now be purchased for £30,000 and occupy the space of two filing cabinets. The inevitable tendency is for information systems to become steadily more complex with the reducing costs of data storage.

USES OF THE INFORMATION SYSTEM

Management will, however, have to continue to ask itself certain key questions.
1. What will management do with faster information if it is made available? Will management actually be able to use the information that is made available effectively?
2. What new types of decision will management be able to take if the information is made available?
3. How flexible should the system be? How many different types of information requirement must it service?
4. What range of inputs will be required to reach the acceptable level of risk?
5. How much internal and external information will need to be included to reach an effective decision?

The range of sophistication required of the information system will therefore be considerable when different companies are compared.

The small firm, for example, might be facing the problem of declining sales. It would perhaps decide that it needed information on where its customers were based, how each of them ordered, the competitive products in the market together with their prices. The first two pieces of information would be available from internal company records; the company would be able to compare the results of the previous year(s) with those of the current in a number of ways (Table 6.1).

Table 6.1. *Different comparisons of results*

	Year A	Year B
Region A	1,000	1,200
Region B	2,200	800
Customer type A	8,500	6,000
Customer type B	1,000	1,250

In this situation, there are two other items of information the company would require: the market share in region A and region B, and the price of the company's products in relation to the competition. Thus, the company would either have to initiate some form of research or attempt to gain access to some already available external information. For example, if the company was operating in a consumer market it would be able to buy information on market share and competitive pricing from one of the major research companies such as Nielsen or Audits of Great Britain (AGB). This information might reveal the pattern shown in Table 6.2.

Table 6.2. *Market share and price analyses*

	Year A %	Year B %
Region A market share	20	18
Region B market share	12	10
Price vs. competition	+5	+8

Combining two streams of information, one internally sourced and the other external, would have certain advantages. It would enable the company to identify clearly where the major problem areas exist – whether it is the changing size of the market, a lack of competitiveness on price or some other more serious product shortcoming which will require more analysis.

In contrast, a larger firm might find that the risks involved in the large market in which it operated demanded a far higher level of investment in some form of permanent monitoring system to monitor the overall effect of such influences as:

- the effect of advertising expenditure on overall sales
- the effects of per capita income on overall sales
- the effects of age distribution in the population on sales.

Readers will be aware that some of this information is normally labelled 'market research'. The division into external 'market research' and internal data often leads to a false understanding of the research process. As we have seen, information needs will differ from company to company. Some will need large amounts of externally generated information to provide data on which to take decisions. Others will rely mainly on the information that is available within the firm for the majority of their decision requirements.

Each decision will incur a level of cost; the greater the amount of data, and the faster the speed of access to it, the higher the cost. Large, sophisticated companies maintain continuous or on-line information systems for continuous monitoring purposes; in a smaller company off-line or intermittent information will be used.

> British Airways has a complex on-line system to handle flight reservations and bookings which can be accessed by travel agents to provide instant seat bookings. The information system also allows British Airways continually to monitor its level of seat loading, determine baggage handling, meal requirements and so on.

> The introduction of EPOS (electronic point of sale) tills in retail outlets is allowing the head offices of the store groups to develop off-line data analysis systems. At the end of the day these will be able to determine what replacement stocks the individual stores will require for the following day. In this instance, an on-line system would be unnecessary, and extremely expensive.

Surveys of the research that companies carry out show that the most frequent are those that rely on internal data. One survey of company research in the United States showed the following descending order of research activity:

1. Determining the nature of the company's customers.
2. Monitoring the level of profitability on a product by product basis.
3. Evaluating and directing the sales force.
4. Evaluating distribution and other potential cost savings in the level of stocks.
5. Providing forecasting information. Though it is part of the management information process, forecasting demands the application of specific techniques and is discussed in Chapter 7. Readers should however be aware of its role in the management information system.
6. Estimating the competitive position of the company products.
7. Analysing the size of the market.
8. Economic research.
9. Measuring the acceptability of new products.
10. Comparing competitive products.

Such surveys underline the fact that the main information requirement for most companies relates to current problems. Very few companies carry out longer-term, more theoretical research. This explains in part the reluctance to carry out investigations into such areas as advertising effectiveness which require long-term analysis for full understanding.

EXTERNALLY DERIVED INFORMATION

There are an increasing number of data sources available to the company. Government and public agencies produce vast libraries of information which may be useful to the marketing team. For example, *Social Trends* is a valuable indication of overall changes in consumer attitudes, Customs and Excise maintain records of imports, the Department of Trade and Industry maintains information on industrial production. The OECD comments on West European economic development, the United Nations and subsidiary organizations publish data on such diverse facts as family planning and food production levels.

In addition to official publications there are an increasing number of commercial databases which allow access to a wide range of specialist information. Indeed, one of the distinguishing advantages of the large multinationals or conglomerates over their rivals is the continuing development of inter-group databases from which any of the operating subsidiary companies can derive consumer or market information which may originally have been commissioned by some other company within the group.

When the firms still wants additional, specific, external information it will have to commission research on the issue itself.

General Foods is an example of a consumer goods organization that spends heavily on market research. For example, it found by specific research that the vast majority of housewives preferred custard in a sachet rather than a carton. Changing the pack led to increased sales.

UK MARKET RESEARCH

Total expenditure on external market research in the United Kingdom was around £150 million in 1984.

The range of activities carried out by market research agencies is extremely wide. The five most important topics with which they are concerned are:
1. estimating the competitive position of the company products;
2. analysing the size of the market;
3. economic research;
4. measuring the acceptability of new products;
5. comparing competitive products.

Studies are carried out by firms in all main areas of the marketing mix, looking at economics, consumer behaviour, distribution structure, pricing, market planning and the like.

There are three main subdivisions.
1. Observation. Measuring how consumers react in specific circumstances.

One of the strengths of the American toy company Milton Bradley is its exhaustive testing procedure by which the company observes the reactions of potential customers – children – to any proposed new product.

2. Qualitative research. This measures, by a process of open-ended, group or individual discussion, attitudes towards a particular product or product field.

Birds Eye, the frozen food manufacturer, found via group discussions that consumers were becoming increasingly wary of additives in frozen food. In the light of these findings it decided drastically to reduce their level in all Birds Eye products.

3. Quantitative research. This attempts to define the total market in detail on which the company can base specific actions or plans.

Syndicated research, where companies share in an ongoing data collection and analysis service, makes up the lion's share of quantitative research. These include consumer panels, trade audits and omnibus surveys. The role of trade audits in test marketing (discussed in Chapter 8) is a vital part of product planning especially for new product introductions.

SURVEY STRUCTURE

Though the company can often use all the internal data that it has at its disposal, external research will demand that it only considers part, or a sample, of the total external data that is available. Some companies will carry out investigations to gain generalized opinions: this is called qualitative research. Of interest to the majority is accurate data on how a particular factor is changing, which is termed quantitative research. The nature of the sample is essential for the accuracy of any quantitative research.

For example, many companies in the consumer goods field rely on the Nielsen company for market share and pricing reports. Nielsen investigates the sales position of a particular market sector on a two-month basis via a sample of all the stores that it could visit (in the UK this would be in the region of 55,000 outlets in the grocery sector). The creation of a sample which accurately reflects the overall market is a vital preliminary for this type of market research.

In every case, the larger the sample the more accurate the results. An analogy can be made with newspaper photographs. In some the grain is very coarse and widely separated – the resulting picture is blurred and indistinct. In others the grain is fine and closely packed producing a much clearer picture. Large samples, in a similar vein, produced more detailed and accurate pictures of the total. A formula relates the size of the sample to the probability that it occurred by chance:

$$P = \sqrt{pq/N}$$

P is the value of the standard error.
p is the number of samples showing a certain trend.
q is the number not showing the same trend.
N is the total number of samples in the survey.

The larger the sample, the greater the cost. Central to the planning process for the survey will be the decision by the marketing team as to how closely the results must reflect the true nature of the market.

A number of approaches have been used to define the sample.

1. Unrestricted random sampling. In the example of the Nielsen two-monthly survey, each store would have an equal chance of being selected for research purposes. The shortcomings of such an approach are obvious – the differences in importance to total sales of a particular product between the results obtained in a corner grocery store and a hypermarket would be immense.

2. Stratified sampling. This approach concentrates on developing weightings for the importance of various groups. In the example of the grocery survey it would address the issues of how many hypermarkets should be included, how many supermarkets and how many corner grocers. One of the criticisms

levelled at this method is that though it reduces the bias of the sample it still relies heavily on judgement to determine the sample structure.

3. Area sampling. A sample where a group, location or cluster of respondents is chosen at random, to reduce the bias of the interview process.

Bias can also occur in questionnaire design. The more opinion that the survey is trying to elicit, the greater the possibility of error. Thus, to the question, 'do you have a freezer in the house?', the answer will either be yes or no. To the question, 'are you religious?', all sorts of misunderstandings will arise.

There are many other pitfalls in questionnaire design. The key issues can be summarized as follows:

1. Language:
   (a) maintain simplicity in language;
   (b) avoid emotional words.
2. Question structure:
   (a) ensure that the possible types of answer are clearly identified, and that the whole range of possible answers is included;
   (b) always include a 'don't know' or 'not applicable' column which does not force the respondent into a choice.
3. Question content:
   (a) ensure that the question does not imply the respondent is of low status. For example a question such as, 'do you read books?', will tend always to be answered in the affirmative, regardless of the reality;
   (b) ensure that the questions can be readily answered without too much strain on the memory of the respondent, which inevitably introduces inaccuracies into the questionnaire;
   (c) ensure that the questions follow a logical sequence.
4. Length of questionnaire. Concentrate on minimizing the length of the questionnaire as many studies show that respondents rapidly lose interest in the subject under discussion.
5. Control questions. The inclusion of control questions that check initial responses can be of great value in complex questionnaires.
6. Training interviewers to minimize interviewer influence (tone of voice may for example affect respondents) and to maintain a high questionnaire completion rate.
7. Initial piloting of the questionnaire. This ensures that the company carrying out the survey will be aware of specific problems that may arise before the main survey is completed.

In the United Kingdom, the majority of surveys are carried out on a face-to-face basis, with very few postal or telephone surveys (these currently only account for less than 5 per cent of total surveys). This is in contrast to the United States where telephone surveys are the norm comprising over 70 per cent of total surveys.

Once the data is collected the firm will often have substantial problems in analysis unless the questions and answers have been properly coded so that the results can be easily analysed. There has been a steady increase in the number of computer packages which can be used to carry out cross referencing of questions and compilations of data which have tremendously speeded up the analysis process.

Summary

The development of a management information system is a vital task for the marketing department, as good, accurate and useful information will allow the firm to respond more rapidly to events or take advantage of opportunities in the market. The most frequent source of information for the firm is internal, drawing on the organization's own resources. However, external market research is vital for many effective decisions. The collection of data poses numerous design problems should the company want a high degree of accuracy from the results – how the sample should be determined, how bias in the questionnaire should be minimized and how the data should be coded for easy analysis.

ASSIGNMENTS

1. You are working for a medium-sized engineering company without an MIS. Prepare a report on what issues are involved, what sort of data should be collected and the types of improvement in operation that should result.
2. Your boss is a small manufacturer of analytical equipment for schools and colleges and has asked you to investigate what low cost research could help him define the company direction more accurately.
3. A company currently based in bus and van maintenance has asked you to prepare a report on the research it should carry out prior to entry into the manufacture of vehicles for the disabled for local authorities and hospitals.

MAGIC MAIL

BACKGROUND

Magic Mail had been established in the late 1960s as a specialized mail order operation concentrating on 'customized' consumer durables and clothes for middle class households. By advertising a limited range of products in premium newspapers such as the *Sunday Times* and *Observer,* and via Barclaycard and Access mailings it managed to grow rapidly into one of the leading specialized mail order outlets. Profits rose from £100,000 in 1965 to £1.2 million by 1974.

The number of customers that it serviced rose from 12,000 in 1964 to 75,000 by the mid-1970s. Analysis showed that the average expenditure per customer was steadily increasing from £15 per head per transaction to £27.50; the total number of transactions per customer was also slowly increasing. Magic customers tended to be fairly loyal, with a 68 per cent chance of repeat purchase in the year following the initial purchase. The geographical spread of business indicated that the majority of the sales were coming from the south or south-east of the United

Kingdom, and what little hard information it had suggested that the buyers were predominantly the older (thirty plus) upper socio-economic households looking for either distinctive products or slightly unusual gifts offering value for money. The gift element meant that there was a high degree of seasonal demand in the Magic range with 55 per cent of sales being achieved from the end of October to the middle of December.

The early success of the limited range of consumer durables such as digital clocks, functional clothing and a variety of bags and suitcases suggested that the company could expand in a number of directions.

A number of problems were identified, however. The first was the increasing cost of maintaining stock with the problems of seasonality and the rising value of the items being offered. Second, the costs of promotion were steadily rising. The company's mailing list had risen from 50,000 to 210,000 by 1974, and with the increasing competition caused by other direct marketing companies the numbers of mailings had had to be increased from two to four per year. Third, it suffered from the classic problem of the direct marketing company – the long planning horizon over which it had to work. A direct marketing company has to plan stockholdings in advance of the catalogue; the catalogue itself takes time to produce, and response from the consumer will often be delayed. This long timescale posed especial problems for the fashion-oriented mail order operation; the products offered would often be out of date by the time the catalogue appeared. This often meant it had large stocks of certain lines which would have to be sold off through the retail trade or slowly at discount through the catalogues, though this last solution lowered the image of Magic as a premium supplier.

MAGIC'S NEW DIRECTION

1. The company decided to establish a number of shops to create a retail presence in the south of England, reduce its dependence on seasonality and to allow it to move obsolescent stock without harming the overall Magic image.
2. The company decided to expand into offering summer products which would further smooth the seasonal demand pattern, and established a garden mail order catalogue.
3. The gift element was identified as requiring specific action to reduce the level of stockholding required. A new catalogue was produced with lower cost items that could be personalized by the addition of gilt names or initials.

MAGIC'S INCREASING PROBLEMS

The new strategy immediately caused problems. Few of the fifteen stores that had been opened appeared to be profitable with the high overhead costs each of them incurred. The new catalogues dramatically increased the level of stock the company had to hold. The additional catalogues added to the cost burden, even though both ideas had been reasonably well received.

By 1979, profits had slumped to £80,000. More worrying were the continual cash flow problems that the company was experiencing. Borrowings had increased over the four years from £200,000 to £460,000 and seemed set to go higher.

MAGIC TAKE ACTION

The management of Magic was aware that it would have to take some drastic action – otherwise the company would face bankruptcy. The initial problem was to determine what information was needed to formulate a decision. The internal information system had not kept pace with the expansion of the group and would need a considerable overhaul to produce some of the necessary reports. Each item of information would therefore incur a cost, which varied according to complexity. Magic management was also aware that it could call on outside research agencies for a wide range of material which might help in formulating policy decisions.

1. Retail sales and growth monitor report for the UK – £1,200.
2. Fashion trends in the UK report – £2,000.
3. Profitability on store-by-store basis – £3,000.
4. Five-year analysis of stock levels on line-by-line basis – £2,500.
5. Profit assessment of individual products – £3,000.
6. Assessment of current Magic customers and socio-economic groups – £5,000.
7. Assessment of current catalogue strategy – £7,000.
8. Detailed assessment of ordering pattern of current Magic customers – £2,500.
9. Forecasting system to analyse demand in main product areas – £10,000.
10. Economic forecast – £2,000.
11. Research report into potential Magic customers – £2,000.
12. Advertising effectiveness analysis over the last five years – £3,500.
13. Postal code analysis to allow the company to target direct mail to higher income groups more accurately – £7,500.

Installing a computer to handle all the company's internal and external information requirements was estimated by consultants to require at least six months before it could be fully operational and even this was not totally guaranteed.

Comment

This case explores the issues of what constitutes necessary information, and how information requirements may change over time.

7

FORECASTING

All firms live and perform in two time periods: today and tomorrow. Tomorrow is being made today. In turbulent times managers cannot assume that tomorrow will be an extension of today.

(Drucker)

As we have already discovered, planning for change involves not only the ability to react rapidly to changes in the environment, but the ability to anticipate major alterations in all factors that affect the firm. The firm must be able to decide where it should be investing and what the rate of return is likely to be. In common with the more general management information system of which a forecasting system is part, the firm that is able to understand the environment better than a competitor is likely to gain a substantial competitive advantage.

Forecasting is all to do with the minimization of risk. One of the largest risks that an organization can face is the inability to foresee rapid change. This can either cause a dramatic increase or decline in demand. Either will cause the company greater problems than it can immediately deal with. Advance warning of these 'turning points' allows the firm to make resources available in other areas of the business – more production, more promotion, or whatever. In a simple environment of one company supplying a long-established loyal customer with a component in short supply, demand is largely predetermined, and there is a minimal risk that the environment will change sufficiently to affect the supplier's production, for even if overall demand drops this will be offset by the shortage of supply. A company in this situation could plan with a high degree of confidence for the future.

At the other extreme a company with a volatile customer base, and a surplus of product available in the market, faces a very different set of demand problems. These will be made even more acute should the sector in which the firm operates face rapid technological, political, economic, or social change, which will be very hard to quantify.

1. Political. What happens if political systems change?

> The decision of the Common Market to introduce milk quotas had a dramatic and severe effect on many small farmers especially those in developing dairy areas such as Wales.
>
> Whether the major debtor nations, Brazil, Argentina and Mexico, would default on their massive debt repayments has overshadowed the planning process in many large banks.

2. Economy. What are the likely changes in economic activity both at home and abroad over the next five years?

> The level at which oil prices will stabilize has been a factor of major importance to many companies. Its sudden collapse in 1986, for example, was predicted by few.

3. Social. What important social changes will take place over the next five years?

> The number of people regularly playing bingo has dropped from 5.5 million in the 1970s to 3.5 million by the mid-1980s. Ladbroke, one of the major operators of bingo halls, has taken the view that this decline will continue; the Rank Organization, which purchased their halls, takes the opposite view.

4. Technological. What effect will changing technology cause over the next five years?

> The introduction of the tape cassette virtually eliminated the market for reel-to-reel tape recorders except for professional applications.

These largely imponderable problems can be remembered by the mnemonic PEST; they are the problems that lie at the heart of many companies' forecasting difficulties.

Some firms consider that the problems these changing trends cause are too severe to combat effectively, and withdraw from any attempt to determine long-term demand.

> The major record companies find it impossible to forecast demand for particular recording artistes. Bands surface for six months, a year, and then mysteriously disappear from the public consciousness. They respond to these extreme fluctuations by keeping as many artistes under contract as possible.

The record companies can adopt this approach because the investment involved is low; groups are paid on a royalty basis after their records sell. For other companies facing similar rates of change the solution is not so simple.

> The Boeing Aircraft Corporation currently faces the problem of assessing the future replacement of the 747. The investment that such a move will require will be immense; the pay-back period well into the next century.

Companies like the Boeing Aircraft Corporation need to develop some system to minimize the risks such investment decisions impose upon them. Any assessment of likely change will inevitably be subjective; in other words the research will be qualitative rather than quantitative, issues which were discussed in Chapter 6.

TYPES OF FORECASTING SYSTEMS

Forecasting systems of both qualitative and quantitative natures have been developed to minimize risk. The relevance of each will vary according to the nature of the problem and the degree of risk.

QUALITATIVE METHODS

Delphi. The Delphi forecasting technique developed by the Rand Corporation attempts to use expert opinion to develop forecasts by an exchange of questionnaires. Members are kept unaware of who else is on the panel and there is no discussion – feedback is maintained by the group leader who analyses the questionnaires and asks individuals who deviate significantly from the group consensus to justify their answers. Companies such as the Lockheed Aircraft Corporation have found this a useful technique to attempt to minimize the problems of change in a rapidly changing technological environment.

Visionary statement. A similar approach, albeit on a more simple level, is to ask individuals within an organization for a 'visionary' statement, an attempt to forecast broad changes that may affect the organization.

QUANTITATIVE METHODS

Even when the environment is rapidly changing the use of current information to forecast will increase the chance of the company identifying turning points within the planning horizon.

Historic projection. The simplest approach is the straightforward historic projection, taking the current level of activity and projecting forward from that base. Such a forecast will be unlikely to identify major changes in the environment as it will be far too affected by short-term fluctuations.

Customer projection. Where the bulk of the business is carried out with a limited number of customers, direct contact with them over likely future demand will often provide one of the most accurate forecasting systems. This approach is very similar to the simple environment discussed in the introduction.

Moving totals. A method of removing some of the fluctuations, such as those caused by high seasonal sales, is to combine the sales for a year or two years adding current months and removing sales which occur outside the time period. This system, which is extremely easy to apply and fairly accurate as a short-term indication of likely trends, is particularly suitable where the change in sales levels is fairly gradual.

Exponential smoothing. Where there are rapid changes in the sales history, recent events will be far more important in explaining the near future than sales of one or two years ago. Introducing a smoothing constant which gives greater importance to more recent sales is one way of overcoming this problem.

The comparison between historic projection, moving averages and exponential smoothing is shown in Figure 7.1.

Figure 7.1.   Comparison between various historic projection techniques

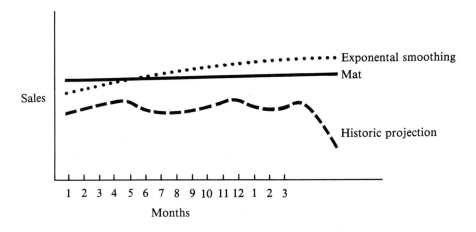

Time series analysis. More sophisticated analyses, such as the Box–Jenkins method, attempt to take a number of elements of the company's sales record and produce a model to explain the underlying trends. Both this system and the more complicated X-11 system produced by the US Weather Bureau require computer assistance and a degree of statistical expertise. Both systems do, however, reduce the element of risk in the forecast process by more accurately identifying possible turning points within a one-year projection period.

Environmental factors. The use of the PLC as a forecasting system has already been commented on (see Chapter 4). This and the experience curve discussed in Chapter 9 are used by some firms as additional forecasting tools.

Causal analysis. The main shortcoming in all time series analyses is the fact that the information used to develop the forecast is internal. The company will not be able rapidly to relate violent change in the external environment to the effect on demand. To do this the firm will need to determine a factor in the external environment which causally related to the demand for the company's products. The example in Chapter 1 of Unilever's detergent policy relating on a worldwide basis the amount of detergent consumption to gross national product (GNP) per head is one such relationship. Rising GNP appears to have an effect on the overall consumption of detergents.

Other relationships that have been found by companies include the level of consumption of consumer durables (on fast-food consumption in the United States) and the level of unemployment (on demand for holidays in the United Kingdom). The advantage of such causal systems is that it allows the firm to predict demand patterns more accurately. The main problem in using causal systems is the complexity of data analysis required, the removal of spurious interrelationships, the critical assessment of what are in fact independent rather than dependent variables. For example, there might be a relationship between the number of miles of motorway and overall ice cream consumption; the real underlying factor would perhaps be increases in GNP. Second, there would be a clear relationship between the number of new cars and demand for number plates; one would be a dependent variable on the other.

At its simplest level, regression analysis of a single factor against another will yield information about underlying demand trends. Often more than one factor will be important in influencing demand and therefore multiple regression techniques will be important for complex sales relationships. In many large companies this is built up into an econometric model which attempts to provide an explanation or a simulation of all the main external factors affecting sales.

> Bowater Scott and Beechams are two companies that have developed sophisticated models to explain the effects of environmental factors upon their leading brands. The logic underlying the model suggested to Bowater Scott that continuous advertising would be highly profitable for the Andrex brand; Beechams that increasing price along with extra promotional expenditure would be the most profitable route for Dettol.

These econometric models at their most sophisticated simulate the external environment; they enable firms to test out hypotheses such as the effects of increasing distribution, lowering price, and raising promotional expenditure on the total market sales.

As forecasting systems become more complex, they tend to become divorced from the operational level and require the services of trained statisticians. The results of such forecasts tend to be treated with a degree of caution, as line managers often feel that the figures arrived at do not accurately reflect the market place.

RELATING THE COMPANY POSITION TO FORECASTING REQUIREMENTS

As risk increases, the need for forecasting investment will grow. Crucial factors will be:
(a) the level of investment;
(b) the speed of return on that investment;
(c) the uncertainty in the environment.

More investment means more risk, as do longer and longer pay-back periods. As the uncertainty in the environment increases, so forecasting becomes more crucial. Figure 7.2 highlights the criteria of forecasting.

Summary

Forecasting is an essential part of any complex business. It enables the firm to reduce the level of risk inherent in all long-term planning. A variety of techniques has been developed to analyse sales records and isolate trends; others exist to handle complex technological and economic forecasting problems. The key issue, the ability to identify turning points in the future demand patterns, appears best served by some form of causal system.

Figure 7.2. Forecasting criteria

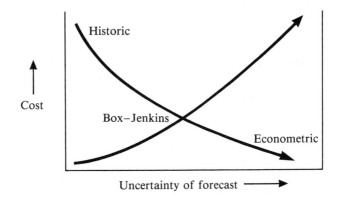

ASSIGNMENTS

1. You are working for a computer software company. Write a memo to the managing director outlining the problems of forecasting product demand.
2. Take the last ten years' admissions data to your college and try to forecast future demand over the next five years. Write a report outlining the issues that would need to be considered.
3. You have been called in as a marketing consultant to advise a firm in the sporting goods sector. Its sales are highly seasonal with 60 per cent of annual demand occurring between March and September. In addition, sales have grown annually at 50 per cent, 10 per cent, 90 per cent, 5 per cent, 23 per cent over the last five years. Write a report analysing the firm's forecasting problem and provide recommendations.

PART 3

THE MARKETING MIX

– 8 –

CONTROLLING PRODUCTS

Where he led he conquered, where he followed he failed.

(A description of the progress of Lord Lever, the founder of Unilever.)

PRODUCT CHANGE

Earlier chapters have underlined the dynamic nature of the interaction between the market and the firm.

Strategies may change, implying that different segments of the market will be addressed; the market segment itself may change, involving additional alteration in the emphasis placed within the marketing mix (Figure 8.1).

Figure 8.1.   Changes in the marketing mix

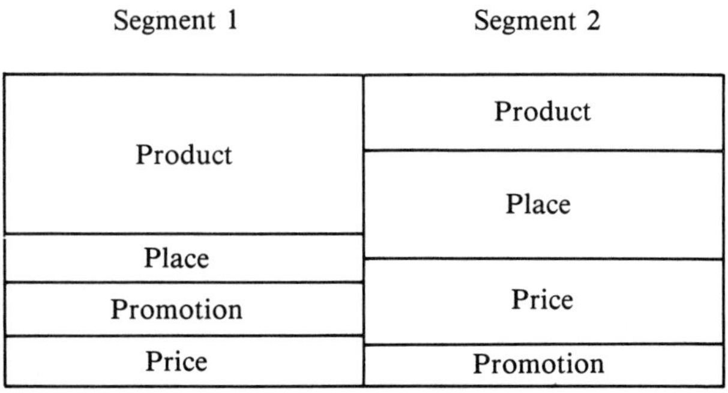

Segment 1	Segment 2
	Product
Product	Place
Place	Price
Promotion	
Price	Promotion

Changes in product emphasis can be considered in the majority of instances as central to this continual realignment process, even though distribution, price, promotion and competitive effects will in some instances be more important.

The company is faced with two broad initial alternatives when it comes to analyse its products; either to abandon the product, or to continue to maintain it in the market.

PRODUCT ABANDONMENT

For the firm to consider abandoning a product it will need to evaluate two often conflicting factors.

The profitability or otherwise of the specific item. The effects of how the fixed overheads within a linked product range are allocated can have a decisive influence on the profitability of the brand. Take three products as shown in Table 8.1.

Table 8.1. *Profitability evaluation example*

Product	Sales	Overhead	Profit
A	150	100	50
B	120	100	20
C	80	100	−20
Total	350	300	50

Suppose the firm decided to abandon product C because it was 'unprofitable'. Table 8.1 would now appear as Table 8.2.

Table 8.2. *Revised profitability evaluation*

Product	Sales	Overhead	Profit
A	150	150	0
B	120	150	−30
Total	270	300	−30

The logic would suggest that product B should then be withdrawn: this would inevitably mean that product A should be scrapped as losing large sums of money. Following this process the firm will have moved from a position of making an overall profit to achieving a substantial overall loss.

Where overheads are shared the products within a particular group must be seen in totality; removal of one will inevitably affect the profitability of others.

The 'service' element. There may be important reasons for maintaining the product in the range for promotional or service reasons.

Gerber the baby food company had a wide range of speciality meals for babies with dietary problems. Though these continually lost money it was felt that the continued presence of them in the range was important as sales of baby food greatly depended on recommendation at maternity hospitals and the speciality products gave Gerber clinical superiority over the other brands.

Service considerations are always an acceptable reason for maintaining a loss-making product within the portfolio provided that they are adequately accounted for; if they are included within the promotional budget this will accurately reflect the reality of the product: it is seen as a promotional item and should therefore be funded as such.

Competitive value. Even though the product may be neither particularly profitable nor provide important support for other products within the company, the maintenance of it may prevent a competitor from becoming established. An increasingly common feature of the retailing takeovers in the high street is the willingness of some chains to continue to maintain two or more outlets in the same location to ensure that no competitor can become easily established.

Withdrawal from the market will involve the firm in taking a number of subsidiary decisions.
1. Can the product be sold to another firm?
2. The speed at which the product should be removed from the product line.
3. The level of service and spare parts that will be needed to maintain the declining product.

To phase out the old style razor blades in its range, Gillette made the offer of replacing all old style razors with ones that would accept the new blades, expecting only a small response. Instead the company was inundated with requests for the replacements.

Meccano, the toy construction company, kept over thirty spare parts of kits it no longer made to service worldwide enthusiasts.

MAINTAINING THE PRODUCT IN THE MARKET-PLACE

Holding current position. Though in periods of recession and severe market depression zero or no-growth budgeting is practised by many firms, in the longer term the lack of direction will lead to the slow erosion of market share and profitability. All markets are dynamic; change in some direction is essential for survival.

Investment. Most product strategies will concentrate on the development of markets and products, which can be summarized in tabular form as:

Market/product	Present	New
Present	Penetration	Product development
New	Market development	Diversification

Market penetration

This product strategy demands increasing share of current products in current markets. Options open in this area would be:

Changing pricing policy. Reduction in prices can significantly increase volume sales.

Changing promotional policy. Redirecting the sales effort in other directions will possibly open up new market areas that have not been currently exploited. Casual clothing such as tracksuits and sports equipment such as running shoes were once purchased predominantly by people actively involved in sport. Manufacturers have now realized the vast untapped market that exists in the area of 'social' sport.

Increasing promotional expenditure. Heavy advertising or consumer promotional campaigns can change brand share over a limited period of time.

Changing distribution methods. Pepsi-Cola, by concentrating on vending machines and other non-standard points of sale, managed gradually to establish itself as the number two cola in the market.

Improving product quality control. This can have a rapid effect on overall demand.

> Jaguar Cars has achieved a major increase in sales largely due to improved product quality control with turnover up from £120 million in 1980 to £500 million in 1985 and profits up sixfold over the same period. The high product quality of the Jaguar range had enabled it to become firmly established in the lucrative United States luxury car market.

Branding. The use of a brand name can be an important vehicle for improved market penetration.

The rewards of successful brand creation are several:
1. Sales. A successfully branded product will have a substantial advantage over the non- or poorly branded product. This is partly because once the brand is well established in the market customers will continue buying it without continually questioning product quality.
2. Customer retention. Branding increases the power of the supplier compared with the end user or retailer by ensuring a built-in level of demand that the end user or retailer has to satisfy.
3. Price. In general a poorly branded product can achieve a moderate premium over non-branded competition; well-branded old-established products can achieve premiums of 20–30 per cent in the grocery area and often substantially more in the industrial market.
4. Profitability. In the long term establishing a brand will tend to improve profitability as the product is more resistant to trade fluctuations and can achieve a higher price in the market.
5. Flexibility to change. The well-established brand can allow substantial changes in formulation/design/packaging while still retaining large parts of its original market share.

> Coca-Cola and Pepsi have long been rivals for the $25 billion American and $40 billion overseas soft drinks market. In the US Coke had been steadily losing market share to Pepsi (22 per cent of the US market in 1984 compared with 19 per cent). The

company has reacted to this by the introduction of 'new formula Coke'. Public outcry led to the reintroduction of the original formula product as 'Coke Classic'. Recent introductions of 'Cherry Coke', a highly successful low-calorie 'diet Coke', 'caffeine-free Coke' and 'caffeine-free diet Coke' have significantly increased the overall Coca-Cola market share in the United States in 1984 (Table 8.3).

Table 8.3. Coca-Cola and Pepsi market shares 1984

	Coca-Cola %	Pepsi %
April	42	35
June	43	33
August	45	32
October	46	29

Branding will be particularly important if there exists a strong difference between the product and others, or when the company is trying to establish one. It has most clear applications when the product is patented or has major differences in quality. It is seen as the key to success by many companies but inevitably carries a level of risk that has to be assessed in the context of the company's strategy. The issues that need to be considered are:

1. What level of investment over what timespan will be needed to develop the brand? (How much money for how long will be required to establish the consumer franchise?)
2. Does the likely return to the company merit this investment? (What likely market share at what price will be achieved by the level of investment?)
3. Should the brand be clearly identified from other products in the range or should they be integrated under the umbrella of company advertising? (Should the products all be included under one roof – Black and Decker for garden equipment, Birds Eye for frozen food – be split into ranges – Penguin, Pelican and Peregrine books, for example – or individually identified – Stork, Blue Band margarine).

Sales integration. The supplier buying the end user can also be a worthwhile route to increased market share. Remy Martin, suffering from distribution problems due to a restricted product range, bought the Nicholas wine shops. Similarly, a firm can buy a competitor in the market to increase market share. Boots, already involved in the sale of household equipment, bought Timothy Whites, a major competitor, and then closed down its stores reducing the distribution outlets for household wares, improving Boots' own share of this business.

Product development

Product modification. This may involve quality improvement – upgrading the ingredients in ice cream; feature improvement – the addition of safety plugs to electrical appliances; or style improvement – changes in design such as replacing steel elements with plastic. The results of product modification policies are all around us. 'Newer smoother taste', 'Easy opening lid', 'Even whiter wash', are common claims seen on a wide range of consumer products.

Product modifications will fall under a number of headings:

1. Physical characteristics. Improving ease of flow, ease of mixing, storage quality, would all be examples.

> The Spillers Homepride campaign based on the more finely ground flour is a good example of a slight product modification leading to substantial increases in market share.

2. Health benefits. Increased vitamin, sugar, fibre.
3. Physical dimensions. Granules instead of powder, shape of item and its packaging.
4. Convenience. Speed and ease of use provided by new packaging or packet top.
5. Subjective characteristics. Smoother flavour, smell, texture would all be examples.

Many companies are continually looking for means of improving profitability and market share by continual small changes in product quality. Detergent companies will, for example, continually evaluate the level of active detergent necessary in washing powders to ensure that the product remains correctly engineered for the market place. Obviously the danger is that the process will go too far and the product will become devalued in the eyes of the consumer; the process needs the most careful monitoring and control.

> Schlitz Beer in the United States attempted to reduce quality of the product to improve profitability. The attempts caused problems in the fermentation process with the result that there were many complaints and much returned product. This caused a significant drop in market share from which the company has not yet recovered.

The crucial question for the company is to define carefully the position of the *just definable difference* where a substantial number of consumers are able to detect a difference, be it ever so slight, between the current product and the proposed modification.

Product addition. Once a brand becomes established there is a tendency to produce new variants, as this can provide additional growth, restrict the shelf space available to the competition, and provide a better customer service. Toothpaste has moved from a single 'regular' size to 'economy', 'family', and 'giant' sizes. Customization of cars is another example of such a tendency – with L, GL, GLS, SR, SRi, hatchback, non-hatchback variants of a single model. Such proliferation, however, has effects on economies of scale, inventory, promotional, sales force, and distribution costs.

> Ranks Hovis McDougall has invested large sums in various areas of product development; the Sharwoods range and biscuits such as Cracottes are examples. One of the most profitable introductions, however, was the development of Bisto granules which gained instant acceptance and increased overall Bisto consumption. So successful was it that it led to the development of a further range of Bisto granule-based sauces.

Line extension. The current product range can be modified to reach different parts of the market, either downward or upward for companies placed at extremes of the market or in both directions for the centrally placed firm (Figure 8.2).

Figure 8.2.   Line extension strategies

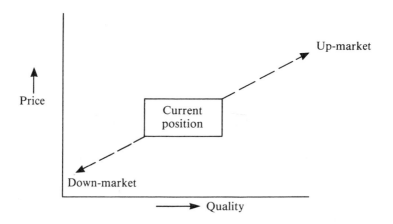

Such a policy will entail risks resulting from lack of resources to cope with the new market sectors, and the problems of confusion between different elements of the product range, unless they are clearly identified.

Nissan entered the UK car market with a limited range of family saloons which built up a reputation for reliability. From that position it has expanded into the small car market (downward) and is now entering the premium market with a range of sporty models (upward line extension).

Market development

The geographic expansion of the firm from its initial market base is an obvious method of achieving growth. The nature of the home market will greatly determine the potential for changing from a small, regional operation into a larger national organization. For a firm in India, Nigeria or the United States, enormous federal countries with huge populations, this will offer far greater market opportunities than those available for the growing firm in the Netherlands or Belgium.

JCB has effectively developed a world market presence with a single product. Though one product (technically called the backhoe loader) makes up 70 per cent of total sales, it is market leader in fifty countries. This market spread has enabled JCB to be one of the few companies in the construction machinery market that has managed to remain profitable from the early 1980s. Growth is likely to continue with an expanding share of the large market in the United States where market share has climbed from 2 to 8 per cent over the last ten years. Currently JCB has 17 per cent of the world market, a share which has slowly but steadily grown in competition with major American groups.

Diversification

Production integration. Many firms see a logical development in the development of operations relating to the primary company activity, in that the company will improve its overall profitability (by not paying the profit margin of its suppliers), and enable the marketing and production expertise to be fully utilized over a wider range of products.

Ford developed interests in batteries and tyres; Spillers, an English baking firm, went from flour to animal feed, from animal feed to petfood; IBM has bought Rohm, a computer micro chip manufacturer; Unilever bought plantations in Central Africa to supply copra for the production of soap; GEC, supplying the electronics for ships, bought a shipyard.

Other companies will look for other uses of their manufacturing expertise. A producer of pressure lamps might consider that the knowledge of producing airtight containers could be developed into a range of vacuum flasks.

The Bic organization has effectively translated production expertise in one area (biros) into another (disposable razors). In the early 1960s Bic had become market leader in the low-cost segment of the disposable pen market by concentrating on simple effective products and utilizing the large economies of scale afforded by volume production. Its manufacturing expertise was in the combination of plastics and metal alloys in small consumer products.

The UK razor market of 325 million blades was dominated by Gillette and Wilkinson Sword who considered that the market for disposable razors rather than razor blades was likely to be limited. Bic entered the market with a low-cost simple product consisting of a single blade and three plastic components. Because of the simplicity of the design and the production expertise in this area it was able to underprice the competition significantly and gain a substantial part of what became a steadily growing market.

Market integration. In this the company identifies possibilities of supplying a totally different range of products to its current customers (commonly termed 'horizontal diversification'). The Airfix case study showed a classic example of this product policy by diversifying into a wide range of associated toy products.

IDV, part of Grand Metropolitan, has successfully grown into one of the major international drinks companies by developing a range of products such as Bailey's Irish Cream, Malibu, and Piat d'Or in addition to sales integration with other successful brands.

Opportunity development. Many companies identify market opportunities which involve them producing diverse products for diverse customers (which can be also termed 'conglomerate diversification').

General Mills saw that the marketing techniques it had developed with great success in its development from a flour manufacturer to branded cake and bread supplier could be applied to another growth area – that of toys – buying Palitoy, Parker Games and Airfix – it has since taken the decision to withdraw from the market entirely.

Associated Paper, initially producing bulk paper, proceeded to buy firms specializing in foil, poster paper, gift packs, air fresheners, and oil purifiers for

Kentucky Fried Chicken. Once established in this area it then sold the initial core activities as they were not meeting the strategic objectives laid down for the company.

WHAT IS THE BEST POLICY?

The best policy is obviously the one best meeting the strategic objectives of the firm. Having made that broad statement, every development will have implications for the allocation of resources and the degree of *risk* that the firm will face. As the firm moves further and further away from its initial base the level of risk will increase – market penetration policies tend to require far lower investment than diversification strategies.

On the other hand, the level of return or reward will tend to be higher in new ventures. Graphically, this can be represented as in Figure 8.3.

Figure 8.3.   Risk/return considerations in product change

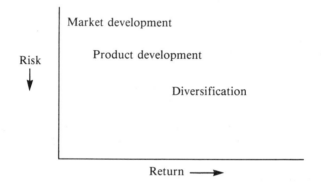

The assessment of risk is however related to strategic requirements and is commented on in Chapter 4.

Research tends to suggest that the most successful firms are those that only move slowly away from their traditional areas of expertise. Rapid change or quick alteration in fundamental strategy tends to cause major problems even for organizations with considerable depths of experience.

NEW PRODUCT DEVELOPMENT

Changing markets will necessitate the development of new products by all organizations, either to maintain their position in the market-place or to achieve their growth objectives.

The investigation, development and introduction of new products is an area of exceptionally high risk. The problems of the Ford Edsel, which failed at a cost of over $350 million, and Corfam, the synthetic leather product developed by Du Pont which is estimated to have cost the company over $275 million, are only the tip of the failed product mountain. It is estimated that around 2,200 new grocery products are introduced into the United Kingdom market every year; of these only five or six are likely to be continuing successes. Where, for example, is the Harvey's Duo-Can with rice at one end and curry at the other? Crocodilo, the competitor to Babycham? Cabana, the coconut and nougat chocolate bar? Dynamo, the liquid washing machine detergent? All have disappeared at considerable cost to the manufacturer.

The number of products that actually appear on the market is the result of a winnowing process which can remove more than 90 per cent of the initial ideas with which the company starts. A typical picture of the new product development process might be as in Table 8.4.

Table 8.4. The new product development process

Stage	No. of products	Chance of success (%)
Idea collection	200	3
Screening	100	10
Concept test	25	20
Physical development	12	30
Test marketing	6	50
National launch	3	60

For a typical consumer product, the later stages of the new product development process will be the most expensive. For example, concept testing of ideas may only cost £5,000–6,000, plant development, test marketing and national launches will be much more expensive, with national launches – even in the United Kingdom for mass market products – often costing over £10 million. Other products will show different cost patterns. For something with a lengthy development process such as a drug, the product development and testing costs can be enormous. An estimate of the average development costs of a drug at each stage is shown in Table 8.5.

Table 8.5. Average new drug development costs

Stage	Cost (£ million)
Drug synthesis	14
Biological screening	12
Pre-clinical tests	50
Controlled tests	5
Final tests	4
Gaining approval	2
Launch	1

The stage-by-stage approach adopted by the majority of companies is designed to reduce the level of failure, by creating points at which the decision as to whether the project should proceed can be taken.

IDEA COLLECTION

Ideas for new product development can be derived from many sources, and the degree of importance attached to each avenue will depend on company circumstances and the nature of the industry.

1. Customer contact. For many firms customer contact will be the most valuable source of new product ideas, especially via the sales force in technical industries, where a client's particular problems will often be discussed during a sales visit.
2. Competitive input. It will be essential for the company to analyse product development trends of the competition. Car companies, for example, buy competitors' new models as soon as they are available, to tear them apart piece by piece to determine engineering and manufacturing advances. Trade literature and exhibitions will be particularly valuable sources of information.
3. Internal sources. There will be a number of ways in which firms can generate ideas internally: from research and development departments, management 'brain storming sessions', suggestion boxes, and quality circles.
4. External research sources. These will include specific market research designed to isolate gaps in the market; for example 'cluster' research (Figure 8.4).

Figure 8.4.   Cluster analysis

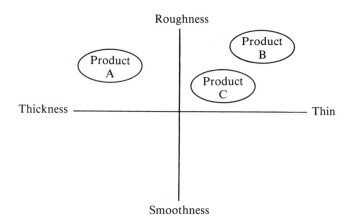

Recently a number of new product development companies have emerged which provide specialist consultancy advice for new products in specific fields.

SCREENING

One approach used by many companies is to develop a range of criteria by which new products can be judged, and measure the probability that the new product will meet these criteria (Table 8.6).

Table 8.6. New product development criteria

Factor	Weight	%	Probability
Uses R & D facilities	3	45	1.5
Fits production	7	80	5.6
Fits management skills	6	40	2.4
Fits distribution	3	80	2.4
Fits market position	7	70	4.9
Long-term demand	9	50	4.5
Patentable	2	20	0.4
Unique selling point	5	90	2.4
Raw material available	8	100	8.0
Safety	4	100	4.0

Such a process, though subjective, is valuable as an initial filter, to define where the major strengths and weaknesses of particular products are likely to lie and for the company to compare the range of possible new products against each other.

Ideally, what the firm should be seeking is the minimum utilization of its resources to obtain the maximum return. By moving away from currently available resources, diversification strategies will only be viable if the return on the proposed activity more than offsets the increased level of resource allocation.

CONCEPT TESTING

For consumer goods there are a number of low-cost methods available to carry out concept tests – members of the public can be recruited off the street to try the product (hall testing), or market research services exist that make sample products availabe to consumers in simulated sale conditions (mini-van tests). Industrial companies face more difficult problems in carrying out concept tests, though by choosing sympathetic customers the same result can often be obtained.

TEST MARKETING

Concept testing is normally limited to the product in isolation. Test marketing investigates the interaction of all other factors in consumer acceptance, price distribution, competitive effects, and promotion.

In order to be successful the test market should meet certain criteria:
- the area chosen should be truly representative of the nation as a whole
- the test should be run long enough for accurate results to be obtained
- the company can achieve adequate distribution within the test market area
- progress can be accurately monitored by objective measurement of actual sales offtake.

Even with such a structured approach many new products still fail. The reasons for product success and failure are legion, but the more important ones are held to be:

1. Inadequate market analysis.
2. Product deficiencies.
3. Lack of clear differentiation from the competition.
4. Poor timing.
5. Poor pricing.
6. Poor packaging.
7. Poor planning and management back-up.
8. Competitive reaction.
9. Technical and/or production problems.
10. Limited investment in support for the new product.
11. Higher costs than anticipated.

Keys to success appear to lie in:

1. Fundamental and distinctive product advantage. The Polaroid camera, oven chips, the Amstrad PCW8256.
2. Distribution advantage. The initial growth of both Avon and Tupperware was mainly due to distribution methods.
3. 'Image' advantage. As the intangible element in products increases this becomes increasingly important. Nike running shoes, Porsche, John Player Special cigarettes are examples in this strategy.

PACKAGING

Part and parcel of the product development process or the introduction of many new products is the attention that should be given to packaging. The importance of packaging to the majority of consumer goods and a substantial number of industrial products should not be underestimated. According to one writer, packaging in Europe accounts for around 3 per cent of Gross Domestic Product, significantly higher than the amount of money spent on advertising, and about the same as advertising and sales promotion combined.

PACKAGING CRITERIA

One can identify four main elements that need to be considered in what can be called the packaging mix: brand, consumer, distribution and production-related factors. A simple example would be a fizzy drink – the nature of the product demands that it be contained within an airtight, relatively tough exterior layer: glass, tin, or thick plastic rather than a polythene bag. The consumer requires not only a hygienic pleasant product but also an increasing quantity of information about calorie levels, contents, volume, and manufacturer's name. The company will have an objective for the development of the product which will be reflected in the packaging, whether it is a premium, medium or low priced item for example. Finally, the retailer or the distributor will place certain demands upon the product. Each of these requirements will introduce an element of conflict into the development of packaging, which the manufacturer will need to develop a policy to overcome.

Brand-related factors

Brand name. It is considered that the brand name should bear some relevance to the product type – Softlan, Downy, and Comfort for fabric conditioners have the right connotation – and should be easily remembered. There are of course numerous exceptions to this ideal – Japanese car names such as Sunny, Cherry, Violet – but nevertheless the underlying concept appears sound. Would, for example, the washing powder Tide have been so successful if it had been called Swamp?

The inapplicability of a brand name developed in one market for another is one of the major problems facing companies attempting to globalize their products.

Vauxhall could not use the name Nova in Spain as it means 'does not go' in Spanish (*no va*).

Rolls-Royce pulled back launching its new car as the Silver Mist when it realized that mist meant 'dung' in German.

A brand of Chinese playing cards was called Maxipuke (*pu* and *ke* are the literal translations of Chinese characters for poker).

The beer Castlemaine XXXX faces severe problems in the United States as Forex is a leading contraceptive brand.

Logo. An easily identifiable logo may have advantages in two respects: if it is used to identify products under a common umbrella (for example the Birds Eye range), or where the company considers sports sponsorship and the accompanying television coverage as effective advertising (for example Nike and Adidas at athletics meetings).

Logos can also cause problems. After 113 years Procter and Gamble was forced to remove its company logo of thirteen stars and a bearded man following five years of unsubstantiated rumours associating it with witchcraft, and hundreds of thousands of dollars spent trying to quell the rumour.

Colour. The use of different colours is held to have a fundamental effect on consumer attitudes. Some of the associations put forward are:
- Black/blue: coolness, distinction
- Red: heat, excitement
- Purple/gold: royalty, richness
- Orange: warmth, movement
- Green: naturalness, softness, freshness.

There is a strong association between the interpretation of colour and culture. White and black have reversed implications in many Eastern cultures – black being a colour of rejoicing and white a colour of mourning among the Chinese. Colour often has important product connotations. For example, butter and margarine are often packaged in yellow containers and coffee in brown, even though there are many exceptions to this.

Numbers. Numbers may also have consumer connotations. A car manufacturer such as Renault produces models typed as 5, 9, 11, 12, 14, 16, 18, but never a

Renault 13 which would probably be considered unlucky. The Chinese would consider the number 7 as lucky; in European cultures the number is neutral.

Symbols. A black cat could be considered lucky or unlucky in different cultures; an elephant associated with memory or with size and bulk, and so on.

Design. The shape of the package can also be an important factor in consumer purchase. Over and above the functional aspects – cans produced in such a way that if you want a can it must be cylindrical – there are behavioural and traditional factors to be considered. The introduction of table wine in lined paper containers has been slow not only because of the technical problems associated with it but also as a result of consumer resistance. Wine should come in bottles not in orange juice containers – or so the consumer thinks.

Differences between countries as to the way in which products are designed go beyond the purely functional requirements of the product. American trucks are therefore held to reflect the 'rugged frontier life style', much German design is considered to mirror the values of thrift, hard work and reliability, whereas much French design is still considered to be derived from an 'idealized agricultural heritage'.

Regardless of whether these differences do in reality exist, more competitive markets will make good product design increasingly important as a means of standing out amongst other products in the market.

There are other elements of design that the company will need to consider:

1. Apparent size. It may be important that the package gives an impression of size consistent with the price being charged. For example: Easter eggs contain very little chocolate; large plastic construction models contain only slightly more plastic than smaller models. As packaging is often regarded as synonymous with price, the larger the item, the higher the price.
2. Visibility. The demands of a particular product will vary: for a consumer product it may be that high visibility is required – the ability to differentiate your pack from others from the end of a supermarket aisle.
3. Distinctiveness. This may be different from the concept of visibility – the level to which the product stands out from its competitors. It also covers the question of memorability – will the package be remembered by the consumer?
4. Display. It may be important that the package offers the ability to provide effective mass displays. For example, Metaxa have developed boxes which when put together in a certain way create a small mural – different boxes of the same product containing different components of the design.
5. Simplicity. The fewer the elements of design on the package, the more effective it is likely to be. Examples include the simplicity of the pack design of Coca-Cola, Colgate toothpaste and McDonald's stores.
6. Consistency. There are two important elements that are included under the heading of consistency. The package should reflect as closely as possible any media or promotional investment, ideally by expanding or complementing the media theme. Second, is the package consistent with the company 'style'?. This may involve the use of particular colours or photographic

techniques, but in certain instances will also be required to reflect 'integrity', 'responsibility' or other attitudes that are important for the company's relationship with its consumers.

Consumer elements

Mandatory information. For each product type and country there will be a differing amount of information that must be included by law. In some it will be necessary to include the full list of ingredients, contents, the manufacturer's and distributor's name. For some products it will be essential for the letters to be of a certain height and in a certain position.

Information. For many products, in addition to the mandatory information there will be a need to provide full and concise instructions as to the product usage. It is often considered that one of the major shortcomings of British goods in foreign markets is the limited amount of information that is included with the pack.

Convenience. It is important that the packaging can be opened and closed easily by the consumer and the in-use product be stored without difficulty wherever it is in use. Whether the theoretical improvements in convenience are actually perceived by the consumer is one of the important questions that should be posed in any packaging exercise. The creation of prepackaged toilet soap was an enormous success; Harvey's Duo-Can (rice at one end of the tin and the meal at the other) an expensive failure.

Safety. The packaging must be able to withstand any of the transportation or climatic conditions it is likely to encounter. It must also meet legal and social requirements in this area. Childproof caps for medicine bottles were introduced in the early 1980s; the Tylenol scare in the United States has caused a further reappraisal of safety standards.

Distribution factors

The co-operation of the retailer and wholesaler is crucial to the acceptance of any new introduction, and their views in certain areas will be very important.

The power of the major retail chains is having an impact on at least two areas: the milk bottle and the tin can. Retailers stock cartons (average cost per pint 2p) rather than glass bottles (average cost 0.2p) because of the problems of recycling the bottles. The growth in aluminium containers at the expense of tin plate for cans is supported by the retailers' search for lighter packaging materials, even though this is more expensive than the other alternative.

In addition to these overall requirements, the packaging will need to meet a number of other criteria:

1. Ease of handling. The packaging should meet the criteria of all stages of the distribution process. Thus, the outer packaging should be designed with the requirements of palletization and containerization in mind. More and more major retailers are delivering from central warehouses rather than allowing direct deliveries, and this will tend increasingly to affect pack design.

2. Retailer information. The pack should give all the retail information necessary, such as whether a special offer is being made and the date of its completion. It should also give the retailer some date information to allow correct stock rotation, and contain the instructions for the correct opening of the carton. More retailers are investing in EPOS (electronic point of sale) equipment to speed up checkouts, improve stock control, and reduce the requirement to price on the shelf: manufacturers need to ensure that the correct bar codes are included on all packs.

3. Display. Products must fit into the shelf space available – non-standard products face impossible exclusion from the retailers' shelves. For example, the development of an E40 size of detergent would mean supplying the pack in drum form to achieve the necessary structural strength; the drum would take up considerable space on the shelf, which would mean resistance to the concept from the retail trade.

4. Simplicity. Again, the outer carton should have the minimum information necessary for the retailer. The use of many colours in the outer cartons, for example, may need to be justified when a one- or two-colour approach may be as effective.

Production factors

The most simple design can easily cause problems in the filling, capping, printing or assembly. These problems are far more easily dealt with before they occur as corrective treatment will be extremely expensive both in money and time.

The issues that the firm will need to consider will include:

1. Efficiency. Does the design use the most efficient machinery possible, or must it be produced on a slower and therefore more expensive machine? For example, a larger pack on a faster machine may be cheaper than a smaller pack which has to be hand filled.

2. Shape. Will the package pass through the current system without causing breakage, and at a satisfactory speed?

3. Strength. Will the package stand up to the rigours of mechanical mishandling and can it cope with the effects of heat, moisture, and sunlight? The last is particularly relevant in the choice of printing inks as some will fade badly on exposure to sunlight. Another important consideration in this context is whether the packaging will last the life of the product without degradation of the contents. Thus, carbonated drinks can be kept in the new PET (plastic derivative) bottles provided the shelf life is reasonably short. For wine or other drinks with a slower rate of sale, the packaging would be inadequate.

4. Components. It is important for certain operations that the components can be easily pre-assembled, and that the sealing operations can be easily achieved mechanically. The interaction of the filling mechanism with the system chosen for sealing the pack is another vital factor in any assessment of whether the product can be easily produced.

5. Cost effectiveness. The relevance of this item will obviously vary from product to product. Within mass market items questions such as the nature

of the material used, and whether savings can be achieved by the use of differing material or a thinner container wall, become crucial.

6. Print surface. The nature of the surface available for print will also vary in importance from product to product and the degree of print finish necessary. Surface irregularities may also deserve consideration, the ability of the printer to achieve correct register, and the combination of colours in a multi-colour process. To cope with the problems that may be encountered with high-speed production, many packs are designed with indented areas to which labels can be stuck and protected from the scuffing the container often receives; another alternative is to leave the labelling until the end of the packaging process.

For many consumer goods it is important that the print surface is such that rapid changes can be introduced ('20p off' for example) to meet sales promotion requirements.

MINIMIZING THE PROBLEMS OF CHANGE

Any packaging proposal should pass through a number of stages:
1. The development of a detailed rationale as to why the packaging should be changed, and the financial benefits that will flow from such a change.
2. The production of a design brief which should include all costing implications.
3. Appraisal of the design proposals put forward by the external or internal team via the use of a structured assessment of the various factors relevant to that particular product.
4. The development of a research programme to test the pack effectiveness, and its evaluation.

Summary

Product policy relates closely to the strategic demands of the company and the segment to which the product is directed. Each option available to the company has a series of implications that need to be evaluated and integrated with other areas of company operation.

Packaging for consumer goods is of great importance; its role in the development of sales is often understated and the complexities little understood.

ASSIGNMENTS

1. Choose two recent product introductions and comment why you think that they have succeeded or failed.
2. You are asked as a trainee manager to develop a test marketing programme for a small range of electrical appliances. Prepare the report that you would submit to your marketing manager.
3. Your firm is thinking of introducing a new brand of dishwashing detergent.

Write a memorandum on the packaging issues that the firm should consider in relation to the main competition in the market.

4.   You are asked by your old school to give a talk on the marketing mix. Prepare your speech.

SPRINT

In April 1981 the Mars Company in the UK launched 'Sprint', a totally new concept in savoury snacks. One of the three largest UK confectionery companies, Mars has an exceptional record in the successful marketing of chocolate confectionery. The Mars bar, developed by the company in the USA, has become something of an institution in itself. In 1953 the company produced the first 'self-server' – the open display unit filled with bars for the consumer to help himself. It was made available to shops on the understanding that it would be placed with Mars products in the front row. The improved accessibility generated a huge increase in sales. Other chocolate-based successes followed: Twix, Galaxy, Marathon, Banjo and the ultimate 'fun size' Mars. In 1980 the company produced 140,000 tonnes of confectionery valued at around £220 million. However, 'Sprint' was a new venture representing a sortie into the savoury snack market.

THE SAVOURY SNACK MARKET

The UK savoury snack market continues to grow and comprises three main product groups: potato crisps, nuts and snacks. It is dominated by three companies – Golden Wonder, Smiths and KP. The value of the market has trebled since 1973 to approximately £400 million in 1980, and Mars believed that the market would be worth £600 million by 1983.

All existing savoury snacks are believed to meet a consumer need for a 'mindless nibble'. The market, however, is dominated by commodity products like crisps or child-oriented novelties like Horror Bags. The opportunity existed for a good tasting, satisfying savoury snack that could be eaten on a wide variety of occasions. Mars believed that it could design a product to meet this need. Pre-launch consumer research tended to support the Mars hypothesis. Those trying the product found the taste good, the snack satisfying and good value for money.

THE PRODUCT

'Sprint' contained a thick layer of creamy filling flavoured with real cheese sandwiched between two thick crunchy wafers, shaped like waffles and sprayed with a savoury flavour to complement the filling. The cheese wafer sandwiches were packaged in foil with excellent protection from light, humidity, spoilage and damage. The bright green package with simple graphics was a convenient pocket-sized shape.

The brand name 'Sprint' was chosen as emphasizing the key qualities of the new cheese wafer: light, crisp, very easy to eat – a perfect quick snack.

The cost of machinery and plant for the manufacture of the product had been reduced by more than 50 per cent: Mars had been able to redesign and modify machinery once used for confectionery production in an unused section of its factory in Slough. The product was also zero-rated for Value Added Tax – unlike crisps and wheat, corn and rice puffed snacks. Mars was therefore able to launch its new product at a very appealing price.

THE TEST MARKET

Mars wanted a good indication of future sales of 'Sprint' on a national scale. For this it chose for a test market the Harlech TV area, which it felt came as near as possible to a perfect cross-section of the whole country. In 1981 there were an estimated 17,000 outlets in the Harlech test market area, all of which were contacted, and well over three-quarters agreed to take orders of 'Sprint' and put it on their shelves from April Fool's Day! They included newsagents, supermarkets, grocery stores, chain stores, pubs and clubs. A strict policy of confining the product to test market boundaries had to be followed for the achievement of accurate results. The test market ran from 1 April 1981 to 1 April 1982.

Delivery of the product for the test market was always on time, cheap and simple, as long as stocks remained in the six Mars depots that were used. All distribution was direct. A temporary sales force was recruited to handle the 'Sprint test market'. Together these methods proved cheap, fast and virtually free of problems.

A television advertising campaign was launched in the test market area on 6 April 1981 and shown regularly throughout the twelve months. In the first twelve weeks of the campaign it was estimated that almost all homes with televisions (98 per cent of the Harlech area) saw the commercial about sixteen times. Posters on 200 sites throughout the test area repeated the TV slogans over a period of one month. To achieve primary consumer trial Mars posted a door-to-door coupon to the majority of homes in the test area. The coupons offered a free 'Sprint'. In addition to this, two further free coupons were obtainable for six 'Sprint' wrappers in the first month of the test launch. Launch bulletins were also mailed to all the Mars major outlets.

THE SEQUEL

After two years of research and development and an estimated £10 million investment programme for the launch of 'Sprint', Mars decided in March 1982 not to launch the product nationally. The returns on the test market were not satisfactory and the company considered that to invest an estimated further £50 million to launch 'Sprint' nationally was not a viable proposition.

With 'Sprint' Mars had entered a totally unknown market although its reputation as a manufacturer of confectionery is unequalled. It appeared that 'Sprint' was developed in order to use machinery that was otherwise idle. Mars, a company that encourages corporate loyalty in its workforce, had, it appeared, own employees for the pre-launch consumer research in order to keep the ~~~~~~ under cover. Their views of the product clearly did not coincide with those of consumers in the test market area. In order to gain an insight into what would happen to 'Sprint' nationally, Mars had insisted that the area chosen for the test market should replicate national patterns. However, in choosing the Harlech TV area it had chosen a region with the lowest consumption figures for savoury snacks in the UK. This may have been further compounded by the test market strategy of covering as many outlets as possible: the figures show that grocers, confectioners, tobacconists and newsagents account for 70 per cent of the market value of savoury snacks.

Comment

This case illustrates some of the problems that companies can experience in developing new products. As a postscript, Nabisco introduced a similar product for the Ritz biscuit range in 1985. Whether this product will be any more successful is, as yet, unclear.

KELLOGG – SUCCESS IN PRODUCT DEVELOPMENT

BACKGROUND

In the late 1970s the growth in cereal consumption in the United States had slowed to 2 per cent per annum from the 7 per cent or so that had been experienced earlier in the 1960s. Traditionally Kellogg had relied on the US market for its profit growth and had three of the main cereal brands in the US market: Corn Flakes, Frosties, and Rice Krispies, all supported by heavy advertising and promotion. These brands were also heavily supported overseas. United Kingdom expenditure on Kellogg's Corn Flakes alone was over £1 million a year in the 1970s making it one of the largest American advertisers in the country, along with Pedigree Petfoods, Procter and Gamble, Mars, Colgate Palmolive, Ford, and General Motors.

This heavy expenditure on advertising has continued in the 1980s. The top five advertisers in 1984 are shown in Table 8.7.

Table 8.7. Top five TV advertisers 1984

Company	Expenditure (£ million)
Procter & Gamble	49
British Telecom	43
Mars	28.5
Kellogg	27
Pedigree Petfoods	25

The figures in Table 8.7 include the high expenditure by British Telecom in the year of privatization and ignore the Unilever companies' combined advertising expenditure of £82 million.

The decline in cereal consumption experienced in the United States resulted from a number of factors:

1. It was partly a consequence of the developing recession, which saw economic growth falter from the 4–5 per cent annual rates previously experienced, reducing American expenditure on many grocery items.
2. It was also influenced by the health movement, especially an increasing awareness of the dangers of too much sugar and too little fibre in the diet. The changing diet has in fact had an important effect on reducing deaths by heart attack from 400 per 100,000 per year in 1970 to 250 per 100,000 by 1982.
3. It was partly a consequence of the end of the baby boom and the changing population structure produced by the steadily declining birth rate, and increasing life expectancy. Older people in the United States eat less cereals – an annual average of 5.4 lb for those aged between twenty-five and fifty, compared with 11 lb for those under twenty-five.

OUTSIDE THE UNITED STATES

Similar trends of consumption were apparent overseas, although overall consumption levels were lower than those of the United States (with the exception of the United Kingdom which historically has always been the world champion cereal consumer – Table 8.8).

Table 8.8.   Selected average per capita cereal consumption

Country	Consumption
UK	12.4 lb
Australasia	8.0 lb
Scandinavia	4.0 lb
Germany	1.0 lb
France	.5 lb
Italy/Spain	.25 lb

The effect of the recession both at home and abroad had also had the effect of increasing sales of supermarket own brands or the plain-packaged generic products. This had been felt most strongly in Western Europe where own-brand market share, relatively small at 5 per cent in the early 1970s, expanded rapidly on the back of the increased strength of the national supermarket chains, Tesco, Asda, and Sainsbury's, until it reached 20 per cent in the early 1980s, and 27 per cent by 1985.

Market share was being lost at the rate of 1.5 per cent per year to these products and the competition of General Foods, Quaker Oats, General Mills and Nabisco.

KELLOGG'S PRODUCT STRATEGY

The strategy developed was to maintain as much as possible of the market share of the three main lines, and concentrate on areas of expertise and, against the declining market, to expand the product range with the emphasis on more profitable products aimed at new consumer groups and new geographical markets. Over 400 staff are employed by the company in the development and analysis of new products in the United States compared with a marketing team of 40.

Products launched included:

1. Nutri-Grain – aimed at the consumer interested in a product with more fibre, less sugar.
2. Country Store – a muesli product aimed at the thirty-five plus market.
3. Just Right –a vitamin and mineral enriched cereal aimed at the housewife.
4. Apple Raisin Crisp – aimed at the over fifties.
5. Fruit 'n Fibre – a mixture of bran and dried fruit aimed at the twenty-five plus health food market.
6. Start – a glucose enriched cereal targeted at the jogger and sports enthusiast.

Relaunches included a reformulated All-Bran to capture more of the high fibre market.

Activity in the traditional children's sector of the market has been less marked with a few product introductions, Coco-Pops aimed at the under-fives being the most recent. On the international front Kellogg has also launched a rice-based product in Japan called Genmai Flakes, and built factories in West Germany, Denmark and Spain to develop sales further in those markets.

KELLOGG IN THE MID-1980s

The fall in market share experienced in the early 1980s has now been reversed, and the United States market share stands at the highest level ever achieved. Although research and development costs have increased fivefold as a result of this dash into product innovation, profit levels have also continued to advance (Table 8.9).

Table 8.9. Kellogg's results 1975–84

Year	Sales ($ billion)	Profit ($ million)
1975	1.25	200
1976	1.4	240
1977	1.6	280
1978	1.8	300
1979	2.0	300
1980	2.1	340
1981	2.2	360
1982	2.25	400
1983	2.4	420
1984	2.6	480

Return on capital employed has always been high, ranging from 35 per cent in 1980 to around 50 per cent in 1984.

It is interesting to compare Kellogg's performance with the far larger Beatrice Foods (Table 8.10) which had followed a wide-flung acquisition policy throughout the late 1970s from a base in food manufacturing (fruit juices, tinned food, speciality flavourings) ending up with a range of companies from Avis cars, Samsonite luggage, kitchen furniture, Playtex underwear, and the distribution company Hunt Wesson Foods.

Table 8.10. Beatrice Foods' results 1980–85

Year	Sales ($ billion)	Profit ($ million)
1980	8.0	300
1981	8.5	300
1982	9.0	400
1983	9.0	50
1984	9.0	400
1985	12.0	480

Return on capital employed has hovered around the 20 per cent mark over the five-year period.

Comment

Kellogg has followed a very successful product policy. Have there been aspects it has ignored?

9

FINANCIAL PLANNING AND MARKETING

Loss is a four letter word, profit is not.

(Anon)

Turnover is vanity, profit is sanity.

(Owen Green, Chairman of BTR)

THE IMPORTANCE OF FINANCIAL PLANNING

Many firms find that they are unable to translate their magnificent, theoretical, strategic marketing plans into profits. This is because they have failed to grasp the financial implications of their plans – a problem especially acute in small firms with limited resources. The profit aspect of marketing is often ignored but companies must pay close attention to the economic aspects of their businesses if they are to survive. Surveys of small companies show that they are most likely to fail for two main reasons:
- the inability to cost accurately the activities in which they are engaged
- the failure to control the flow of funds into and out of the company.

Research also indicates that there is a close correlation between long-term growth and the overall level of profit achieved. Companies with small margins of profit have far less ability to weather problems in the external environment – a healthy profit margin provides the corporate body with a degree of fat to withstand hard times!

COSTING

Every product or service will have a price at which it is sold and a cost at which it is produced. The gap between the two is the return to the firm. If it is positive the firm makes a profit, if negative a loss. From this profit figure the owners of the firm can calculate the level of return on capital employed (ROCE) (Table 9.1).

Table 9.1   ROCE calculation

Sales	1,000	750
Cost of sales	600	550
Profit	400	200
Capital	4,000	3,000
ROCE	10%	6.6%

This is straightforward and obvious when a single product is considered, when all the costs of production will be allocated to a single item. It becomes more complicated when the number of products increases and the business is faced with dividing the costs between products. The normal approach is to separate the costs into 'direct' and 'fixed' costs and allocate all direct costs to the product plus a proportion of the fixed.

Direct or variable costs are those that are directly involved in the production of the item as they vary directly with the quantity produced.

Typical variable costs are:

Labour

Raw materials

Power

Inventory costs

They will all vary with the amount produced – inventory costs referring to the cost of maintaining stocks – the higher the level of sales the higher the required stock cover.

Fixed costs are present at all levels of production and involve the total output of the factory.

Typical fixed costs are:

Rent

Capital equipment

Rates

These can be grouped under the heading of 'base production costs', costs which would still be incurred if for example the factory was on strike or unable to produce due to some other disturbance.

Firms will have developed some method of allocating these fixed costs to the range of products or services produced by the organization, either on turnover, floor space that the process occupies, the percentage of time that the production comprises in the total company operation, or some other approach.

Allocation of costs will inevitably produce artificial distortions as to the true profitability of any particular product.

This is further complicated by the fact that there are certain costs which can be considered as either fixed or variable, and as the profitability of different products often depends on how they are considered, it is important that they are correctly assigned.

Though discounts are related to volume and, therefore, can clearly be identified as variable costs, it is quite logical to claim that sales force costs are essentially fixed. It is often thought that all promotional expenditure is a variable cost but in many instances it can be considered as fixed, with a large proportion of the money spent – in production of an advertising campaign, for example – before sales are achieved. Costing approaches in companies will therefore often vary according to the accounting convention followed. The important fact from the marketing viewpoint is to understand the nature of the costing system employed and to make allowances when developing and analysing the true profitability of any marketing plan, to consider the *reality* of the marketing environment: is it realistic to consider advertising and sales force costs as fixed for the particular product line, or not?

THE ROLE OF COSTING SYSTEMS

Research shows that the majority of firms base their prices closely on the underlying costs either by:
1. adding a percentage to the overall cost (cost plus) – a procedure used by 60 per cent of firms;
2. setting a required level of return to cover overheads and profit requirements (overhead recovery) – used by perhaps a further 30 per cent of firms in any market;
3. setting prices by what can be charged in the market (market-place pricing) – a technique employed by 10 per cent.

Costing systems based on either cost plus or overhead recovery approaches tend to develop a standard production cost for each product which holds true for the entire year, based on a forecast level of sales, and which will ensure that all costs are being covered. Unfortunately they produce an inflexible system which cannot react to changing market conditions and ignore the reality of the costing environment – that return on capital is highly volume-sensitive.

Creating a costing system that allows for such short-term flexibility, and which also identifies the effects of increasing advertising expenditure or promotional effort, is central to the firm's ability to react to the market.

Let us consider three different levels of activity for a product and show how a marketing approach to a costing system can provide a greater level of control over costs and volumes (Table 9.2).

The level of sales will affect the level of price reduction or discounting. Materials and labour will tend to follow directly the quantity of product produced, as should the level of inventory cost. One can consider the level of advertising expenditure and the expenses of the sales force as a fixed cost, as it will tend to be committed at an early stage in the year. Similarly, each product will have a level of fixed cost attached to it: machinery and space necessary for its production which will need to be paid for whatever volume is produced.

Using such a system, the profitability of various levels of production, price, and promotional expenditure can be rapidly calculated to find the most profitable return on capital employed (ROCE) or to evaluate the effects of an introductory price and high advertising expenditure.

Such a marginal costing system will also help to identify products that appear profitable on the surface with a considerable gap between cost and price, but due to a high level of fixed cost are in reality far less attractive than others with a lower profit margin but considerably lower fixed costs.

Table 9.2   Costs related to activity levels

| | Activity levels | | |
	A	B	C
Sales (£000)	600	650	750
Variable costs:			
Discounts	60	65	75
Inventory cost	10	12	15
Materials	120	130	150
Labour	60	65	75
Fixed costs:			
Ad/sales spend	90	100	110
Base production cost	50	50	50
Profit	210	228	275
Capital	500	500	500
ROCE	42%	46%	55%

THE ECONOMIES OF SCALE

As we have outlined, there will be an element of fixed and variable cost at all levels of production. However, as the total number of units increases the proportion of fixed cost will obviously decline, the rent of £10,000 might be spread over 1,000 units (£10 per unit) or 20,000 units (£0.50 per unit) and the variable cost will also tend to decrease as the plant becomes more efficient. Graphically, this leads to the concept of 'economies of scale', that is the greater the volume of production the lower the unit cost, and if the product continues to sell at the same price, the greater the unit profit (Figure 9.1).

Such considerations are especially important for large-scale enterprises with a high level of capital investment such as petrochemical complexes, detergent

Figure 9.1.   Economies of scale: relationship between fixed costs and sales revenue

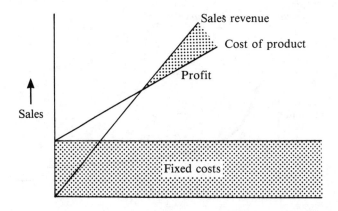

plants, superstores and car factories. Economies of scale are far less important where fixed costs are low: perfumery and high fashion clothes are examples.

Breakeven point

Where the combined cost (fixed and variable for an individual product) meets the sales revenue achieved for that product, it begins to make a profit for the firm, a stage which is known as the breakeven point.

The breakeven point can be calculated with a simple equation:

$$\frac{\text{Fixed costs}}{\text{Gross margin per unit}}$$

For example, a product costing £15,000 in fixed costs with a gross margin of 50p per unit would need to sell 30,000 units to break even. Cost control of overheads will in consequence be seen to be of crucial importance to the profitability of any product and any marketing department will need to concentrate on trying to reduce overheads to lower the breakeven point and improve profitability.

Serck Audco, one of the largest UK valve manufacturers, was taken over by the conglomerate BTR in 1982. Against a background of declining market share of UK suppliers, the company has steadily improved profitability.
- the 400 employees produced in 1985 more than the 700 in 1981
- new machinery has reduced the production time for the normal valve from 24 to 14 weeks
- flexible raw material purchasing policy has reduced inventory costs
- concentration on higher margin products has further reduced the breakeven point.

EXPERIENCE CURVE

A further important factor in the economies of scale is the effects on cost of long-run production. It has been found that the greater the accumulated total volume of production of any one item, the lower the unit production cost, which has been called the 'experience' or 'learning' curve (Figure 9.2).

Figure 9.2.   Experience or learning curve

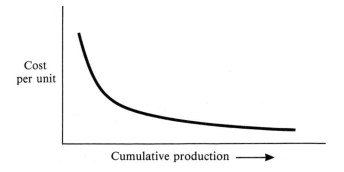

Some industries have found that doubling the volume produced leads to a 30 per cent decrease in production costs; other studies suggest that the effect will be much smaller, around 6 per cent.

Most manufacturing industries can, however, provide examples of the learning curve in operation. A similar colour television set has a labour content of £6.50 in Japan but over £10 in the UK. Similarly, the production cost of the hundredth Tornado aircraft has been estimated to be only 50 per cent of the first ten, the management and labour force having learnt how to produce the same product far more efficiently.

THE RELEVANCE OF CASH FLOW

The nature of the investment and the speed at which profit will return to the firm also need to be carefully considered. This is the concept of 'cash flow'. The firm must ensure that the flow of cash in at least balances the flow of cash out – obviously the ideal position is for the company to have a positive cash flow. Increases in research and development, changes in production and inventory levels, heavy advertising or promotional expenditure, can all have effects on the company cash flow, and marketing planning needs to ensure that the financial health of the firm is being maintained within the confines of the overall company strategy.

Many small businesses with basically healthy market positions fail to realize the importance of cash flow and in consequence run into severe difficulties; money going out for expansion and development is not returning to the organization quickly enough. All businesses require to retain a level of liquid funds to pay for stock, rent, rates, distribution, labour, and so on. This money is the firm's working capital. Many marketing decisions will have an impact on the level of working capital that the firm requires. For example, the launch of a new vending machine is accompanied by a hire-purchase package for firms to buy the more expensive machine. This would mean that the profit on the sale of the equipment would come back to the firm far less quickly; in other words more capital would be tied up in financing the sale of the product and the firm would need more working capital.

There are a number of other areas where the marketing department can have a major impact on the working capital requirements of the firm:
1. Effective forecasting of demand will reduce to the minimum the level of finished stocks that the firm holds.
2. Setting and maintaining rigid quality control standards will minimize the level of product returns, which also tie up large quantities of capital.
3. Major expenditures on product launches and large advertising campaigns will also significantly affect the level of working capital requirements.
4. It will be important for all companies to control discount and credit levels to minimize working capital requirements.

The effects that marketing decisions can have on the financial well-being of the organization are, therefore, considerable and demand that the marketing department accurately plans the effects of what it is intending to do and how this will affect the flow of funds within the organization. The flow of activities needs to be structured to ensure that they will have the least impact on the working capital requirements of the firm.

METHODS OF MAXIMIZING CONTROL OVER INVESTMENT

Decision trees

The timescale of any investment decision will be crucial. Should the firm invest at the present period, or wait until the market has developed? Each path will have opportunities and risks associated with it. Promotional costs to enter an established market will be higher but the risk that the market will be short term will have disappeared. Such considerations produce a 'decision tree' so named because at each decision point there will be a number of alternatives or branches (Figure 9.3).

Figure 9.3.   Decision tree

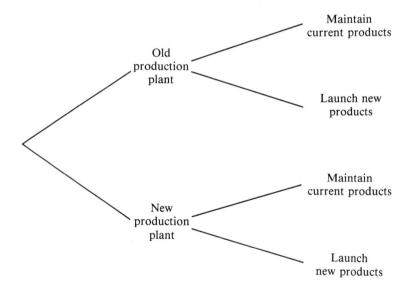

Developing a decision tree will require management to:
1.   Identify the points of decision and alternatives at each point.
2.   Estimate the probabilities of each event occurring.
3.   Evaluate the costs and benefits of each outcome.
4.   Analyse the alternative routes to determine the best outcome.
    The use of decision trees inevitably involves a high degree of judgement, and is similar to the risk return analysis of strategic paths.

Network planning

Each marketing activity will therefore affect the cash flow, but many activities will require far greater investment than others. There will be for each product a sequence of necessary steps: for example, steel rods cannot be produced without the required raw material, machinery and labour being available. From such a list of items, when they need to take place, and which item is dependent on the completion of another, a grid of interlocking *events* can be created connected by *activities*, with estimates of the shortest time in which the event can occur (earliest event time or EET) and the latest time by which the event must have taken place for the project to be successfully concluded (latest event time or LET). The difference between the two timings is the amount of time that the event can be allowed to slip, or 'slack time'. Where there is no slack time, where the EET is the same as the LET, the correct progress of the event is *critical* to the success of the project. Connecting up these events produces the activity path that requires the closest attention: which is in fact the *critical path* for the success of the project.

In the very simple example in Figure 9.4 the critical path is clearly definable as being the development of artwork, and the printing of packaging; the accurate arrival on time of the packing machinery and the raw materials is not crucial to the final production deadline.

In larger projects this concept has evolved to systems involving the use of computers such as the Programme Evaluation and Review Technique (PERT) which also produces an analysis of the shortest, most likely and longest times that

Figure 9.4. Critical path analysis

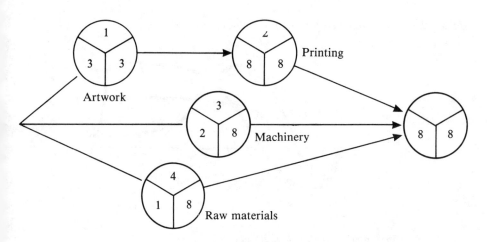

any activity will require to provide a spread of likely times for the project completion (Table 9.3).

The use of these techniques will enable the impact on the company cash flow to be accurately measured in the short term, and define the working capital requirements of the organization.

Table 9.3   PERT analysis

Activity	Shortest time	Most likely	Longest
A	5 days	8	13
B	17	34	45
C	22	28	34

DISCOUNTED CASH FLOW

Marketing is not concerned only with the short-term effects of the marketing plan on the company but must also consider the long-term investment problems that certain plans will entail. It is clear that investments in different areas will pay back at differing speeds. There is a need for a way of evaluating whether one strategic development will be more effective than another option.

The most commonly used system is the concept of 'discounted cash flow'. Investments with low initial and rapidly increasing returns can be compared with investments yielding a standard rate of return over the life of the project, and those with a high initial but declining rate of return.

If one compares three projects A, B and C, as in Figure 9.5, it will be seen that the total return from all three is identical but project A generates the majority of the income in the early years. This will mean that the investment will repay more quickly and the money may be used elsewhere. To evaluate any given project the firm needs to apply a discount rate to the flow of funds (i.e. the rate at which the value of money is being eroded) (Table 9.4).

Figure 9.5.   Discounted cash flow: three alternatives

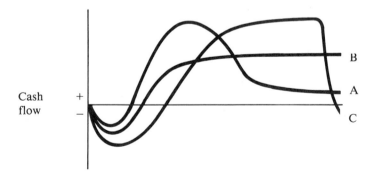

Table 9.4   Discounted cash flow: evaluation

End of year	Discount at 10%	at 16%
1	.909	.862
2	.868	.802
3	.829	.738

Summary

Marketing often ignores the financial implications of the plans that are developed. An understanding of the way in which costs can be decided, and the budgetary planning process, is essential for effective competitive action.

ASSIGNMENTS

1. You are asked by your managing director to allocate the cost of the firm's computer department to the main departments within the organization: marketing, accounts, sales, production and distribution. Comment on the methods you might adopt and their advantages and disadvantages.
2. Your firm is considering entering the shampoo market from its current base in toiletries. Attempt to develop a decision tree to deal with the various issues involved.
3. You are working for a small housebuilding company which, after astute promotional work initiated by yourself, is given the opportunity to take a contract to build fifty houses, double the normal level of activity. Write a note to the managing director outlining the financial implications of the proposal.
4. Your firm is in the process of implementing a plan to enter the computer educational market with a range of small software packages designed for the small business. Due to problems at senior level, the project has fallen six months behind schedule. Develop some form of network analysis to show the managing director how such a project should be controlled.

MONTAUBAN

Charles Edwards, the new owner of the Montauban hotel following the death of his father, was reviewing development plans for discussion with the bank manager in the following week.

TOWN SETTING

The Montauban hotel was a small hotel situated in a quiet cul-de-sac two hundred yards from the Cathedral Close in Eastchester and six hundred yards from the busy shopping centre. The Eastchester Cathedral with its famous statue of St Robert de Montauban, depicting his death surrounded by Saracens in one of the early Crusades, its beautiful rose window from the thirteenth century, and the largest Norman crypt in Europe, received thousands of overseas visitors every year, particularly from North America. Eastchester itself had an affluent population of around 50,000. Though there were large numbers of ethnic restaurants in the city centre there was a shortage of those serving traditional cuisine, and this was one of the commonest complaints tourists made about the town.

The Montauban, with its Tudor reception area, was one of the oldest hotels in the town, though modern competition – Holiday Inn, Novotel and Post House hotels – had been built on the ring road on the outskirts of the town which was some 250 miles from London, a five-hour journey by road or six (intermittent) hours by rail.

THE HOTEL

The Montauban, which had been valued for probate at £200,000, was currently a one-star hotel with twenty bedrooms:
(a) eight single (without bath) at £14.50 a night (not including breakfast);
(b) eight double rooms (without bath) at £26.00 a night;
(c) four double rooms (with bath) at £32.00.
The Montauban took most of its business during the early part of the week, with very few rooms being occupied over the weekend (Table 9.5.)

Table 9.5 Montauban: weekly occupancy

% occupancy by day of the week						
Mon.	Tues.	Wed.	Thurs.	Fri.	Sat.	Sun.
20	20	20	15	15	5	5

Similarly, there was considerable variation throughout the year, with occupancy reaching a peak 70 per cent during the summer, but being much lower during the winter months (Table 9.6).

Table 9.6 Montauban: monthly occupancy

Month	% bedrooms occupied
January	25
February	20
March	20
April	25
May	40
June	45
July	60
August	70
September	60
October	50
November	25
December	15

Occupancy rates at the other hotels were considerably higher: the Holiday Inn and Post House were full during weekdays throughout the summer months and had substantially higher occupancies during the winter thanks to the special deals that they were able to offer. Though the Montauban was conveniently situated for the centre of town and had a large car park, the lack of amenities in the bedrooms meant that the tourist trade largely avoided it, and the main users were the older type of commercial traveller, and this market was becoming smaller and smaller as the years went by. Looking back over the last three years' bookings it was apparent that occupancy rates were dropping at the rate of 10 per cent per year.

COSTS

Hotel

Overheads for the hotel were currently estimated as follows for the year:
Rates: £8,000
Labour consisting of two maids, one part-time receptionist, one part-time barman: £8,500
Heating/lighting: £2,800
Hotel maintenance: £3,000
Miscellaneous (telephone, laundry, furniture, cleaning materials, breakages, insurance): £2,800
Van costs: £2,000
In addition to these overheads Charles Edwards had had to borrow money from the bank to pay the inheritance tax resulting from the death of his father – £60,000 at the current interest rate of 14.5 per cent.

Bar/food

Currently the hotel provided a cooked English breakfast (cost of ingredients 70p) at £2.50 to a small proportion of its overnight guests. Charles Edwards also served small quantities of food at lunch time and evenings (Table 9.7).

Table 9.7   Montauban: meals cost/selling price

Type	Raw material cost (£)	Price (£)
Starter	0.30	0.80
Main course	1.50	4.50
Sweet	0.40	1.00

On average demand was limited to five people in the evening and a couple at lunch. All the cooking was done by his wife; they found that the bar and its food broke even over the year, though they did serve coffee (raw material cost 5p) at the normal price of 30p. Charles had thought of stocking wine which he could buy at an average price of £2 for resale at £5.50 but considered that the likely demand would be minimal.

The dingy nature of the bar, and the clientele consisting largely of retired army officers, had prevented it becoming more used by the business community either at lunch or in the evening.

THE PROPOSAL

It was obvious that the hotel was steadily becoming less and less profitable; neither Charles nor his wife were taking anything from the business and this was unlikely to improve. The bank had indicated its willingness to lend up to another £60,000 on the security of the hotel for renovation work.

Charles had identified two areas in which investment could lead to dramatically improved profitability: upgrading the bedrooms, or building on a restaurant at the rear of the hotel.

Bedrooms

The investment of £60,000 would just allow the Montauban to upgrade all rooms to produce twenty newly decorated double rooms with attached bathrooms. This would allow it to be upgraded from one to three star in line with the out-of-town competition and allow its room rates to rise to £48 per night.

Occupancy rates would be expected to rise to those of the other hotels as well; Edwards thought that a 50 per cent increase in occupancy would not be a difficult target to achieve within eighteen months of completing the building work. This would be done in two stages: the ten bedrooms on the first floor would be out of use for three months, followed by the ten on the second floor. Because of the financial problems of the Montauban, all builders were demanding that payment for the works should be in two stages in advance.

There would be some additional overheads associated with the change in bedrooms: the heating bill would probably increase by £500 a year; insurance would go up by £250; a full-time receptionist would need to be taken on at an additional cost of £2,500 per annum.

As an additional bonus it was thought that at least 75 per cent of the new visitors would take the English breakfast which could be charged at £3.50 per head at the same ingredient cost as previously.

Restaurant

Alternatively, the money would provide for and fully equip a new kitchen and enlarged restaurant with room for fifteen tables each seating four. The building work would take four months to complete; again, payment would have to be made in advance.

Close scrutiny of the competition suggested that though the current raw material costs of the menu items would have to be slightly increased the final price charged could be significantly raised (Table 9.8).

In addition most people would take coffee (40p per head) and one table in two would probably purchase wine. A 15 per cent service charge would also be possible.

Table 9.8   Montauban: revised meals cost/selling price

Type	Raw material (£)	Price (£)
Starter	0.50	1.50
Main course	1.80	6.50
Sweet	0.40	1.20

The numbers using the restaurant would, in Charles's view, rapidly increase and he would hope to be filling 80 per cent of the tables for dinner within three months of opening. A businessman's set lunch at £4.95 (raw material cost £1.20) would probably draw around fifty people during weekdays; a Sunday lunch at the same price around twenty families or eighty people.

The restaurant would significantly add to the overheads:

Heating/cooking: £1,500

Breakages/replacement equipment: £400

Wages (cook, two waiters, washer-up):   £14,000

Extra rates: £800

Maintenance/insurance: £350

Comment

This case reviews a number of issues: discounted cash flow, the issue of breakeven point; product development policy; and the problems of forecasting demand.

10

PRICING

Look after the pennies and the pounds will look after themselves.

(Anon)

The price that a company charges, or attempts to charge, for its goods or services interacts with many elements in the planning process. Obviously it directly affects profit, but it will have strategic, promotional, distribution and product implications as well. Manufacturers with high levels of fixed costs need to pay particular attention to pricing levels as poor pricing will mean that overhead expenditure is never recovered, but an understanding of pricing is essential for all firms. Surveys show that the level of gross margin that a firm charges has a direct effect on its long-term survival potential: within any industrial sector those firms with the highest gross margins are more likely to survive than those with low, as was commented on in Chapter 9.

One can identify a number of general factors that affect the way a company considers its pricing policy in addition to those that are related to specific products in specific markets.

GENERAL INFLUENCES ON PRICING

STRATEGIC

Legal implications of pricing policy. Where a company is charging too high a price and is in a dominant position in the market, it will run the risk of government action to control pricing. Governments may also affect the level of pricing by laying down acceptable rates of return on capital employed for an industry sector. Finally, in times of economic problems the government may become centrally involved with the imposition of price control measures as were maintained during the 1970s. Governments can also by inaction allow a pricing policy to become established in a particular industry sector.

Oftel, the Office for Telecommunications, was set up to control the pricing structure of British Telecom following privatization. A year after privatization it was already reviewing the pricing policy that had been initially laid down.

The Monopolies and Mergers commission took action in 1986 to control the prices set by British Salt which has a 50 per cent share of the £19 million UK market.

The pharmaceutical industry has the level of prices that it can charge its sole customer for prescription drugs, the National Health Service, effectively set by an 'acceptable rate of return on investment' determined by the Department of Health.

British car prices have for many years been higher than those in other countries of the Common Market which has led to the development of a thriving import business. It is thought that this may be as a consequence of the British government's desire to improve the profitability of nationalized British Leyland.

Trade agreements. Trade agreements may be an important factor in determining the pricing structure in the market. An example is the book market where only remaindered books are sold at a discount to the full price in retail outlets.

Return on investment. The level of pricing will affect the speed at which the company gains a return on its investment which will be a feature of the product and the industry. Fashion industries traditionally show rapid fluctuations in product demand (commented on in Chapter 3). A company will have, in these situations, to evaluate carefully the likely overall payback period at various prices in conjunction with the level of promotional expenditure.

In contrast, a company which is endeavouring to earn a return on investment over many years faces a different strategic emphasis. It may be prepared to operate at a loss for the first few years so that it will become established in the long term.

Introductory pricing strategies have been part of the successful expansion overseas by Japanese industry. Low initial pricing enabled many sectors to become firmly established in overseas markets.

Social factors. There may be social as well as legislative pressures in restricting the prices that a company can achieve in the market.

The introduction of admission charges to main museums has always been a hotly debated issue. Should citizens of a country be denied access to publicly owned (and maintained) collections unless they pay?

Degree of competition. A company with a unique, greatly demanded product is in the satisfactory position of being able to charge a substantial premium. Substantial competition will tend to have the effect of forcing prices downwards. Where there is considerable competition a company may, for example, have to provide additional incentives to intermediaries in the distribution channel (discussed in Chapter 11).

Relationship with buyers. A company that is poorly established in the market will face a substantially different pricing environment from one which is well established. This is a particular problem of small businesses when dealing with large; they are required to pay their bills rapidly but are quite often not in the position to demand rapid payment themselves in a competitive environment.

Companies may need to reconsider their pricing structures should they need to maintain a certain level of market share. Where a major outlet only stocks the leading three brands it will be vital that the company ensures that pricing levels are carefully monitored, so that market share does not drop below the level at which they remain stocked.

> Independent wine distributors find it very difficult to become established in the United Kingdom as only the major groups, such as Bass, IDV, Allied Breweries, have a sufficiently extensive range to negotiate effectively with major multiple chains as they can spread promotional and listing expenses across a broad range of products.

Financial strength is also a relevant factor. The company that is financially sound is in the position to be more demanding on price than one with a strong cash flow.

Nature of industry. The type of market in which the firm is operating will also be an important influence on the pricing. As is discussed in later chapters, companies operating in the service and industrial sectors of the market find that price is often not as central a determinant of demand as within the consumer sector (discussed in Chapters 13 and 14).

Economic state of the market. Companies will have to consider the economic level of activity in price setting. Affluent West Germans, for example, are often willing to pay more for the same item than the poorer British consumer. Changes can also occur on a micro-environmental level.

> The collapse of the oil price from $30 to $15 in 1986 rapidly changed the pricing environment of Aberdeen. Most obvious was the almost immediate drop in house prices, but changes occurred in other areas such as the price of restaurant meals.

PRODUCT

Product life cycle position. The product life cycle with all its limitations (discussed in Chapter 3) provides valuable indications as to the approach that the company should adopt at each stage of growth, maturity and decline. In general terms for the normal consumer, product pricing should be low at the early part of the cycle to encourage trial and increase as maturity is reached.

Product range. Where a single product extends across several market segments each product variant will need to be priced differently or segmentally.

> The VW Golf is a good example of segmental pricing. The VW Golf GTi with a more powerful engine and minor changes in accessories commands nearly double the price of the Golf C at the base of the range – the one appealing to the 'sports' car sector the other to the family car market.

Quality/image relationship. Pricing has always been associated with often intangible quality elements. In many markets consumers associate quality with price and low priced products, even of superior quality, will often be ignored. Premium pricing for many products will therefore be an essential prerequisite of establishing a particular market position.

The development of the successful Croft Original sherry which, from a negligible sales base in 1974, now vies for market leadership with Harveys Bristol Cream in the UK sherry market was at least in part due to the close pricing relationship established between Croft Original and the market leader.

PROMOTION

Expenditure/price relationship. Promotional expenditure will interact with the price the company charges relative to the competition in the market to determine the penetration of the product and the profit that it achieves. Four possible combinations exist:

1. Heavy promotion and high price. This approach is often termed market 'skimming'. It is particularly appropriate for fashion products where rapid return on initial investment is essential.
2. High promotion and low price. This is particularly appropriate for companies that are seeking rapid increases in market share as such a combination should ensure a high level of trial and repeat purchase.
3. Low promotional expenditure and high price. Yields a slow market penetration but high profitability, and is particularly appropriate for products in short supply.
4. Low promotional expenditure and low price. Commodity products such as flour, nuts and bolts fall into this category.

Promotional material. The nature of the promotional material chosen may have some impact on the level of price that can be achieved. 'Exclusive' items can only be exclusive if access is limited – a fact on which many dress designers survive.

DISTRIBUTION

Price will be an important part of the way in which a company builds up strength within the distribution channels it is using.

Nature of the distribution process. Where a company is heavily dependent on intermediaries such as wholesalers the discount and credit structure will need to reflect this importance.

Maintaining loyalty. It may be important for supplier companies to maintain certain outlets as sales outlets, and provide special prices to ensure it.

Woolworths, as one of the initial stockists of Airfix construction models, received a special discount to continue stocking a wide range of models. This policy remained a very successful one for the Airfix group which gained in return large shelf areas in the major Woolworths outlets.

SITUATION SPECIFIC PRICING FACTORS

COSTING SYSTEMS

For many companies the prime determinant of price will be the costing system.

As the previous chapter identified, three pricing systems appear to exist.
1. cost plus pricing;
2. overhead recovery pricing;
3. market-place pricing.

  As the last is by far the least common, most companies will initially set
price by reference to production cost.

ELASTICITY OF DEMAND

Economic theory suggests that there will be a fairly clear relationship
between demand and price; that as relative price rises, demand will fall.
Demand is in other words elastic and primarily affected by price (Figure
10.1).

Figure 10.1.   Elasticity of demand and price

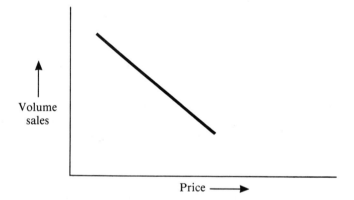

  Price elasticity curves can be established for each market over specific time
periods. Crucial to the formulation of a price elasticity is an understanding of the
average relative price in the market; inflation and market share will change the
actual prices seen in the market from year to year. Relative price changes to the
average price weighted by volume sold in the market will establish the nature of
the relationship between price and market share (Table 10.1).

Table 10.1   Price elasticity calculation

Product	Market price	Market share %	Weighted price index
A	20	25	500
B	25	20	500
C	15	40	600
D	22	15	330
Total		100	1,930
Average market price (weighted for volume)			19.3

Price elasticities are most acute for commodity products such as flour, sugar and butter, where elasticities of ten have been reported. This means that a 1 per cent movement in relative price can lead to a 10 per cent drop in market share. Put in the context of butter in a supermarket, this means that for a 250g packet of butter a 1p increase in price (on the assumption that the weighted average for the butter market was around 110p per 500g) would lead to a 10 per cent decrease in market share. Such reactions to price may seem severe to the reader, but they reflect the normal purchasing habit in the supermarket – to buy the cheapest butter available.

Where a product has more intangible qualities (being more associated with image rather than specific product qualities) price elasticities become less severe. Thus, though price elasticities for catfood may be around five, for whisky around two to three, the elasticity curves for Rolls-Royces and Joy perfume will be much flatter (Figure 10.2).

Figure 10.2.   Varying price elasticities

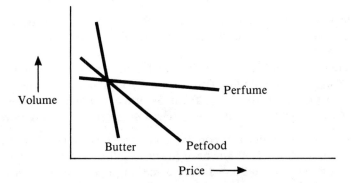

Figure 10.3.   Changes in price elasticity outside normal range

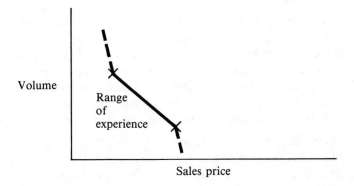

The use of price elasticity as an aid to management decision-making does present certain shortcomings. First, price elasticities rely on historic data, and the environment is always changing. Second, the elasticity will only hold true for a limited area of the price/volume relationship. At either end of the graph within which the company has experience, the elasticity may be significantly different (Figure 10.3).

PSYCHOLOGICAL FACTORS IN PRICING

The behaviour of particular markets also supports the view that consumers are not acting in a wholly straightforward fashion to produce a linear relationship between the relative price of a product and the volume purchased. Markets may, for example, show a dramatic decline in sales at one particular price, which could not be explained by classical economic theory.

> Black and Decker, the home DIY appliance manufacturer, found that sales of one of its Workmate range dropped by around 30 per cent when it tried to increase the price past a particular point over a three-year period.

The Black and Decker example illustrates that there are many behavioural factors that have a major influence on the ability of the firm either to set or change prices.

A considerable number of behavioural factors that can influence a firm's pricing policy have been identified within various markets. The author has attempted to put them into some form of order of importance based on the frequency with which they appear in discussions of specific pricing problems.

Price points. Consumer markets contain a number of examples of products which have sold well at, say, £1.99 but have failed to sell satisfactorily at £2.05, even though such an effect could not be predicted on price elasticity considerations. The more expensive the product, the less likely that this will occur, and rapid price inflation is likely to make the phenomenon far less important. It will, therefore, be most marked in low priced, frequently purchased items in periods of economic stability, and is an important technique for many retail chains, and direct marketing organizations.

Historic pricing. The example of the Heinz company and the link between the price of baked beans and spaghetti, mentioned in Chapter 2, neatly illustrates the point of historic or reference pricing. Consumers may become habituated to either a relationship between product groups or between brands – Cadbury's Dairy Milk always being more expensive than Yorkie, for example. Providers of goods and services will have to be aware of such issues as they will affect the perception of the product and the price that consumers are prepared to pay.

Perceptual differences in pricing. There is a large body of evidence to show that the individual is unable to differentiate between items which are closely but not exactly priced. This again will vary from industry to industry, but in general terms it would appear that price differences of around 10 per cent are the limits of awareness. Thus, a product priced at £3.25 may easily achieve the same sales as one at £3.55. The effects of perceptible difference in pricing are often ignored by small mail order firms in the fashion industry who in consequence miss an opportunity to improve margins substantially. Perceptual differences will vary considerably from market sector to market sector.

Halo effects. When consumers are purchasing a range of products from the same source the prestige or acceptability of one item can spill over on to other items, the logic being that if some S is proven all S must be proven. Many retail chains have managed to build up a tremendous consumer franchise and achieve impressive profit margins on this basis, such as Marks and Spencer in England, which succeeds in selling fresh fruit and vegetables at a considerable premium over that obtainable in the local greengrocer.

Price effects of risk. Every consumer is aware that each purchase contains an element of uncertainty, that is, the product will not meet their expectations. An unknown product will carry a higher risk than products which have previously given satisfaction. For each market there will be a discount rate operating which offsets the risk factor by a lower price. For petrol or butter this discount rate will be small or non-existent. For technical products the discount level will have to be substantially higher.

> Computer hardware companies find it very difficult to compete with IBM in the corporate sector because of the security that dealing with IBM allows the purchasing manager. A company attempting to become established in this sector faces a major risk pricing problem.

Risk pricing will obviously be more important in the industrial sector, and is discussed as one of the specific problems faced in the industrial environment.

Convenience effects. Products offer varying levels of convenience and there will be a pay-off between the product/service and the amount of time that it saves over competitive products, and the price that it costs. Thus, there has been a dramatic growth in the take-away food market due to the combination of minimal time taken and costs of food.

> Shower gels and toothpaste pump dispensers are two examples of products that have been fairly unsuccessful in crossing the Atlantic. Though the British use of showers is lower, per capita consumptions is below that which might be expected on the American model. British consumers do not appear to be willing to pay the extra premium for the convenience that these two products provide.

> Canned wine products such as La Sonnelle have failed to make a major impact on the UK wine market in contrast to wine boxes, convenience and price being of crucial importance.

'Morality' issues in pricing. Manufacturers may have to consider the social implications of the products or services they supply. Baby food manufacturers for example would need to consider the pricing of their range in this respect as would drug companies and school textbook publishers.

Range pricing. When a manufacturer produces a range of complementary products, decisions as to how the various items should be priced may affect overall success. Problems of this nature may be particularly important for products with replacement parts such as vacuum cleaners. The interrelationship between the price of the original item and the spare part may be crucial to ensure repeat purchase of the entire range.

Summary

Pricing is one of the most important elements of the marketing mix affecting success or failure in a number of ways. Consumers do not react in a straightforward fashion and the understanding of the exact price relationships in the market shows that accurate pricing is a complex task.

ASSIGNMENTS

1. The diversified company for which you are working has asked you to consider the pricing issues it would need to consider for the launch of its new range of programmable calculators.
2. As a marketing consultant you are asked to prepare a plan for the introductions into the UK of a new banana flavoured liqueur. The product is to be launched with minimum advertising and you are asked to write a report on what pricing issues the company would need to consider.
3. The chairman of the local regional health authority has asked you to prepare a short memorandum on pricing of privatized services within the large local hospital.

11

DISTRIBUTION IN THE MARKETING MIX

Four and twenty ponies, trotting in the dark,
Lacies for a lady, baccy for the clerk.

(Kipling)

THE IMPORTANCE OF DISTRIBUTION FOR THE FIRM

The role of distribution in gaining competitive advantage is often ignored by many companies: advertising and packaging are far more visible and therefore tend to receive considerably more attention, but it is when viewed in relation to their overall contribution to the cost of the organization's goods or services that they are relatively insignificant.

Distribution costs make up a far more significant proportion of the final price than might be expected. A recent survey in the United States showed this in relation to many industries (Table 11.1).

Table 11.1   Distribution costs as a percentage of price

Industry	Percentage
Food and food factors	29.6
Machinery	9.8
Chemicals	23.1
Paper	16.7
Primary metal	26.1
Wood products	16.1

The average across all these industries was 19 per cent. The main cost components were administration, transport, storage or warehousing costs, the cost of the stock that the company holds (inventory), order processing and raw materials or handling incoming goods.

Of the average 19 per cent distribution cost, the contribution of the various factors would be as follows:

Administration: 2.4
Transport: 6.7
Warehousing: 3.8
Costs of stock (inventory): 3.7
Order processing: 1.2
Cost of incoming materials: 1.7

KEY DISTRIBUTION CRITERIA

A number of issues will affect the level of distribution costs and determine the competitive position of the firm in the industry.

1. Strategic factors:
    (a) the level of distribution required to meet strategic requirements (the required service level of distribution);
    (b) the way the company reaches the consumer (channel decisions);
    (c) the level of control that the company needs to maintain over distribution to meet its strategic requirements.
2. Product factors: physical nature of the product (size, weight, freshness, frozen etc.), value, security.
3. Logistical elements:
    (a) where the company produces its product (production and supply alternatives);
    (b) how the company stores its product (warehousing options);
    (c) the way in which the company moves its product (transport).
4. Service factors:
    (a) the level of stock the company needs to maintain (inventory);
    (b) the way in which orders are received and despatched (communication).

STRATEGY

Strategic requirements

All industries will demand the investment in distribution systems to meet the required level of supply; some companies will perceive an opportunity to gain competitive advantage by offering an improved level of distribution.

> ACS, Automatic Catering Supplies, became one of the largest catering supply firms in the United Kingdom by offering a rapid door-to-door delivery service.

These companies will in consequence need to invest more heavily in the distribution network than the industry traditionally requires; delivery on a daily basis might mean that the investment in vehicles and drivers would be 40 per cent higher than one operating a twice-weekly service.

There will always however be a pay-off between the level of service the company offers and the demands upon the system, and it will become progressively more expensive for a manufacturer to service smaller and smaller customers; for most companies 80 per cent of the business is generally achieved with 20 per cent of the customers, and reaching progressively smaller businesses will be disproportionately costly (Figure 11.1).

Figure 11.1.   Market coverage costs

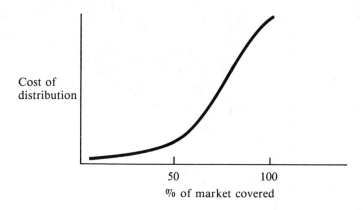

Cost of
distribution

50   100

% of market covered

> Nineteen thousand grocery retail outlets (or 16 per cent of the total UK grocery outlets) account for 67 per cent of total grocery turnover.

Deciding on the level of service that a firm should provide will be an important factor in the marketing mix. High levels of service will not just involve a higher level of investment, they will often reduce the level of out-of-stock goods at the end user and allow a far higher level of market coverage, which will mean that the consumer is practically guaranteed to find the particular item in any outlet.

> One hundred per cent distribution is particularly important for the manufacturers of impulse buy items, such as sweets and chocolate bars, to ensure that their product is on the counter as well as the competitors'.

Channel decisions

Organizations will also need to consider as part of their service the way in which it reaches the final consumer. In broad terms, two possible approaches exist: sending goods straight to the consumer or end user (direct distribution), or using an intermediary (indirect). A typical intermediary would be a wholesaler or a franchisee. Some writers would include the sales force as an intermediary in the distribution process (Figure 11.2).

In order to determine whether direct or indirect distribution is most appropriate, firms will need to evaluate the needs of the market on certain criteria (Table 11.2).

Figure 11.2. Distribution intermediaries

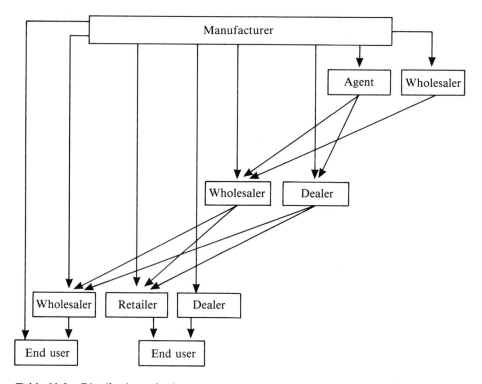

Table 11.2 Distribution criteria

Factor	High	Low
Geographical concentration	Direct	Indirect
Number of buyers	Indirect	Direct
Complexity of product	Direct	Indirect
Unit price	Direct	Indirect
Standardization	Indirect	Direct
Servicing requirements	Direct	Indirect
Price negotiation	Direct	Indirect
Frequency of purchase	Indirect	Direct
Financial strength	Direct	Indirect
Payment problems	Indirect	Direct
Strategic control	Direct	Indirect

For example, a chocolate bar is low in price, purchased frequently by large numbers of consumers, is standard and requires no servicing or installation. The manufacturer of the chocolate bar needs to ensure that the widest possible distribution is achieved and will use wholesalers and other intermediaries to achieve it. Contrast the supplier of turbines for power stations. The product is not standard, requires a large amount of attention to installation and servicing, and distribution will be direct from manufacturer to end user.

Other factors may also be important. Should the organization be in a bad financial state it may prefer to use wholesalers rather than deal direct with large numbers of individual companies, and where there are complex legal issues the use of intermediaries may also be advisable. The importance of the role of agents and distributors overseas is commented on elsewhere; they are vital to overcome legal, currency and cultural problems within the distribution chain.

Strategically, the use of intermediaries reduces the level of control the manufacturer has over the distribution process; the firm will be less clear as to where the product is being sold and at what price. Different markets will show different levels of usage of intermediaries: for example, the grocery wholesaler sector is dominated in the UK by the cash and carry outlet, a relatively unimportant feature of the American distribution system.

Direct selling by mail order. Many firms in the consumer goods sector attempt to bypass the distribution process by selling direct to the customer via mail order. These include large organizations such as Great Universal Stores, Freemans and Grattans, and many firms providing specialized products – it is estimated for example that over 45 per cent of computer games are bought via mail order.

There are both advantages and disadvantages for the firm involved in mail order.

Advantages include:
1. Complete control over where the product is distributed.
2. Reduced selling expenses – the entire country can be covered without the expense of the sales force.
3. Improved costing as there will be no need for expensive high street locations or to provide intermediaries with sales margins.
4. Manufacturer can receive rapid feedback on product acceptability without the confusing effects of intermediaries' stockholdings.
5. The manufacturer can often receive payment before the goods are despatched, thus improving the firm's cash flow.

Disadvantages, however, are:
1. Catalogues must be planned months in advance, severely reducing the ability of the manufacturer to reflect market trends accurately in rapidly changing markets, such as high fashion.
2. Prices once established are fixed until the next catalogue.
3. Forecasting is crucial to success or failure of the operation; too little stock and the firm loses credibility in not being able to meet orders; too much will cause cash flow problems.
4. Products will need to be sufficiently distinctive from those currently available in the retail outlets unless there is a significant price advantage.

Channel conflict

In all industries there will be competition or conflict within the channels of distribution. Currently there is considerable friction between the retailers and the suppliers of consumer goods. Retailers are steadily becoming more powerful as buying power becomes more concentrated; this is defined as vertical conflict. An example of this power is seen in the steady reduction in the time a new product is allowed to establish itself in the market. The majority of large retailers now state that three months is the benchmark for success or failure, compared with previous bi-annual or annual reviews.

Retailers themselves fight for market share; this is defined as horizontal conflict. Finally, there may be examples of companies outside the traditional distribution channel competing for the same market. Makro, the wholesaler, is an example of this inter-channel conflict. Whereas in theory only businesses are able to obtain cards to use Makro, there is in reality quite a wide spread of use, and in many instances Makro will be seen to be competing with other retailers. In Belgium this now means that Makro is estimated to have around 9 per cent of the retail trade in fast moving consumer goods. In the United Kingdom the Dee Corporation, owners of the Gateway, International, Fine Fare and Carrefour chains of stores, has been active in trying to build up a dominant position in the wholesale sector by a series of acquisitions; it considers this an important way of increasing purchasing power with the major suppliers and a useful diversification.

Channel rigidity

In an established industry the way the distribution channels operate may create major barriers that prevent new firms entering the market from becoming established.

The popular music record industry would appear to be one in which new companies can rapidly become established, with over 3,000 independent labels in existence in the mid-1980s. With costs of production low and margins high, fragmentation would appear to be inevitable. In 1972 six companies held 60 per cent of the market. In 1983, even after eleven years of rapidly changing fashion in music, seven companies (the same six plus one newcomer, Virgin Records) held 66 per cent of the market. Distribution has remained the key to market domination. While new, successful groups will be signed by the small independent labels for their first disc, the major record producers will be able to offer guaranteed promotion on the radio (70 per cent of purchase decisions are made following radio 'plugs') and the widest distribution throughout the record trade. Such incentives mean that the successful group will move from the independent label to the major label, reinforcing market strength of these companies. Virgin Records has come to join these major companies because it concentrated on building up its own retail chain which could provide instant distribution for its own artistes, allowing it to hold on to successful groups.

Legislation can also have an effect on maintaining channel rigidity. Drug wholesalers in the UK are prevented from buying standard branded drugs from other EEC countries, where prices are often lower, by a government licensing requirement that all drugs must be obtained from licensed suppliers.

Managers of 'tied' public houses were required to purchase all their catering requirements from a single source until a court ruling in the 1980s.

Channel control

The marketing strategy followed by the company will be important in determining the amount of control it will have over the distribution process. This can be seen as an investment process. To achieve high levels of control the firm will have to invest heavily; this will either take the form of promotional expenditure, the acquisition of the company's own outlets (or by a franchise process ensuring maximum control over them), investment in physical distribution and/or an extensive sales force.

> Wall's Meats established a van sales force which enabled it to gain impressive distribution of its products against the competition which relied more heavily on wholesalers.

The degree of control that a company is able to exert will therefore tend to vary with the degree of investment.

Low or nil investment. Different manufacturers offer end users large numbers of competing and unknown items in a product category. As there is no specific demand for any particular manufacturer's product the end users can freely substitute the goods without fear of losing sales. The ability of the end user or retailer to replace one supplier with another will have the effect of reducing the prices that the supplier can achieve and will minimize their independence from the end user.

> The industrial fasteners market (discussed in the AMC case study in Chapter 5) is an example of limited investment by manufacturers in controlling the distribution channels with over 300 companies in the market.

Increasing levels of investment. Consumer or end user demand begins to be generated. Retailers or end users must stock the product to achieve sales. Suppliers manage to increase distribution without making major concessions on price. Supplier independence is increased.

Heavy investment. Products are carried by almost all end users or retailers. Demand continues to increase, leading to successful suppliers achieving major economies of scale. For the major suppliers the percentage of sales revenue spent on promotion will start to decrease in line with their considerably expanded distribution. Competition will become steadily more intense between suppliers effectively controlling prices. The suppliers will now have considerable independence unless similar developments are taking place within the end users or retailers, that is, they also become larger, fewer and more powerful.

> Though the overall share of supermarket own brands in total grocery sales has steadily increased (by 1985 accounting for 27 per cent of total sales), certain market sectors show much slower growth. Own-brand petfood for example only accounts for 9 per cent of total sales, roughly the same level as toiletries and detergents. The variation in the figures may well reflect the level of investment the firms in this area have made to maintain their position within the distribution channel.

THE NATURE OF THE PRODUCT

Physical constraints will play an important part in determining the structure of the distribution method that the company needs to employ.

1. Perishability. The increasing amount of frozen food consumed annually has led to the development of specialized distribution systems catering solely for this trade.
2. Size. Large items will pose different problems from those products that can be stored in standard cartons.
3. Security. The needs of security may similarly change the nature of the distribution process.
4. Value. The higher the value of the product, the more quickly and securely the firm will want it to be transported.

LOGISTICS

Production and supply alternatives

There will be a number of interrelating factors that affect the choice of where the company manufactures.

Economies of scale. As has been mentioned elsewhere, the greater the volume produced, the lower the unit cost of the production. It may be in the interests of the company to concentrate production in one site.

Vulnerability. Concentrating all production in one site may make the entire company vulnerable to political and economic upheaval.

> The multinational car companies such as Ford and General Motors are increasingly moving towards multi-sourcing of components within Europe following the serious problems caused by strikes in the late 1960s and early 1970s.

Flexibility. Large production plants cannot easily or cost-effectively cope with small volume production which may be demanded by a change in the market.

> Courage, part of the Imperial Tobacco company, concentrated in the late 1960s on investing in large production units to maximize economies of scale in the beer market, producing a small range of keg beers for national distribution. The overall decline in the beer market, matched by the steady switch to real ale and regional beers, increasingly stresses the importance of small-run operations for which the Courage plants are not ideally suited.

Cost of transport. Each of the production points that the company chooses will have an effect on the distribution costs; the more widely spread the manufacturing sites the lower the distribution costs on average.

Warehousing

The location of the warehouse, the way in which both incoming and outgoing product is handled, and the way in which product is stored will all have an impact on the distribution costs.

Warehouse numbers. One of the more important decisions that the growing company has to take is whether to increase the number of warehouses it uses to service its customers.

Many of the costs will increase (such as the cost of stock, which will need to be substantially higher in five separate warehouses compared with one central operation) but some will decrease (transport costs, for example, will decline when comparing the use of regional depots for deliveries, rather than a central national depot). Other costs may grow initially and then decline or vice versa. The best option for the expanding company would therefore be where the combined costs would be minimal. This is outlined in Table 11.3.

Table 11.3   Comparative costs of one or more warehouses

Factor	Warehouse numbers						
	1	2	3	4	5	6	7
Warehouse costs	10	15	20	25	30	35	40
Transport costs	60	45	35	28	25	22	20
Costs of stock	20	30	35	50	60	70	80
Obsolescent stock	5	7	9	11	13	15	17
Customer service cost	12	8	7	8	9	10	11
Supply alternatives	18	14	10	9	7	5	8
Communication cost	2	3	4	5	5	5	5
Totals	127	122	120	136	149	162	181

As the number of warehouses increases it can be seen that:
(a) the costs of warehouse construction and maintenance increase steadily;
(b) transport costs to the individual customers decline steadily as warehouse numbers increase but not in a linear fashion;
(c) the amount of stock that the company needs to maintain steadily increases;
(d) the level of stock held in the depots which is slow moving will increase as the numbers of warehouses increase;
(e) the additional costs of providing the strategic level of service on which the company has decided decline initially and then increase;
(f) the costs of using different sources of supply decrease initially and then increase as the number of warehouses in the network expands;
(g) each additional warehouse will increase the costs if a single source of supply is being used;
(h) the costs of administering the receipt and despatch of orders will increase initially and then plateau.

For this firm, the current cost environment would suggest that three warehouses would provide the most cost-effective solution to its warehouse requirements. Different firms in differing markets with different cost and service criteria would reach other conclusions.

Warehouse organization. The way in which the warehouse is organized can make a substantial difference to the efficiency and costing of the operation in a number of ways.

1. Traffic flow. Warehouses that can separate the unloading and loading processes are generally more efficient than others where the two areas are combined: reductions in labour cost of 15 per cent have been reported by firms.
2. Mechanization. The introduction of fork-lift trucks and containerization has done much to reduce the levels of labour and to increase the speed at which goods can be transferred with the consequent effect on cost.
3. Automation. Large-scale investment in product handling equipment can lead to substantial reductions in the labour force and speed of assembly.

   Fiat maintains an automated warehouse to handle all spare part delivery throughout Europe. The introduction of automation reduces the time taken to despatch spares from four days to two; inventory levels have declined by 40 per cent.

4. Packaging. Well-designed packaging which can be efficiently stacked and moved can substantially increase the speed of warehouse operation. Many products are now stacked on wooden platforms or pallets; a well-organized batch of cases on a pallet will hold together like an interlocking wall, allowing the pallet to be stacked high up on warehouse racking systems.

Transport issues

The manufacturer has a number of options available to achieve the target distribution levels:

- Rail
- Road
- Air
- Water (both inland and sea).

Each will offer a level of speed and security coupled with a level of cost which will when combined decide the most appropriate transport system for the organization. In addition, the firm will need to consider the inventory cost for each transport option as part of the overall equation. For example, to supply the Middle East overland with consumer goods will take around fourteen days; by sea around five weeks. The additional cost of financing the three weeks' stock required for delivery by sea would be a potential saving if the company changed from sea to road which might offset the higher transport costs.

Rail. The advantage of rail transport is the ability to move large quantities with fair speed and at low cost. However, the system is inflexible, often requires special containers, and is vulnerable to disruption. In consequence many firms no longer use rail for transport unless they are immediately adjacent to a railway line.

   News International, printers of the *News of the World*, the *Sun* and *The Times*, switched to road delivery following the industrial dispute consequent on their move to new premises in east London. Road delivery was far less open to industrial action by national unions and in consequence the majority of circulation was maintained.

Road. Road has become the preferred method of transport for a wide range of consumer and industrial goods. It offers the advantages of fair flexibility with good security, and is much less vulnerable to disruption. There are higher costs to be considered, and substantial legislation governing the length of time that drivers can work, the maximum weight of vehicles and many other constraints. For the firm many of these problems can be solved by contracting transport rather than owning a fleet of transport vehicles. This further improves the flexibility offered by the use of road transport, but for a large firm will often be the more expensive option. The point at which it becomes more cost-effective for a firm to own and operate its own vehicles will vary according to the nature of the industry in which it operates and the level of service that it is trying to supply. In the late 1960s the point at which it was economic for the average firm to employ its own drivers was around eight vehicles; it has since risen to twelve as independent transport operators have become more cost-competitive.

Air. Air transport provides an extremely rapid and secure means of transporting product, thereby minimizing inventory and packaging problems. Though it is the most expensive option available there has been a steady growth in its use and it now accounts for around 5 per cent of total freight movements.

Water. Inland water transport in the United Kingdom is very limited, accounting for far less than 1 per cent of total freight movements. In Europe the advantages of river transport, low cost and flexibility, have continued to maintain a healthy level of investment in barge transport, particularly on the Rhine in Germany.

Central to the method of transport that the firm chooses will be the pay-off between the cost of maintaining stock and the cost of the transport method. As inventory costs rise, it will be more advantageous to pay for a more rapid method of transport (Figure 11.3).

Figure 11.3. Interaction between inventory and transport costs

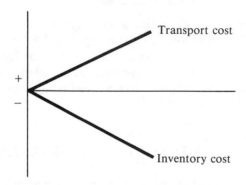

Inventory control

The level of stocks that the organization needs to maintain will be a result partly of the level of service it is trying to offer, and the fluctuations in demand within the market. The firm will need to establish three levels of stock; 'buffer stock', reorder levels at which a new production run will be required, and maximum stock levels (Figure 11.4).

Figure 11.4.   Stock movements over time

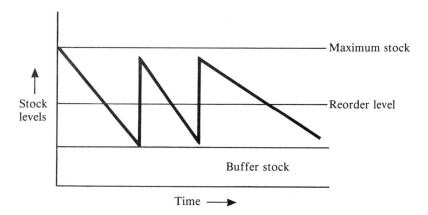

The firm can easily calculate the optimum number of orders per year, the optimum level of stock required for each order and the optimum level of stock cover that should be ordered.

Control over obsolescent or redundant stock will be vital in minimizing the amount of working capital the firm needs. By efficient organization and forecasting, firms can also significantly reduce the amount of raw material stocks held with additional improvements in working capital.

SERVICE

Communication factors

The speed at which orders are processed will affect the level of inventory and transport costs. The introduction of computers has greatly increased the efficiency of many distribution systems. In Germany the issue of computers to certain sales forces has reduced the time from receipt of the order to despatch by up to three days; an example of how effective technology can be in improving the distribution process.

IMPORTANT FUTURE TRENDS FOR DISTRIBUTION

Increasing concentration of buying power will influence the distribution process towards larger and larger loads, with greater and greater palletization and automation in the manufacturer's warehouse.

Buyers will be more demanding on the speed of delivery which will further change the balance towards road and air; this will be emphasized by steady increases in the value of goods shipped.

Computerization will improve the speed of reaction both at the customer end of the distribution channel and through the manufacturer's ordering process.

More accurate controls will enable both end user and manufacturer to operate on progressively lower levels of stock.

ANALYSING DISTRIBUTION

Reassessing the distribution system can provide large savings for any company. Dupont, the major American chemical concern, managed to save over $350 million by a careful reappraisal of its distribution system.

The firm will need to evaluate:

1. Present distribution:
   (a) frequency of orders;
   (b) size of orders;
   (c) product lines per order;
   (d) overall annual demand per order.
2. The seasonality of demand.
3. The geographical spread of orders.
4. Strategic policy.
5. Costs by type and product group.
6. Variation in cost of different transport systems.
7. Cost of owned compared with hired transport.
8. Warehousing – manning, equipment, design.
9. Inventory costs – maximum/minimum.
10. Order processing: systems alternatives and current costs.
11. Packaging implications.

RETAILING

The retailing sector is not only becoming a more and more important employer within the economy, but is also having a steadily greater influence on the distribution of products especially in the consumer goods sector.

CONCENTRATION OF RETAILING

1. Grocery outlets. In 1983 in the UK, multiple groups accounted for 67 per cent of all grocery turnover, with the top 2 per cent of shops accounting for 49 per cent in Belgium. In the UK five groups, Sainsbury's, Tesco, Asda, Argyll and hypermarkets accounting for 70 per cent of grocery sales in France and 75 per cent in Belgium. In the UK five groups, Sainsbury's, Tesco, Adsa, Argyll and Dee, control well over 50 per cent of the total grocery market: in Belgium one group, GB, controls 22 per cent alone, and with two other groups – Delhaize (12 per cent) and Colruyt (11 per cent) dominates the Belgian retailing scene.
2. Clothing. Marks and Spencer, C & A, BHS, Burtons and Next make up a substantial element of British clothing retailing.
3. Electrical goods. Dixons (including the Currys subsidiary) and Comet make up a substantial part of total electrical retailing.

4. DIY. B & Q, Do-it-all, Homebase and Texas Homecare are the major outlets for DIY products.
5. Department stores. House of Fraser, Debenhams (now part of the Burton Group), Sears, and the John Lewis Partnership make up most of department store retailing.

Similar trends are occurring in other retailing areas. Petrol sales are concentrated in a few hands, estate agent chains are becoming increasingly established.

RETAILING STRATEGIES

Market development

Currently the movement is towards larger and larger stores, with 404 stores in the UK having more than 25,000 sq ft of selling space. Table 11.4 shows the principal groups.

Table 11.4   Principal grocery groups

Group	Number of superstores
Asda	85
Dee	17
Fine Fare	41
Sainsbury's	29
Tesco	96

This concentration on large stores has meant impressive economies of scale in the retailing industry with the normal superstore achieving double the sales per square foot of the smaller independent or co-operative store, figures for 1983 show the sales per square foot per year as: multiples, £377; co-ops, £232; and independents, £186.

Profitability in superstores is achieved not only by the considerable buying power they are able to exert, which extends to the length of credit they can obtain – compare the independent grocer obtaining stock from a cash and carry and the superstore with sixty days' credit, which gives the superstore the ability to pass lower prices to the consumer – but is also due to the high level of stock turnover that they are able to achieve. For example a superstore may only make 4.5 per cent profit margin on sales but will make this profit around thirty times a year as they turn their stock over every eleven days. Independent stores' profit margins will be higher but they will turn stock over far less frequently.

Whether there will be a continued growth in the importance of the superstore is open to question. In France their share of the market has recently fallen in favour of smaller supermarkets nearer the town centre, especially the Intermarche and Leclerc groups with 600 and 400 stores respectively. This is seen as an example of what is known as the wheel of retailing – innovative groups dominate the market with a new concept, become fixed in their approach to the market and are then replaced by new types of retail outlet.

The process in the United States has seen the growth and then partial decline of:

- department stores
- mail order houses
- chain stores
- supermarkets
- out of town superstores
- centre of town convenience stores
- shopping malls.

Market penetration

Retailers have steadily expanded geographically from their original bases: Sainsbury to the north of England and Asda to the south are two examples. In addition some retailers have developed the concept of parallel retailing where they maintain a number of partially competing outlets in the high street. The best example of this is the Burtons group with different outlets specializing in clothes for different market sectors.

Some retailers have started to expand overseas. Marks and Spencer has developed an operation in Canada; Laura Ashley is successful in the United States; Benetton has become well established throughout Europe from its Italian base; Safeway, the American supermarket group, has a small presence in the United Kingdom grocery market, with Woolworths another example of an American group that managed to develop internationally but eventually had to become re-established as a purely national group (Woolworths in the UK is a totally independent group from Woolworths in the USA). Successful international development of retailing appears to require an ability for management to respond effectively to local conditions, which may mean significantly altering policy decisions which are successful in one country, and to invest heavily to achieve the level of coverage in an overseas market that they have built up over a number of years in their home countries.

Product development

Retailers have become increasingly important in developing new product ranges. Health food and new ranges of convenience food are good examples (Marks and Spencer being especially innovative in this area), and retailers are also concentrating on the development of own brands, which now account for 27 per cent of all grocery products and a much higher percentage of clothing.

Diversification

Retailers are expanding into new fields of activity as growth in their original fields declines.

Options include:

1. Vertical integration. Sainsbury's has bought vineyards, the Argyll group a biscuit manufacturer.
2. Market diversification. Laura Ashley diversifying into curtains and wallcoverings would be an example. W. H. Smith has steadily expanded its interests in specialist bookshops.
3. Other retailing ventures. Sainsbury's has expanded into DIY, Asda had developed interests in carpets with Allied Carpets, and merged with MFI in 1985.

RETAILING AND THE MARKETING MIX

Retailers face many of the problems experienced by service companies (discussed in Chapter 15) even though they provide a very tangible service. In consequence, large retailing organizations will have to pay especial attention to a number of additional factors in the marketing mix.

Personnel. The retail organization will need to consider carefully the training, payment and evaluation of the staff in its employ.

> Dorothy Perkins, part of the Burton Group, instituted staff training in an attempt to improve turnover. The emphasis was placed on finding out customer requirements and on range selling – adding blouses to skirts, belts to trousers, and so on. The company found that the comparison between matched stores, one with trained personnel and the other without, showed a 6 per cent increase in turnover, an extremely profitable investment in staff development.

Environment. The nature of the store, where it is situated, the style of the furnishings, the colour, layout, noise levels, and heating can all have an important effect on the profitability of the operation.

1. Location. A number of site location mathematical models are available to define the most effective area in which to establish to maximize the catchment area.
2. Provision of car parking. Central to the superstore concept is adequate (and free) car parking facilities.
3. Internal design. There is a substantial body of research on the effective design of supermarkets. First, customers need to be persuaded to use trolleys rather than baskets, as use of the trolley can increase purchase levels by around 20 per cent. This means that the store needs to provide large quantities of trolleys and persuade customers to use them by, for example, placing bulky special offer items near the entrance. Second, individuals tend to buy product close to eye level; sales of product either high or low on the shelf tend to be restricted. This suggests that the most profitable items should be placed close to eye level. The width of aisles also has an important effect on how easily product can be seen and purchased. The height of the ceiling has been shown in some studies in the United States to be important for a large number of consumers; should the ceiling be too low the length of time spent in the store will be reduced compared with the store with a higher ceiling.

4. Heating, lighting and colour. Sales in overheated stores will be substantially lower than those with air-conditioning; bright but not too harsh colours have been found to be most effective in maximizing sales.
5. Atmosphere. Research has shown that in certain stores the use of appropriate music can increase sales by 13 per cent. Even smell has an important bearing on overall sales levels: the introduction of bakeries into many superstores has been influenced at least in part by the finding that the smell of fresh bread can increase overall demand for food products.

Process. The way in which the store operates will also have an important influence on whether the consumer will repeat the purchase. Speed, reliability and efficiency of operation will often be crucial factors.

A key factor identified by many wholesalers is the speed at which clients can pass through the checkouts: increasing the number of checkouts at one wholesaler increased sales by 18 per cent. Marks and Spencer has recently introduced its own credit cards in response to growing demands for speedier payment methods; many stores are experimenting with electronic funds transfer (EFT) both to speed up payment but also to improve cash flow for the store.

Summary

Distribution makes up a very large element of the cost equation in any firm's final selling price. It is an area where the marketing department is able to make a major contribution to improving the overall profitability and competitive ability of the firm by relating the distribution structure of the firm to its long- and short-term requirements.

ASSIGNMENTS

1. Currently, the responsibility for the distribution system in your company lies between the sales, marketing and production departments. You are asked to prepare a report defining how a centralized distribution department could help the company which is engaged in the manufacture of domestic and industrial pumps.
2. As a marketing consultant you are asked to prepare a report on the changing nature of the distribution process and how it is likely to affect a company producing low-cost industrial cleaning products.
3. Because of financial difficulties your company is considering changing from selling direct to retailers to predominantly using wholesalers. The sales manager has asked you to write a report on the issues that are involved.
4. Currently your firm is a manufacturer of rubber tyres. It has the opportunity to buy a chain specializing in tyre sales to the public. Outline the problems it might encounter.

TANKARD AND WAREHOUSES

Tankard–UK, part of the US brewing and entertainment conglomerate, is seeking to rationalize its distribution and warehousing. The company was giving particular attention to deciding on the numbers of warehouses required to satisfy best the needs of its customers without affecting profitability.

BACKGROUND

The demands of UK superstores made action on distribution problems a matter of urgency. There are currently about 405 superstores accounting for 27 per cent of grocery turnover and it is expected that thirty or more superstores per annum will be opened in the next two to three years. Historically Tankard had achieved the majority of its sales through public houses and bars (the on-trade) but there was an increasing shift towards consumption of alcohol at home which was reflected in far higher purchases in supermarkets and specialist stores (the off-licence trade). The superstores required more rapid and more frequent delivery of product. Tankard currently worked on a weekly delivery cycle for both the on-trade and off-trade but the large stores were now wanting delivery every 48 hours. Sales through these outlets had grown from 20 per cent of Tankard turnover in 1974 to 45 per cent in 1984.

More recently, the company had initiated a capital investment programme of some £60 million to boost the company's competitiveness against the growing numbers of real ale brands in the UK. In the last ten years the real ale share of the beer market had grown from 5 per cent to 8 per cent. In the £7,750 million a year beer market, supermarket own brands were also gaining momentum, and were now believed to account for around 12 per cent of beer sold through supermarkets.

Tankard was also interested in the possibility of exploring alternative production sites. Currently it produced in Birmingham for the entire country. Only 20 per cent of national sales were achieved in the Birmingham area while 45 per cent were achieved in the south-east, 15 per cent in Yorkshire and the remainder in Scotland. Transport costs worked out at £3 per mile for a full lorry. As part of its investment plan it might be able to share production in a brewery in the London area and one in Scotland.

The superstore retailers had made it clear to Tankard that other companies were able to meet their requirements. The excess delivery time and excess variability in delivery time would all result in lost sales.

TACKLING DISTRIBUTION PROBLEMS

Tankard considered that there were a number of clear advantages to be gained from changing its warehousing arrangements. It was looking for improved profitability from better market coverage. Delivery could be provided far more rapidly to the superstores. There should be benefits from the improved economics of minimum drops: if a lorry has to travel a long way to deliver a small amount of stock it is less profitable than if it has to travel a short way to drop the same amount of stock. In order to calculate the total number of warehouses required, Tankard was examining the issue of total costs in order to gain some insight into the potential impact on profitability.

The first step involved consideration of the distribution-related factors and their effect on total costs. It was intended that the analysis would yield guidance on the number of warehouses required to service the superstores adequately at the lowest cost and the maximum profit possible.

THE FACTORS INVOLVED

Warehousing costs. Current warehouse costs were estimated at £0.5 million capital cost and £0.25 million running costs per annum, the warehouse having a staff of five. Increasing the number of warehouses would not imply the same level of cost: additional service warehouses would cost around £0.2 million and £0.15 million to run.

Transport costs. The cost of transporting product from factory to warehouse worked out at £650 per full load delivered, and was increasing by 10 per cent a year. The average round trip was 200 miles but this hid vast discrepancies between .Scottish deliveries and Midlands servicing. Currently Tankard was delivering 400 full loads nationally every day, or the equivalent of 1.2 million pints. Changing the number or location of warehouses would obviously affect the transportation costs but the relationship is not necessarily linear. The company assessed that while an increase in the number of warehouses may initially reduce total transportation costs the cost could reverse if more frequent deliveries to superstores meant less than full lorry loads. With the increasing superstore demands, Tankard management considered that the likely daily lorry movements would have to increase to 520 for the same volume of product.

Inventory. Tankard estimated that the value of stock in warehouses would go up as the number of warehouses increased. These would include a rise in the costs incurred for inventory insurance, pilferage and custodial services estimated at about 15 per cent of average annual inventory value. While customer service would be improved by keeping stock at more warehouses close to retailers, the total cost of the stock and the cost of carrying it would also go up. Currently there was about £0.25 million of stock in the warehouse.

Obsolescence. The cost of old stock, stock control and data processing the order was estimated at about 1 per cent of every lorry load. Past experience had revealed that, if at a given level of sales total inventory is increased to provide better customer service, then inventory turnover is decreased. There was concern that the turnover of stock would slow down, the greater the 'pipeline fill' in the distribution system. This increased the risks of obsolescence especially with foods having a limited shelf-life.

Economies of scale. Currently, with all beer produced at the Birmingham plant, the cost per pint averaged at 10p net of duty for the three main products Tankard produced, two bitters and one lager. The move towards a wider range of beers suggested by the market would increase costs to around an average 15p per pint. Production in London and Scotland would be more expensive at 17p per pint.

OTHER FACTORS

Other factors that Tankard needed to consider were: the costs of order processing; the benefits of minimizing out-of-stock customers; the improved market coverage in small accounts; and the possible improvement in profit margins which might accompany more frequent deliveries.

Comment

This case illustrates some of the key distribution issues that a firm in a competitive environment will need continually to monitor and optimize.

LAURA ASHLEY

Popularly regarded as one of the great British clothing and design success stories, Laura and Bernard Ashley began by printing tea towels and scarves in their London flat in 1953. Today the group has two textile and wallpaper printing and eleven making-up plants, 219 shops in twelve countries, and employs some 5,000 people in manufacturing and retailing its own clothes, home furnishings and related products throughout the world.

DISTINCTIVE STYLES

Distinctive styling was an important element in the success of the company and continues to be a major policy influence.

Laura Ashley prints are usually described as romantic, classically English and reminiscent of the countryside. They were developed from the initial designs prepared by Laura Ashley herself, derived from motifs and patterns used in historical designs which she studied in London museums and elsewhere. The first designer to assist Laura Ashley joined the company in 1968, and since then design teams have been built up for clothes and related products and home furnishings, with freelance designers also being used. Laura Ashley remained closely interested in all design matters affecting the company until her death in September 1985, although her son Nick Ashley had succeeded her as design director in 1982.

As the group's activities had expanded, Laura Ashley had created and trained teams of designers to continue and develop her work. It was regarded as an important element of continuity that her concepts should be thoroughly understood throughout the group. The vertical integration of the group – embracing design, fabric printing, clothing manufacture and retailing – provides significant advantages in this respect allowing it to maintain control over the integrity of the designs and the quality of the finished products. In-house printing of both textiles and wallpapers is therefore regarded as crucial to preserving the design quality of Laura Ashley products.

A further aspect of this policy is the group's determination to protect the Laura Ashley designs. It is the group's stated policy to pursue those attempting to copy its designs by every means at its disposal.

The Laura Ashley Design Centre at Clapham – moving to Fulham in spring 1986 – is responsible for design, fabric and print research, styling, sample pattern cutting, sample making and some artwork. The Fulham centre encompasses an expansion of these activities and includes the group's central marketing activities.

GROWTH

Initially Bernard and Laura Ashley's first company, Ashley Mountney Limited, formed in 1954, sold the printed tea towels and scarves to department stores. When Bernard Ashley developed a continuous textile printing machine and curing oven to fix dyes, the company began to supply dress and furnishing fabrics again mainly to department stores. In the years that followed, sales continued to grow and the first export orders were achieved. By the end of the decade the expansion of the business led the Ashleys to move it to Carno in Powys, Wales. By 1966 the company had a staff of nineteen and sales of around £1,000 a week. At about this time, Laura Ashley designed the first clothing items, two housedresses retailing at about £2 each. Encouraged by the success of exports and of a small selling operation near Carno, the Ashleys became convinced that their products had a wider market than they had reached through selling to department stores and speciality shops. The first Laura Ashley retail shop opened in 1968 in South Kensington. This shop drew attention for the first time to the highly individual designs and style of Laura Ashley.

The subsequent growth and development of the group has stemmed from this move into direct retailing. Demand was such that within two years the company had withdrawn from wholesaling to concentrating on producing goods for sales through its shops. The basic structure of Laura Ashley as a vertically integrated business, embracing design, fabric printing, clothing manufacture and retailing, was thus established.

Over the next few years, other shops were opened in the UK and by 1973 the company had opened its first overseas shop in Geneva, followed by others in Amsterdam, Paris and Düsseldorf. In late 1974 the first shop in the USA opened in San Francisco and was a near disaster. In a city hit by the recession the company had attempted to adapt UK sales methods to the highly competitive American market. The shop was too large, on the wrong site, and opened at the wrong time of the year. However, by 1984 almost half the company's sales were made in the USA. An analysis of 500,000 names on Laura Ashley's US customer list revealed that 10 per cent were in the top demographic category (i.e. super-rich). In the USA the company has successfully exploited the appeal to 'life style', which leads shoppers to dress themselves, their children and their homes in a homogeneous fashion.

To meet the growing demand in the shops, production capacity for textiles and wallpaper was steadily expanded at the original factory site at Carno and more making-up plants were opened in the Welsh border counties. In 1977 a second printing factory was acquired in Helmond, in the Netherlands, to support the expansion of retailing in continental Europe.

PRODUCTION

The Laura Ashley Group and its subcontractors currently manufacture about 85 per cent by value of the products sold. Outside manufacturers produce items such as ceramic tiles which the company does not wish to produce itself. Periodic increases in production demand may also be met outside the group. Quality standards are established by a central technical department, which also carries out regular factory audits to monitor performance.

In-house printing of both textiles and wallpaper is regarded as being of great importance in preserving the design quality of Laura Ashley products. This is reflected in the product division's considerable investment in machinery. Carno and Helmond are capable of producing broadly similar products. The need for increased production capacity has led to a new plant being built at Newtown, 11 miles from Carno, which will have the capacity to produce 12 million metres of fabric, more than doubling the normal capacity at Carno, and 10 million metres of wallpaper. The group also plans further extension of its Helmond plant. Fabric for clothes is cut at Carno according to computer-graded patterns developed from the final designs. The cut fabric, ready for sewing, is then sent to one of the group's eight garment making-up plants within approximately 80 miles of Carno. A similar operation in Dublin is used for exported clothes. Fabric, with lay-plans is also supplied for third party manufacture in Kentucky where garments are made up under contract for Laura Ashley. Home furnishing accessories are made up at two further plants.

DISTRIBUTION

The group is expanding its Newtown warehouse to form the distribution centre for both clothing and home furnishings which, until 1985, were shared between warehouses at Carno and Newtown. A smaller warehouse at Greenford, Middlesex, is used to service the London shops. Overseas there are warehouses at Helmond and Mahwah – the latter completed in August 1985 at a cost of $6 million to include office space as well.

Clothing and home furnishings are supplied directly to each UK shop by lorries owned by the group. Clothing and home furnishings for Europe are sent via the Helmond warehouse, whence they are distributed either by group transport or through arrangements with local carriers. Clothing for North America is despatched weekly from the Newtown warehouse by airfreight to each shop. Home furnishings are sent by sea to Mahwah and then distributed.

RETAILING

Although the presentation of merchandise in each Laura Ashley shop reflects local customer preferences, these retail outlets are designed to create the same look and atmosphere throughout the world because they are seen as important in projecting the Laura Ashley image. Shop fronts are 'Paris Green' and high-quality wooden fittings are a standard feature.

In its shops in the UK and USA electronic point of sale systems are in operation providing daily sales figures for each shop by product line. These figures feed into the group's computers enabling it to respond quickly in the areas of stock control and production planning. A similar system is planned for Europe. A special role is given to catalogues, also used for mail order. They are produced for home furnishings and clothing collections including bridal wear. The catalogues vary in emphasis between the different national markets. Advertising is largely in magazines with some additional newspaper advertising, the focus being on innovation in product ranges. Point of sale material is used extensively by the shops, often to support particular promotions and in-shop promotions are co-ordinated with window displays, press advertising and the timing of catalogues. Printed material is designed to ensure consistency with the style of Laura Ashley products.

UK outlets

Table 11.5 shows Laura Ashley's growth during the first half of this decade.

Table 11.5   Laura Ashley: UK outlets 1980–85

Year	Shops	Homebases	Sales (£ million)
1980	25	—	12.7
1981	27	2	16.7
1982	34	5	20.4
1983/4	41	14	29.2
1984/5	49	23	39.7

Originally, priority was given to the selection of buildings in retail areas like Bath and Winchester which were considered harmonious with the traditional country image of Laura Ashley. This is still important, especially in the choice of building, as many shops are of historical interest in themselves, but in places like Peterborough and Brent Cross the best sites have been in new shopping precincts.

In 1981 the group was invited to open a 'shop-in-shop' within the first Homebase home and garden centre established by Homebase Limited, the Sainsbury subsidiary. The twenty-seven separate and clearly differentiated shops are in prime positions within each store and are operated and staffed by the group. They now account for 20 per cent of the group's home furnishing sales and have given it access to the increasingly important do-it-yourself market served by out of town sites.

Mail order accounts for 3 per cent of turnover in the UK and is handled by the mail order centre at Newtown.

European outlets

Table 11.6 shows the group's European position.

Table 11.6   Laura Ashley: European outlets 1980–85

Year	Shops	Sales (£ million)
1980	34	9.0
1981	35	9.0
1982	39	9.7
1983/4	42	10.0
1984/5	43	13.4

The main contributors to sales in 1984/5 were France (nineteen outlets – 38 per cent); West Germany (nine outlets – 20 per cent); and the Netherlands with seven shops attaining 21 per cent of European sales. Generally there have been higher garment sales in the Netherlands, Switzerland and West Germany, and higher home furnishings sales in France and Italy.

Most of the group's free-standing shops were originally in secondary locations. In the early 1980s, to maintain sales, a number of shop-in-shops were opened in Galeries Lafayette and Au Printemps stores in France. A programme of relocation of existing free-standing shops is being undertaken, and from 1986 no further shop-in-shops are planned. The group is concentrating attention on France and Germany, which are its major markets, and all new shops will be situated in prime sites.

In 1984/5 mail order sales represented 9 per cent of European sales turnover.

American outlets

Table 11.7 shows Laura Ashley's rapid expansion in the US.

Table 11.7   Laura Ashley: US outlets 1980–85

Year	Shops	Sales (£ million)
1980	11	3.0
1981	15	7.3
1982	28	12.9
1983/4	43	25.2
1984/5	55	40.1

The American consumer regards Laura Ashley as a high quality, exclusive designer label with a specially English appeal. Sales of clothing represented about two-thirds by value of total sales in the United States throughout the five years – a much higher proportion than other markets. This reflects the fact that in the USA a much higher proportion of consumers use professional interior decorators and designers. As a result the group has established Decorator Collection Showrooms to sell to interior designers and specialist centres. A specialist consultancy service to provide a complete interior design service for clients in their own homes has also been established.

Rapid expansion has also been facilitated by the relatively low capital costs of establishing shops in the USA. More than two-thirds of Laura Ashley shops are located in modern shopping malls. Rentals are generally turnover-related and Laura Ashley is attractive to mall developers as a tenant because of its high sales per square foot.

Catalogues are similar to those used in the UK and are used to generate interest in the shops but, with nearly two million distributed in 1984, they serve to increase general consumer awareness of the Laura Ashley name. They are also used for mail order, which is based in Mahwah and accounts for about 3 per cent of USA sales turnover.

Licences have been granted to a number of manufacturers in the USA. Chief among these is that to Burlington Domestics which has the exclusive right in the USA to manufacture and sell bed linen and bathroom accessories the design of which is under the control of Laura Ashley. Other licences have been arranged with Henredon Furniture Industries Inc, which manufactures and sells in the USA a range of furniture upholstered in Laura Ashley fabrics, and with Raintree Designs Inc which produces furnishing fabrics and wall coverings. In the year to January 1985 these and other licensing agreements produced royalty income of about $2 million.

Pacific Basin

By October 1985 there were eleven shops in Australia and one in Japan. The group has a joint venture with Japan United Stores Company under which a shop was opened in Tokyo, in 1985, selling home furnishings and clothing made up locally from printed cloth supplied by Carno. The Tokyo shop was conceived as a test market operation.

Other retailing

In addition to shops in Canada and one in Dublin, Laura Ashley has arrangements with retailers chiefly in countries where the group is not otherwise represented. These arrangements are either franchises or designated stockists to which the group supplies Laura Ashley products.

PROFITS

In the year to 26 January 1985 the UK contributed 37 per cent of operating profits. This includes not only profits from retailing but also contributions from the manufacturing operations in the UK for products supplied to the retailing outlets and third parties. Ireland contributed 3 per cent of operating profit. Five per cent of total operating profits in 1984/5 was achieved in Europe. As in the UK, this included a contribution from manufacturing operations. The USA has become the largest contributor to the group's operating profits accounting in the year to January 1985 for 55 per cent.

Profit before taxation and extraordinary items has increased from £875,000 in the year to 31 December 1980 to £14.1 million in the year to 26 January 1985.

– 12 –

PROMOTION

Half of the money that I spend on advertising is wasted. I wish I knew which half.   (Lord Lever)

Promotion includes personal selling, public relations and media advertising, which are often referred to as the 'communications mix'.

The amount of money spent on both sales promotion and display advertising has continued to grow more rapidly than the rate of inflation, with an average year-on-year real increase of about 4 per cent (Table 12.1).

Table 12.1   Media advertising expenditure 1982–84

Media type	1982	1983	1984
		(£ million)	
Press	1,297	1,436	1,626
Television	928	1,109	1,245
Cinema	124	137	150
Radio	70	81	86
Posters	18	16	16
Sales promotion (est.)		4,200	5,000

Press continues to be the most important media channel chosen, but television is growing in importance. For many companies faced with a hostile competitive environment the importance of public relations should also not be underestimated.

To spend money effectively on promotion, the company will need to understand:
1. How advertising works, and what it can or cannot achieve.
2. The strategy of the company and how promotion relates to it.
3. The type of promotional material available and what best fits the requirements of the company.

4. How the company should structure the promotional investment during the year.
5. How the company should decide on the level of expenditure for the promotional campaign.
6. The way in which the company should measure and improve the effectiveness of the promotional expenditure.

HOW ADVERTISING WORKS

Individuals receive information about products or services from a number of sources:
1. Personal contact: family, friends and business acquaintances. This would also include the sales representative as a source of information.
2. Pack information: the product will itself convey valuable information to potential new customers – the pack on the shelf, the new car on the road, for example.
3. Editorial comment: information on the product from 'unbiased' sources such as consumer group magazines, and expert comment in specialist magazines, for example.
4. Paid promotional activity, which will include advertisements on television, press, radio and cinema.

The importance placed on each will vary according to the individual and the nature of the product, and the nature of the information required to take a decision.

In any market a customer will have available a number of products that can be considered for purchase. For example, one individual might normally buy own-brand soaps, though occasionally buying Lux for visitors. Another might buy

Figure 12.1. Product portfolio: an example in toilet soap

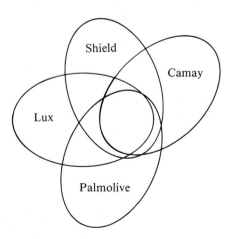

predominantly premium soaps while sporadically buying Camay when unable to make a journey into a major town. In other words each buyer will have a portfolio of products which he or she will consider buying (Figure 12.1).

The consumer will switch between these products from purchase to purchase, and the nature of the portfolio will change over time with new brands being introduced, prices altering, stores closing or personal circumstances changing. The rate at which the consumer switches between products will vary on a market and an individual basis. Consumer goods markets tend to show very high levels of brand switching, industrial markets far less. If all else is equal, such as price, distribution and product quality, the system will be in some form of equilibrium with the numbers of individuals switching to a competitive brand being matched by individuals switching from competitive brands.

Each bit of information that an individual receives affects his or her propensity to purchase a particular item. Promotional information will cause a shift in favour of the company's product and away from competitive products. A fundamental distinction appears to exist between media investment (which is often called above-the-line expenditure) and sales promotional expenditure (below-the-line) as to the long-term effects of promotional expenditure. Most studies suggest that media expenditure will cause a long-term change in the relationship of competing products whereas sales promotion will shift the equilibrium that exists during the promotional period (Figure 12.2).

Figure 12.2. Effects of different promotional expenditure

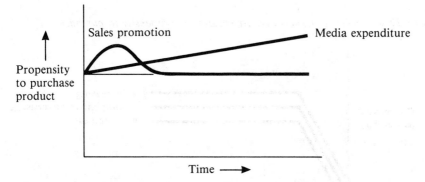

With the Homepride brand in the 1960s Spillers gained considerable market share with its television commercial 'The flour graders – graded grains make finer flour'. Budgetary considerations led to ending this campaign. To maintain sales against the competition of standard own-brand flours and the stoneground/wholemeal varieties that were steadily becoming more popular, the company spent money on short-term promotional activity. In order to combat the growing specialist flour sector the company reintroduced television advertising in 1985 for a new wholemeal variety, using the 'flour graders' theme once more.

The speed at which advertising takes effect in established markets, and the amount of investment that is required to achieve the maximum effect are still subjects of considerable dispute.

Research in the United States tends to suggest that there is no threshold below which advertising is ineffective, and that for consumer goods the maximum effective impact is achieved fairly rapidly with the customer receiving two or three advertising messages over the space of one month (Figure 12.3).

Industrial goods and services such as insurance require a far higher level of continued advertising to achieve the overall effect, as do new products in all sectors.

Figure 12.3.   Plateau effect of consumer advertising

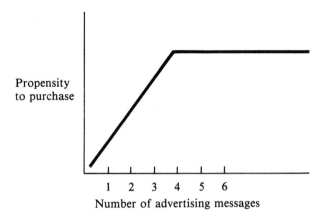

Figure 12.4.   Effect of competitive advertising on propensity to purchase

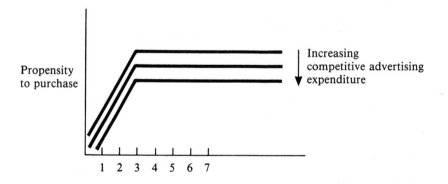

The problem is further complicated by the speed at which individuals forget information they receive. Most research suggests that around 30 per cent of the content of an advertising message is forgotten month by month; for new products it is often much higher.

The effect of competitive expenditure on advertising is to reduce its effectiveness on stimulating brand-switching (Figure 12.4).

THE STRATEGIC ISSUES OF PROMOTION

Speed of return on promotional investment

Investment in media expenditure is a fairly long-term exercise. Whereas sales promotion will achieve rapid, though transitory, increases in volume, after the sales promotion is over the market equilibrium becomes re-established, as was shown in Figure 12.2.

Where the company is seeking short-term volume it will need to concentrate on sales promotion; for long-term market development it will need to concentrate on media investment.

Relation to strategic objectives

Firms will need to evaluate the promotional expenditure in relation to their strategic objectives. As commented in Chapter 3, the options facing the firm will be:

- to invest
- to maintain
- to withdraw slowly
- to delete.

Each of the paths will have promotional implications. Promotional expenditure patterns will be part of the investment decision process on the growth or decline of a product.

> Lever Brothers maintained the detergent, Omo, for many years without advertising as a part of conscious long-term policy that led eventually to the product withdrawal.

Restrictions

Different markets place differing restrictions on the use of advertising material, and this will control the way firms view their promotional investment. The most obvious example is the effect of limitations on tobacco advertising which helped to raise expenditure on sports sponsorship to £191 million in 1985.

The Advertising Standards Authority, a non-statutory body, also has a major influence on the way in which advertisements are designed, by acting as an industry watchdog to ensure that all advertisements are 'honest, decent, and truthful'.

Cultural factors may also act as a restriction on a particular approach or level of promotional expenditure.

The stage of the product life cycle

The product life cycle curve can be a useful method for defining product promotional requirements, though as has been pointed out in Chapter 4, the use of the PLC can be a self-fulfilling prophecy, the withdrawal of support ensuring that the product collapses.

The level of competitive expenditure

Where there is a high level of competitive expenditure, the company may decide that it will have to increase its own level to match that existing for other companies.

The nature of the industry

Different industries have different structures and one culture may differ significantly from another in its promotional systems. Any organization will need to consider this in the planning process.

> In some markets, such as the pop music industry, editorial comment is an essential part of the promotional plan; record promoters with contacts in the industry are employed to gain editorial coverage.

> For many specialized markets the individual approach of the sales representative may be most cost-effective and/or acceptable in the culture. For example, a large proportion of cars are sold by door-to-door salesmen in Japan – a complete contrast to Western Europe. As the complexity of the product and its unit price increase there will be a greater emphasis on the need for personal selling.

> In contrast to other retailers which are heavy users of media, especially television, Marks and Spencer had concentrated on pack information as a means of promotion; placing the product in the store with sufficient information on the nature of the product to achieve an acceptable level of consumer purchase. The recent move into furniture has been supported by their first major advertising campaign.

The acceptability of the industry or otherwise may also affect the degree to which the company considers that it needs to invest in corporate or 'social acceptability' advertising.

> The advertising campaigns run by Shell Oil are a good example of a company attempting to overcome reservations in society. The company emphasizes the minimal environmental damage it causes, and the contribution that it makes to the economy.

Nature of the information

Different products or services will require varying levels of complexity of information. For example, compare the information requirements of the village fête with those of buying a new £5 million generator for a power station. Broadly one can discern four main types of information that the firm could consider:

1. Basic. This would cover dates, times and places. 'Turn right at the lights for X store' data.
2. Information to act as a reminder. This is to remind consumers of a product in the market they may have forgotten – 'you enjoyed X once, so try it again'.
3. Encouragement to trial. Information to persuade customers that a particular product should be added to the portfolio of current brands. 'Why not try it, and amaze your neighbours.'
4. Thought provoking. Information to upset preconceived ideas about particular products or services – 'You never knew you needed it, but this is why'.

These differing promotional approaches will demand different types and levels of investment.

Distribution

The nature of the distribution channel and the amount of control that a company can exert will have important consequences on the nature of the promotional expenditure. This is clearly seen in the UK grocery market where expenditure on consumer goods promotion is shifting away from media expenditure towards sales promotion, largely as a consequence of the demands of the major multiple chains.

The relationship to price and profitability requirements

Promotional expenditure will interact with the price elasticity operating in any market, by shifting the curve to the right (Figure 12.5).

This will mean that the company will either be able to sell more product for the same price or the same volume for a higher price.

As has been mentioned, the interaction between price and promotion will affect the speed of development in the market and the level of profit that a firm wishes to achieve (see Chapter 11).

Figure 12.5. Effect of promotion on price elasticity

'Image' requirements

The firm will also need to relate the promotional requirements of the product to the desired position in the market. Premium products maintain their position at least in part as a consequence of their exclusivity, which is a reflection of which media channel is chosen for promotional expenditure.

IMPLEMENTING PROMOTION – THE ADVANTAGES AND DISADVANTAGES OF VARIOUS OPTIONS

Each method of promoting the product to the end consumer will need to be evaluated in a number of ways.

Coverage

Does the method allow cost-effective coverage of the sector of the market at which the promotional effort is targeted? Media expenditure is usually measured in cost per thousand, that is, the cost of reaching one thousand end users. This simple calculation is often complicated by the amount of multiple readership that can exist for certain titles.

> *Punch*, the humorous magazine, claims a high level of multiple readership, which is in part supported by its wide distribution in doctors' and dentists' waiting rooms!

Frequency

Some media will be more appropriate to provide rapid build-up of the advertising message as they appear more frequently than others.

Production costs

Different media will have vastly differing production costs. For example, an average television commercial will cost in the region of £40,000, artwork for the local newspaper £10–50.

Ability to transmit technical information

Certain media are more effective in their ability to handle large amounts of information than others.

Movement/colour

Certain media are much more effective in dealing with movement and the use of colour than others.

Colour in advertisements is thought to improve impact and make the product more recognizable and more attractive.

Impact

Certain media are more effective at achieving a high level of impact. Naturally this is associated partly with the size of the advertisement. It has been shown that response to newspaper advertisements increases as a square root of the increased space; doubling the size of the advertisement increases response by a factor of 1.4.

Flexibility

Some media are more flexible than others, allowing a more rapid management response than others.

Specificity

Media will range in their ability to deal specifically with a particular target audience, even though the individual cost may be higher than more general media. One feature of the majority of media is the low level of switching between alternative media that exists. Listeners to radio will only choose one or two stations from the wide variety available; similar trends can be seen in magazines and newspapers.

Ease of evaluation

Certain media will be far easier to evaluate than others. For example, the effectiveness of direct mail is easy to measure; the effects of posters extremely difficult.

Ease of control

Different media will provide different levels of support and in many cases a multi-media campaign will not only achieve a higher level of coverage, it will also allow the company to transmit more information about the product.

The ability of each of the media to meet these criteria is shown in Table 12.2 and summarized below.

Table 12.2 *Effectiveness of differing media*

	TV	Radio	Cinema	Poster	Magazine	Press	Exhibitions	Direct mail
Coverage	✓✓✓	✓	×	✓	✓✓	✓✓✓	×	✓
Frequency	✓✓✓	✓	×	××	✓	✓✓	×	✓✓
Production cost	×××	✓✓✓	×××	×××	✓	✓	×××	✓✓✓
Technical information	××	××	✓	×××	✓✓✓	×	✓✓✓	✓✓
Movement colour	✓✓✓	××	✓✓✓	×	✓	×	✓✓✓	×
Impact	✓✓✓	✓	✓✓✓	✓✓	✓	✓	✓✓✓	✓
Flexibility	✓	✓✓	✓	××	✓	✓	×	✓✓✓
Specificity	×	××	×	××	✓✓✓	×	✓✓✓	✓✓✓
Ease of evaluation	××	××	×××	×××	✓	×	✓✓	✓✓✓
Ease of control	✓✓	✓✓✓	✓	××	✓✓	✓	✓	✓✓✓

Press

There are four distinct categories of press advertising:
1. national newspapers;
2. regional newspapers (including the freesheets that are steadily growing in number);
3. consumer (or general interest) magazines;
4. business and technical journals.

Table 12.3   Press advertising split

Category	Share (£ millions)
National press	566
Regional press	388
Consumer magazines	236
Technical	226

Each accounts for varying levels of the total percentage of advertising committed to the press for 1984 (Table 12.3).

Costs and coverage will vary enormously from title to title, and advertisers can choose from an enormous range of specialist titles (over 3,000 in the UK alone).

Television

The two independent UK channels, ITV and Channel 4, provide the potential advertiser with opportunities to concentrate on either regional or national advertising. The Independent Broadcasting Acts lay down strict guidelines on the nature and volume of advertising, restricting stations to a maximum of six minutes per hour. Though costs of commercial time and production costs are both high, the level of coverage is the highest of all available media. In an average week it has been found that 86 per cent of adults look at commercial television for at least fifteen minutes.

A poll in 1981 found that a majority of viewers preferred the commercials to the programmes.

The nature of television advertising is undergoing fairly rapid change. The introduction of Channel 4 has made it more cost-effective to use television for specific products directed at small markets.

OTV Rentals, a company specializing in the sale of ex-rental TVs and videos was one of the earliest companies to concentrate on the use of Channel 4 in the London area to promote its products.

The introduction of more cable television stations and eventual satellite transmission will further segment the television market.

Posters

Posters, or more accurately the whole field of outdoor media which includes hoardings at sports grounds and panels on the sides of taxis, have always proved a difficult medium to measure effectively. They have the advantage of being able to provide considerable impact on either a national or a local basis. Their cost-effectiveness has long been disputed, the main expenditure on posters being derived from the tobacco and spirits suppliers both of which face restrictions on their use of other media.

Radio

The availability of radio as a promotional medium has steadily grown with the expansion of the local radio network. Audience research shows that only a small minority of individuals (about 15 per cent) are paying specific attention to the radio message: the others are using it as background noise to some other task. This has considerable implications for the nature and the style of radio advertising and the type of firms that use the media.

Cinema

Steadily reducing audience numbers have made cinema an unattractive media choice for many products. However, the audience profile of mainly young and affluent consumers makes it an ideal promotional channel for some products.

Non-media methods of sales promotion have become increasingly important. These include:

Direct mail

For many industrial markets direct mail is the most cost-effective way of reaching potential clients even though the rate of return from mail shots tends to be low at about 1–1.5 per cent.

Direct mail has the advantage that large amounts of technical information can be supplied to the potential customer at low cost. In addition to individual companies developing their own material and mailing lists there are a number of organizations that provide an omnibus mailing service for specific market sectors such as education, office equipment, office management and the like.

With the development of more sophisticated methods of targeting consumers, such as ACORN, there has been a steady increase in the number of companies using direct mail in the consumer sector particularly for financial services. By 1984 the total volume of items reported was 1,262 million (though this is probably an underestimate).

Tele-marketing

The use of the telephone as a promotional method is far more prevalent in the United States than in the United Kingdom, reflecting partly the difference in telephone ownership (the difference in attitude towards the telephone is also shown by variations in its use for market research discussed in Chapter 6).

Personal selling

This is a major element of the promotional spectrum and, as the problems that it raises are often distinct from other promotional factors, it is discussed separately in Chapter 13.

Exhibitions

There are wide differences in the nature of exhibitions, from local limited displays to national exhibitions such as those at the National Exhibition Centre or in London. Costs vary accordingly.

Leaflets

Leaflets are most effective as sources of information to explain product benefits, introduce competitions or special offers.

Firms face a bewildering variety of leaflet formats from folded A4 sheets printed in colour on both sides to single-sheet A3 printed in one colour. Complicated artwork, any variation from a standard page format, the use of colour will all increase the cost. As the level of sophistication increases it becomes more necessary for the firm to produce larger quantities to reduce the overall unit cost. For example, a typical costing to print 10,000 leaflets (excluding artwork) is shown in Table 12.4.

Table 12.4   Index of leaflet printing costs

Specification	Index
A4 four colour folded	100
A4 four colour unfolded	90
A4 two colour	60
A4 black and white with perforated coupon	60
A4 black and white	35

Catalogues

Catalogues are most appropriate to provide detailed and full explanations of the features and the benefits of the entire product range. Many firms fail to appreciate the role of good catalogues to aid the establishment of a large product range with the customer. It is quite useful to compare the investment that holiday companies make in brochures to persuade families to book a holiday costing £1,000 – many companies expecting a much greater level of orders from a customer will provide a far inferior catalogue.

Point of sale displays/merchandising material

This will include:
1. shelf 'talkers' – promotional material attached to the shelf to draw the attention of the consumer to the product;
2. shelf strips;
3. mobiles – displays that move in the air, attached to the ceiling near the product emphasizing a particular product benefit or feature;
4. 'dump bins' or special racks for displaying and selling the product.

A specialized form of point of sale material is the 'tent' card used in restaurants, cafés and bars to promote particular items available within the outlet. Other specialized material of this nature would include drink mats, ashtrays, and mirrors with product information.

This material is increasingly difficult to use in the majority of British retail outlets, as the 'Big Five' (Sainsbury's, Asda, Dee, Argyll, Tesco) do not allow promotional material to be displayed in-store.

On-pack material

This will include all material that is attached to the product in some form or fashion to improve sales:
1. 'Flash' packs – packs specially printed with promotional material, which may be competitions, self-liquidating offers, money-off offers or additional product. An example would be '30 pence off next purchase'.
2. 'Banded' packs – material such as free gifts attached to the pack. Twin-packs with promotional material is another possibility, the two packs to be sold at a special promotional price. The dishwasher packet that includes the rinse aid would be an example.

The findings of a survey of preferences for special packs are shown in Table 12.5.

Table 12.5   Index of special-pack preferences

Type	Index
Extra quantity packs	100
Reduced price offers	92
Free gifts	49
Free mail-ins	42
Self-liquidating offers	38
Games and competitions	32

Directories or year books

For many companies, particularly in the industrial sector, maintaining entries in the relevant directories or year books will be an important method of acquiring new customers.

Audio-visual material

With the advent and worldwide spread of the video, a substantial amount of promotional material is now being provided on video. This is particularly relevant for exhibitions and the promotion of complex and expensive technical equipment.

Trade promotional items

There is a wide range of promotional items produced to provide reminders to trade buyers of the company's products. Examples would include keyrings, notepads, pens, ties, cufflinks, badges, certificates, wallets, diaries, calendars, executive toys and other desk-top items. Often this material is very expensive and of dubious value in achieving any sales objective. The Pirelli calendar became a status symbol, but did it sell any more tyres?

STRUCTURING PROMOTIONAL EXPENDITURE

Many promotional plans do not pay sufficient attention to the way in which the expenditure should be managed across the year, which can often be crucial in determining how effective it is overall.

There are a number of issues that need to be considered:

Required investment to reach the level of maximum effective response

This issue of promotion, discussed earlier in the chapter, will be of great importance in defining the way in which the company should spend the money available. Should the threshold be low, high levels of promotional expenditure at any one time will be largely wasted (in providing more than the required number of messages).

Advertising forgetting rate

The rate at which the advertising message is being lost will also have an effect on the structure of the advertising campaign. Should the rate be low, maintaining a low level of continuous advertising will be most cost-efficient (Figure 12.6).

Frequency distribution

As the amount of advertising investment changes the total number of advertisements that individuals see *on average* increases. However, the relationship is not totally straightforward. For most promotional methods (except direct mail, for example) certain individuals will receive far more advertisements than others. Research companies such as AGB can provide

Figure 12.6. Advertising forgetting rate

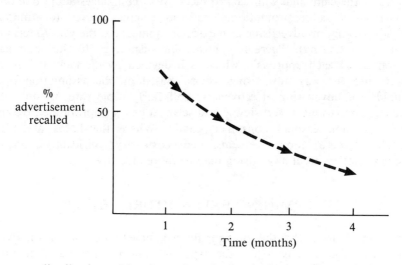

frequency distribution tables that relate the level of expenditure within a month to the percentage of the population that will see the advertisement once, twice, thrice and so on (Table 12.6).

Table 12.6 Frequency distribution table

Expenditure (TVR = television rating points)	Cover					
	1 +	2 +	3 +	4 +	5 +	6 +
100 TVR	56	38	12	4	—	—
200 TVR	70	45	26	16	6	4
300 TVR	80	60	45	28	15	12
400 TVR	92	75	62	35	26	18

Note how increasing expenditure leads to an increased percentage of the population receiving more advertising messages, though in a disproportionate fashion.

Frequency distribution tables differ according to the nature of the media and the chosen target group.

Product seasonality

The effect of advertising is proportional to the sales level of the product. It is fairly self evident that a company should not advertise sun-tan lotion during December, but it would be equally effective for a coffee company to advertise in June or October as the total demand for coffee varies across the year.

Media costs

Pre-Christmas advertising rates are significantly higher than those in February, and any promotional plan will need to take account of media costs.

For any company therefore there will be a degree of conflicting demands that the structure of the campaign will need to meet. Most companies adopt one of two approaches – spreading promotional expenditure across the year (continuous or 'drip' advertising) or advertising at particular moments of the year (intermittent or 'burst' advertising). There is considerable dispute as to the comparative effectiveness of each approach, which is bedevilled by the lack of long-term research into the way advertising works. Based on the assumption of low thresholds for advertising effectiveness, and fairly rapid rates of advertising forgetting, continuous advertising would seem to be the appropriate investment method for non-seasonal consumer goods. Where thresholds are higher, seasonality effects are more severe, and media costs vary significantly at one stage of the year, intermittent advertising may be more effective.

DETERMINING EXPENDITURE LEVELS

The amount of money that the company has available to promote each individual product will significantly affect the type of publicity material that can be considered. Most firms do not regard advertising as an *investment* issue – that promotional expenditure can and should be regarded as similar to expenditure in plant, buildings or personnel all of which are necessary to achieve profitable sales development.

Three common approaches exist to define promotional expenditure, all of which tend to ignore the investment aspect of promotion.

The affordable method

This considers advertising as an afterthought within the company planning process, a form of insurance perhaps. Such a process might follow that shown in Table 12.7.

Table 12.7   The affordable method

Sales	£150,000
Variable costs	£60,000
Fixed costs	£60,000
Income	£30,000
Net profit required	£20,000
Advertising (what is affordable!)	£10,000

The drawbacks of such a method are obvious; the level of promotional expenditure will fluctuate from year to year and often from quarter to quarter. Cynics within the advertising profession notice that marketing managers working for large companies often spend a large proportion of their advertising allocation in the early part of the financial year – perhaps to ensure that it is not taken away from them later on!

The percentage of sales method

This considers that advertising should be viewed as being generated by sales: each case sold can provide for a unit of advertising revenue. Though such an approach has accounting advantages by ensuring that excessive advertising expenditure will not run out of control, it ignores the investment concept of advertising: that some products in some markets will produce good returns, whereas expenditure on other products in other markets will merely be wasted effort, and that initial investment in promotion may be essential to achieve trial and market penetration.

Competitive parity method

This is the 'keeping up with the Joneses' syndrome. It suggests that the competition knows the industry better than management within the company and that the competitors have the same objectives in every market. *Promotional expenditure is all about trying to gain competitive advantage* – what is the competitive advantage in doing exactly what the competition does?

More valuable is to define the investment criteria that the company is using for each particular product, and use these to arrive at the required budget level, continually monitoring performance to see that targets are achieved.

By defining strategic requirements for the product followed by profitability and return on investment, the firm will be able to set targets against which the achievements of the investment can be judged.

MEASURING PERFORMANCE

Advertisements on television, the cinema and radio can either be tested before or after they have been used, or by a combination of the two. This pre- and post-testing will be based on either a comparison between two possible advertisements or recall tests to ascertain what percentage of the population can remember a particular advertisement and what aspects can be recalled.

Other advertisements can be tested by the inclusion of direct response material such as reply-paid coupons. By accurately recording how the advertisement was designed and in what media it was placed, coupon return provides some measure at least of the effectiveness of the media in provoking a positive response.

Sales response to a particular advertisement is more difficult and time-consuming to measure. Companies will have to establish test market regions and because of the small difference in the sales level that will exist between the two regions, the test will have to run for many months – often for over a year – before statistically reliable results can be obtained.

THE ADVERTISING AGENCY

An important element of promotional expenditure in large companies is the use of specialized advertising agencies that take charge of the creation of commercials and the booking of space in the various media. Agencies will vary in sophistication from full service agencies that provide a complete management service, to those that specialize in certain areas, such as design or print and media buying. The full service agencies receive a commission on the size of the advertising budget, often 15 per cent, whereas specialized agencies are often paid on a fee basis. Table 12.8 shows the functions of the various agency personnel.

Table 12.8   The advertising agency

Job title	Function
Account director	Has overall responsibility for the creation and management of client accounts
Account executive	Works with the account director and is the main contact of the agency with the company. Liaises with other departments within the agency to ensure that jobs are completed on time. Transmits the briefing the agency receives into actions that other departments need to carry out
Creative director	Has overall responsibility for graphic design and execution of the design work that the agency carries out
Copy writer	An individual who works with the creative director turning the advertising brief into material that can be used in commercials
Visualizer	Another member of the creative team whose responsibility includes graphic design; the visualizer may also be responsible for the completion of artwork – the finished form of the designs
Media buyer	The individual who ensures that the necessary advertising space for the campaign is made available
Film director	The individual who has overall responsibility for carrying through any photographic work that the campaign may require – hiring outside artistes, booking studio space, ensuring all dubbing and other editing work is completed

PUBLIC RELATIONS

Public relations can be defined as the favourable presentation of information concerning the product or the company in media that has not been paid for. It aims to create a climate of opinion that is favourable to the company by drawing attention to its services to the community. It is therefore more diffuse than advertising which may be used when there is a special controversy, as in the case of concern about industrial pollution of the environment or about nuclear power stations, as additional back-up for the public relations effort. A public relations strategy will depend heavily on providing accurate information about the company and what it is doing.

Public relations will operate at two levels, the visible and the private.

Visible public relations channels include regular press briefings, usually in the form of press releases supplying information about items deemed 'newsworthy': new products, technical innovations, senior executive appointments, penetration of new markets, sponsorship of events, and so on.

IBM, the American multinational, emphasizes the contribution that it makes to the United Kingdom economy.

Shell, the Anglo-Dutch oil company, describes how little damage it causes to the environment.

British Nuclear Fuels Ltd concentrates on describing the benefits of nuclear energy and promotes its view of the safety of the industry.

Private methods may include lobbying of politicians and government departments – for the overseas firm this will mean the leaders involved in overseas trade, foreign aid, and foreign affairs.

It should be clear from this description that, for the majority of companies, public relations will tend to be secondary to other main promotional tools. As public relations tends to be non-specific in its coverage, the majority of consumers of a specific product will tend to miss public relations coverage. Public relations will, however, be a very important factor that large international corporations need to consider in relation to their proposed expansion or contraction of activities overseas.

Summary

The development of promotional plans is a complex management task requiring knowledge of the effects of promotion, what methods are available with the advantages and disadvantages relating to each, and how promotion interacts with strategic and tactical requirements.

ASSIGNMENTS

1. You are working for a firm which produces a wide range of consumer household goods which are promoted in women's magazines and on radio, with a combined budget of £2 million. Write a report on how the promotional activity should be monitored and what advantages are likely to be obtained from such a programme.
2. Write a memorandum on two recent advertising campaigns and why you believe they have succeeded or failed.
3. You are involved as an assistant product manager in the launch of a new range of industrial lubricating oils, and are asked to define the possible methods of promoting it with your recommendations as to the best course of action.

JIF RELAUNCH

BACKGROUND

During the late 1960s and early 1970s heavy enamel baths and basins were increasingly replaced by stainless steel and plastic, for which the current range of cleaners, such as Vim and Ajax, consisting essentially of powdered rock, were far too abrasive. The Unilever company in France developed a new product consisting of a suspension of a far less abrasive mineral dispersed in a cream solution. This product, called Cif in France was launched in the UK as Jif, and became brand leader in the cream scouring market with nationwide distribution. By the early 1980s, though it still maintained an impressive brand share of an estimated £30 million market, Jif was having to compete not only with the branded competition of Ajax Cream and Liquid Gumption, but also an increasing number of supermarket own brands which were considerably cheaper. It remained one of the more profitable Lever products and was expected to remain so until the late 1980s when additional new products would have to be considered.

It was decided by 1982 that the brand should be relaunched to hold on to the current market position, with a slightly new formulation, new perfume and redesigned packaging.

THE OBJECTIVES OF THE RELAUNCH

1. To persuade the target audience, defined as ABC1 housewives to try new Jif.
2. To reach the majority of store managers and buyers with the information that Jif had been reformulated and repackaged.

THE BUDGET

An amount of £890,000 at full rate card prices (this is the full list price that media charge before discounts are arrived at) was allocated to support the relaunch. With Unilever's substantial buying power the discounts achieved would probably be of the order of 40–50 per cent off list price.

TIMING

The relaunch was timed for January 1983.

THE MEDIA

Lever Brothers had to decide on how to allocate the budget between the different media and when it should be spent in order to achieve the objectives set for the media strategy. The following options were available.

Television. At peak viewing times ITV's share of audience was around 50 per cent, Channel 4's around 5 per cent. During 1983 the average number of hours viewing per household was 5.5 hours per day. Table 12.9 shows the regional cost for thirty seconds' peak time.

Table 12.9   TV advertising rates by region

Area	000 households (excluding small regional markets)	30-second peak cost (list price £) ITV	Channel 4
London	20	12,400	750
Midlands	16	6,000	350
North-west	12	5,000	200
Yorkshire	11	5,500	350
South	10	3,750	250
Wales	9	2,850	160
East	7	1,500	250
Scotland	6	3,675	100
South-west	3	1,600	40

As a percentage of the total population in those areas, 21 per cent of ABs lived in the London area, 21 per cent in the South, 17 per cent in the East, 15 per cent in the South-west, 14 per cent in both Scotland and Wales.

Cinema. Cinema advertising is available on a TV region basis. The Cinema Audience Delivery Plan guarantees one million admissions for a 30-second cost of £12,800. The average audience profile of cinema admissions was: AB 25 per cent; C1 35 per cent; C2 25 per cent; and DE 15 per cent.

Posters. One poster site costs around £300 a month, according to location; campaigns can be run on a weekly basis. A minimum national campaign based on 800 sites would cost £30,000, a minimum weekly campaign based on 5,000 sites, £75,000 – both including quantity discounts.

Leaflet distribution. Using shared distribution with other leaflets, any particular area could be covered at the cost of £8.25 per 1,000 homes. There are 18.5 million households in the United Kingdom.

National newspapers. Newspapers naturally vary considerably according to their socio-economic readership. The standard population profile is 39 per cent ABC1, 61 per cent C2DE. This compares with the percentages given in Table 12.10 for the different daily and weekly journals.

In addition to the national newspapers there is a wide range of regional newspapers that could be considered to support the relaunch, with full page black and white rates working out on average at £15 per thousand of the population.

Magazines. These can be divided into general weekly (GW), general monthly (GM), specialized weekly (SW), and specialized monthly (SM). Details of readership and advertising rates are given in Table 12.11.

Table 12.10 Readership profiles and advertising rates for national newspapers

Title	Readership (000s)	ABC1 (%)	Cost per page/colour if available (£)
Sun	4,084	24	22,000
Mirror	3,400	25	21,000
Express	2,000	51	14,000/40,000
Mail	1,800	55	14,000/30,000
Star	1,600	18	8,575/22,000
Telegraph	1,235	80	22,400
Guardian	472	77	14,000
Times	457	85	10,000
Financial Times	214	88	16,000
Sundays			
News of the World	4,698	23	22,610
Sunday Mirror	3,489	27	22,000
Sunday People	3,200	26	20,000
Sunday Express	2,500	60	34,000
Mail on Sunday	1,600	56	14,750
Sunday Times	1,260	78	26,000
Observer	744	75	17,500
Telegraph	713	75	18,000

Table 12.11 Readership profiles and advertising rates for magazines

Title	Readership (000s)	ABC1 (%)	Cost per page/colour (£)
TV Times (GW)	3,200	41	11,000/18,000
Radio Times (GW)	3,200	48	11,000/18,000
Reader's Digest (GM)	1,537	50	8,000/11,000
Woman's Own (GW)	1,180	n.a.	11,000/16,000
Woman (GW)	1,150	n.a.	10,000/15,000
Woman's Weekly (GW)	1,300	n.a.	6,000/ 9,000
Woman's Realm (GW)	600	n.a.	4,000/ 6,000
My Weekly (GW)	700	n.a.	2,500/ 3,800
Family Circle (GM)	550	n.a.	4,000/ 6,500
Woman & Home (GM)	625	n.a.	4,000/ 6,500
Living (GM)	422	n.a.	2,500/ 4,000
The Grocer (SW)	50	n.a.	331/ 1,400
Supermarketing (SW)	22	n.a.	1,400/ 2,000

Comment

The relaunch of Jif can be used to explore some of the issues that promotional policy and media planning involve.

13

SALES AND SALES MANAGEMENT

Everyone lives by selling something to somebody.

(Stephenson)

SALES

Personal selling is part of the promotional process, and is part of the way in which the firm develops a co-ordinated approach to the market. In common with other aspects of the marketing mix, the sales task will be affected by, and affect, many other areas.

INDUSTRY STRUCTURE

The nature of the industry will have a crucial impact on the way in which the firm organizes its selling effort.

First, it will define the type of selling and personnel that is required. As industry demands become more complex, the level of skill required increases. The sales task will vary in complexity from:

1. The van salesman essentially acting as a delivery service but with some order-taking involvement.
2. The salesman whose main task is to gain repeat orders from established customers for non-technical products (the classical picture of the consumer goods sales representative).
3. The sales representative facing the task of initiating purchase of technical equipment in industrial markets.

The differences in the nature of the selling task influence their importance in the marketing mix of both consumer and industrial markets. As the product becomes more complex the percentage of the firm's promotional budget that will be spent on the sales force will steadily increase (Figure 13.1).

Figure 13.1. Role of personal selling in relation to product cost/complexity

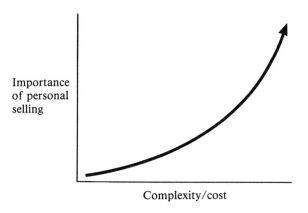

Complexity/cost

Such considerations do not solely affect the industrial market, as firms operating in the consumer market with technical or complex products will face similar investment decisions – double-glazing and insurance companies are two examples.

CUSTOMER/PRODUCT INTERACTION

The breadth and complexity of the products within the firm will have implications as to how the company structures its salesforce.

Geographical coverage. This creates a team of sales representatives each dealing with all products and all customers within a defined territory.

There are a number of advantages for such a system:
- it is cost effective
- it develops detailed knowledge of area and customer potential.

However geographical divisions fail to allow for:
- wide and/or complex product ranges
- customers with specific service requirements.

Product coverage. This approach divides the product range on a geographical basis between two or more teams of sales representatives. It is most common among wholesalers with extensive product ranges. It has the advantage of improving the ability of the company to promote a wide range of products, but the disadvantages that customers can become confused with two or more sales representatives calling from the same company, and considerable increase in expense.

Customer coverage. This approach divides the market on the basis that specific customers will have common problems which can be solved by combinations of products within the company's range – in other words it is problem-specific rather than product-specific.

ICL, the major British computer firm, has a policy of dividing its salesforce on a customer basis. There are education, defence, office and health service divisions, for example, each developing a detailed understanding of specific problems within each market sector.

Though the customer division overcomes the customer confusion inherent in the product division, it is an extremely expensive way of organizing a sales force.

National accounts organization. With the concentration of buying power developing in many areas of the economy, such as the major retailers and the multinationals with branches throughout the country, many companies have had to respond by developing sales forces specifically to deal with these accounts on a nationwide basis.

PRODUCT CHANGE

The way in which the firm is attempting to develop will have an effect on the way in which the sales force is directed and controlled.

Each of the five product options mentioned in Chapter 8 will have consequences for the sales force:
1. product abandonment;
2. market penetration;
3. market development;
4. product development;
5. diversification.

Product abandonment will require the company to keep the sales force fully informed of the planning implications, when and where the product will be phased out, and what implications exist for the provision of spare parts of current products.

Apricot Computers' withdrawal from the personal computer market in 1986 posed a problem for the provision of spares and software to the existing user base. With the large number of existing customers this gap will be filled by independent companies.

Market penetration strategies will require the sales force to concentrate on expanding demand mainly within existing customers. It will need to develop skills to handle sales promotions and concentrate on the most productive customers.

General Foods has pioneered the concept of field marketing for its Maxwell House sales force. This allows the sales force to develop promotions locally with individual superstores and provides it with budgets to advertise these in local newspapers.

In contrast, market development strategies will demand that the sales force is directed more towards finding new customers than expanding sales from the current customer base. This task is called 'missionary' selling and requires different types of expertise from the development of repeat purchase.

IBM has recognized the difficulties inherent in combining market penetration and market development in a single sales force and has established two different sales forces which can concentrate exclusively on the two tasks, one to build up established customer sales and the other to develop new customers.

Product development strategies will involve a high level of new product introduction or reintroduction. The activity of the sales force will need to be accurately controlled to ensure a balance between normal selling tasks and those required to develop the sales of new products.

Diversification strategies will often require a total change in the nature of the sales force, recruiting new individuals with skills relating to the new industry.

NATURE OF THE DISTRIBUTION CHANNELS

The nature of the distribution channels and the amount of control the company exerts within the distribution process will have implications for the sales force structure and organization. Increasing the number of sales representatives will be one means of expanding the company's control over the distribution process – it can more accurately determine where the product will be sold and at what price. Where the company relies heavily on wholesalers or distributors for distribution, the nature of the task for the company sales force will be substantially different – it will be more involved in a training rather than direct sales role, providing support for the independent distributors or intermediaries which the company is using.

The investment the firm makes in the sales force allows it far greater control over where the product is sold than might otherwise be the case.

> It is important for many perfumery companies to ensure that exclusive products are only stocked in prestigious stores. A directly employed sales force will ensure that this limited distribution is maintained, whereas the use of a distributor might widen the distribution beyond these limited number of stores as it would be in the interests of the distributor to achieve as large a sales volume as possible.

LEVEL OF SERVICE

In addition to the demands of the product range and the nature of the customer, the firm will need to decide the percentage of the market to which it is directly selling. This will often relate to the number of customers to which the firm is directly distributing (see Chapter 11) but may in certain conditions be a separate issue.

As the number of accounts increases, the sales force numbers and cost will also escalate, in common with the pattern that exists for distribution costs (Figure 13.2).

High levels of service from the sales force, in common with high levels of distribution coverage, enable the firm to gain a competitive advantage in the market. However, the increase in competitive advantage must be judged against the steadily increasing cost.

PROFITABILITY

What products are sold and to which customers will largely determine the level of profitability the company is able to achieve. The direction of the sales force will be vital in this respect.

Figure 13.2. Cost and market coverage in the sales force

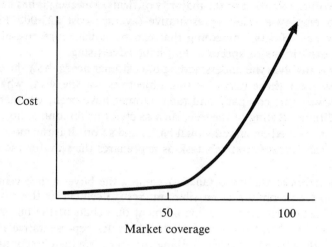

A small firm found that by changing the direction of the sales force away from concentrating on two major lines towards other areas of the range it was able to double profitability from the same level of sales revenue.

PROMOTION

The nature of the industry and the product demands will affect the promotional policy that the firm adopts. The degree of promotion required to support the sales force in generating new accounts will be an important aspect of the promotional policy for many firms in the industrial and service sector; other supporting material such as catalogues and descriptive leaflets will also often account for a substantial element of the promotional expenditure in many industrial and service-based organizations.

PRICE

The sales force will have a very important role to play in the control of pricing in the market by the degree of freedom granted to establish discount and credit terms.

THE SALES PROCESS

There are several mnemonics which describe the sales process. The most common is PAIDA which identifies stages of:
- Preparation
- Attention
- Interest
- Demand
- Action.

Some authors would put a further introductory phase, that of prospecting, before these other factors. For the majority of firms, however, it has become very expensive to employ a sales representative (average cost £25,000–£30,000) to prospect for new clients, something that can be much more cost-effective by direct mail, exhibitions or specialist magazine advertising.

Preparation involves the understanding of customer needs, how the company's products can meet those needs, setting objectives for the visit, what the past relations between the company and the customer have been, whether there are special conditions relating to the sale, such as credit or discounts, how the buyer should be approached on an individual basis, and so on. It is the most important facet of the sales representative's task as it prepares the way for the discussion that follows.

Attention refers to the importance of gaining the buyer's involvement in the product on offer as rapidly as possible; interest to cementing this involvement; demand and action to a positive commitment on behalf of the buyer. Of great importance to the final outcome will be the sales representative's ability to ascertain exactly what the buyer is looking for, handling the objections that may exist about the product (especially problems of price) and then closing the discussion and getting the order.

SALES MANAGEMENT

The control of the sales force relies on a number of management techniques which are common to the rest of the organization.

1. Job and work loading design. There are a number of methods of defining the numbers of sales representatives required and the way in which their territories should be designed. Accurate job specification ensures that the company has a clear concept of what is involved in the sales task, and how above or below standard job performance should be measured.

2. Recruitment. Well-organized recruitment policies will not only ensure the right individuals for the relevant sales task, it will also reduce labour 'turnover, minimize discontent and unrest, and ensure that the individuals can respond well to the training process.

3. Training. Because of the complexities of the industrial sales task individuals receive far more training in these companies (on average twenty-eight days) compared with the consumer goods sales training figure of four days. Successful companies such as IBM identify training as one of the most important contributions to a high level of sales achievement.

4. Appraisal. Companies with structured methods of evaluating their sales representatives, and defining their strengths and weaknesses, will be more able to define and control the changing nature of the sales task and what training is required, or what other alterations need to be made.

5. Motivation. With the wide range of differing sales tasks, the company will face varying problems in encouraging the sales force to improve

performance, or to concentrate more heavily on certain aspects such as new product development or repeat business.

Motivational methods divide into two broad areas. The first is monetary and includes the payment of commission on overall business achieved (the most common method of motivation), competitions, awards, bonus schemes for particular achievement levels, or profit-sharing schemes. Non-monetary methods include sales conferences, meetings, inter-group comparisons, promotion or job reclassification.

6. Sales support. Improving the levels of sales support with more accurate information on current customers, reducing the amount of time that sales representatives spend on non-essential activity such as credit checking, dealing with distribution problems, appearing at exhibitions, and preparing documentation will all improve the cost-effectiveness of the sales force.

Summary

The role of personal selling in the promotional mix of the company will depend on a combination of factors such as the nature of the industry and the level of service that a company is trying to provide. The sales force will have an important impact on other aspects of the marketing mix, pricing and control over distribution in particular.

ASSIGNMENTS

1. You are working for a company which concentrates solely on achieving sales volume of its range of soft drinks. Write a memorandum outlining the problems this might cause the company in the short term.
2. You have recently been appointed as assistant sales manager for a company expanding from the north of England to the south and have been asked to write a report on the sales management issues that will need to be considered.
3. As a management consultant you are asked to advise on how a wholesaler should handle a steady increase in the range of industrial components that are sold by its sales force, with the breakdown of product and customer shown in Table 13.1.

Table 13.1 Data for Assignment 3

| Range | % sales by customer type | | | |
	A	B	C	D
A	10	30	40	20
B	35	15	25	25
C	60	5	15	20
D	15	45	5	35
E	5	25	25	45

VITATOT

BACKGROUND

During a particularly severe winter in Kentucky in the early 1970s, a stud owner, David Lilley, found that when his horses were fed on a certain type of alfalfa, they became restless and agitated. As an ex-vet he investigated the source of this product and found that it was imported from a small area in the Peruvian highlands due to the shortage of fodder in the mainland United States. Closer investigation after the winter found that the grass was apparently able to raise the metabolic rate of the horses with no obvious side effects. The metabolism rapidly returned to normal after feeding on the grass, though for about a week after removal of the feed the horse's metabolism was slightly but significantly below normal before returning to equilibrium.

Chemists at the nearby Clydesdale Institute in Kentucky were eventually able to isolate and synthesize the active ingredient – a complex sterol with the formula $C34H68OH$ – which appeared to be present in minute concentrations in normal horse blood, and appeared to be involved in some way controlling lactic acid build-up in the fast-running horse, enabling it to metabolize glycogen and other energy reserves more effectively. It also seemed to improve the ability of horses to withstand some infectious diseases. As an easily soluble powder it could be added to the horses' drinking water or sprinkled on their feed.

The discovered product, which appeared to function only in horses, was given the name vitamin L and was patented by the Clydesdale Institute as having considerable potential commercial possibilities because, as a naturally occurring product within the horse, additional vitamin L would not count as a stimulant or a drug even though it would have that effect. At the premier Washington International horse-race, Jasmin Lace – a 50–1 outsider, and the only horse in the race to be fed additional quantities of vitamin L – won, and this guaranteed a steadily rising demand for the product throughout the mainland United States. There was, however, considerable resistance in many quarters of the racing world to the introduction of the concept of vitamin additions, and this feeling was especially strong in Europe even though the racing authorities there were on record as stating that the product was permissible.

Having patented the product and registered the brand name Vitatot, the Institute began to ask for proposals from agents in each of the main potential markets as to how they would propose to cover the market effectively.

FASTRACK UK

Fastrack UK had for many years specialized in the design and manufacture of all-weather surfaces for training horses both in and outdoors. It also distributed a range or riding accessories such as whips, spurs, leather boots, helmets and saddles. It was the UK agent of the Australian company which produced all-weather race-track material similar to that used for football and baseball, called Flexitan. As Fastrack had failed to persuade the Jockey Club of the advantages of converting British race tracks to all-weather surfaces, it was interested in the possibilities of Vitatot to provide growth opportunities for the company, especially as the product was highly profitable to the distributor who realized 30 per cent of the selling price in commission. Currently, the company maintained a fully occupied sales force of three, each of whom cost the company around £25,000 in pay, commission and expenses, as a large amount of travel was involved.

THE PROSPECTIVE MARKET

Fastrack had identified a number of possible markets for the product each with their own particular problems.
1. The racing stables. It was estimated that there were 350 stables in the United Kingdom with around 6,000 horses in training. These stables included both National Hunt and flat-racing stables, the horses in which raced at different times of the year. As potential purchasers they were probably at the top of the list, as the daily cost of Vitatot at £1.60 would only increase current annual costs of training a horse by around 5 per cent. Geographically these stables were fairly concentrated in a number of areas: around Newmarket, Newbury, and Yorkshire.
2. Studs. It was believed that there were around 900 studs in the United Kingdom ranging from the extremely large to those producing two or three foals a year. The large studs accounted for around 40 per cent of the total, and had on average twelve horses each. Geographically, the majority of studs were to be found in the southern counties but they were fairly widely distributed.
3. Riding stables. There were around 1,000 riding stables in the country with an average nine horses each. Geographically they were widely spread.
4. Private individuals. It was estimated very roughly that there were 65,000 horses kept by individuals in the United Kingdom. This market would be very difficult to identify easily.
5. Specialist retailers/wholesalers. There were 420 specialist retailers and wholesalers in the country. These outlets were currently visited by the Fastrack sales force with its range of accessories and the addition of Vitatot to the range would not pose any problems.
6. Veterinary surgeons. Though Vitatot did not have to be prescribed, it was clear that vets would have an important influence on the sale to many potential buyers who would feel reassured by professional support. Though there were 40,000 vets in the country, only around 4,000 had substantial expertise with horses and their advice would be an important element in the decisions of potential purchasers.

THE ISSUE

Fastrack was aware that many individuals and stables bought products from the wholesalers and retail specialists, though some of its competitors in the tack business sold direct to large stables, but would its current distribution system serve adequately to penetrate the potentially large market for Vitatot? As the company had limited financial resources it had to ensure that any investment in a new sales force would be rapidly repaid; it would need to set clear targets for sales force achievement as part of the proposal to be sent to the Clydesdale Institute. Currently the sales force spent around twenty minutes on each sales call with established clients, and forty minutes on average travelling between each call (including lunch breaks). It was believed that the amount of time required for each call to introduce Vitatot would be at least forty-five minutes, and that established customers would have to be revisited once a month for repeat orders. Due to the notorious lack of punctuality within the racing world, the amount of dead time (time waiting for appointments) would considerably increase and might add twenty to thirty minutes a call. Using a telephone sales system would not be possible in this highly individualistic market. What type of customer would be economically viable for the sales force to call upon, and which would have to be handled via the specialist retailers and wholesalers, was one of the issues that Fastrack needed to identify clearly. Second, the type of selling involved should it decide to go direct to the main potential buyers would be very different from the skills of the current sales force, and this would be especially true if the sales force were to be involved in discussions with veterinary surgeons; where should Fastrack look for recruits, and how many should be employed?

Comment

This case study explores the issue of profitable sales management and the necessary controls that need to be developed for it.

PART 4

SPECIAL TOPICS

14

CONSUMER AND INDUSTRIAL MARKETS: SPECIFIC ISSUES

Every company will claim with some justification that the problems it faces are encountered by no other, as only it has the same type of product, competition, and legislative environment. Though this is true in detail, businesses within the same sectors of the market tend to encounter the same type of problems that they need to overcome to be fully competitive.

The broad divisions that exist, namely:

1. consumer product companies that sell either direct or via retailers to the general public;
2. industrial product companies that sell components or finished products to other manufacturers or organizations; and
3. service companies that sell either to the consumer or the industrial sector:

all exhibit the same problems in developing effective marketing strategy and plans; but they do so in different degrees; issues that are crucial for some companies are less severe for others.

As has already been stated, the service-based organizations pose especial problems in the definition of the marketing mix, and are dealt with in Chapter 16. Though consumer and industrial companies are both involved in the manufacture and distribution of products, the nature of the market and the buyers makes for a differing emphasis within the strategy and marketing mix that each will need to adopt.

THE NATURE OF DEMAND

Many consumer products face considerable variations in seasonal demand; 85 per cent of port is bought in the November–December period; large numbers of new cars are bought to coincide with the new registration period starting in August;

most ice cream is bought in the summer, and so on. In addition to this seasonality some consumer products show longer-term fluctuations in demand; the demand for sink units, for example, will relate partly to the number of new houses being built, which is often a feature of a longer-term trade cycle.

Industrial product companies tend to face fewer problems of seasonality; the demand for machine parts, for example, follows the total number of machine hours. In consequence the demand for replacement parts will show a more even spread across the year than the demand for ice cream. Demand will derive from the consumer sector and will tend to be fairly inelastic. However, many industrial sectors show longer-term cycles of replacement and renewal; the machine tool industry, for example, is said to follow a three-year cycle with the majority of firms replacing equipment at the same period.

DIVIDING THE MARKET/SEGMENTATION

The consumer market often presents complex segmentation problems. It is often difficult for the consumer goods company to decide who is the potential consumer and how he (or she) can best be reached, and it is also easy for the company to miss potential market segments in such an analysis.

> When colour television sets were first introduced, it was felt that most of the demand would come from the AB socio-economic groups because the sets were relatively expensive. Instead it was found that demand was initially most concentrated among manual workers.

In consequence, the segmentation exercise that is carried out for many consumer products will only indicate the broad nature of likely consumer demand. This will often make demand for new products a complex problem as it will not be clear which group is likely to buy the product.

> Black and Decker found that its lawn raker was far more successful than initially anticipated because it came to be accepted as an important part of lawn care by a wider element of the gardening public than had been initially considered.

> Sinclair Research experienced a far larger demand for its early home computers than anticipated, showing that the product was creating interest in sections of the market which had not even previously considered the purchase of a computer.

For the industrial company the segmentation exercise poses different problems. Though the potential consumer for industrial paints will be fairly easy to identify, as will the potential purchasers of vending machines, from trade directories and similar sources of information, the likely level of demand from each prospective customer is less easy to define as it will be a function of a number of factors. These will include:
1. the degree of technology used by each customer;
2. their level of price sensitivity;
3. their market position;
4. the degree of competition from other suppliers;
5. the way in which the customer carries out its purchasing policy.

In consequence, forecasting demand for a new product will often prove to be more difficult. Complexities will also arise when there is a degree of overlap in product usage. For example, a number of industrial markets will make use of overhead projectors and display methods, and it will be more difficult to define likely demand for new products in this area except by comparison with previous products in the field.

> Semperfresh was a product newly developed to prevent one of the main problems in the cutting and transport of pineapples, that of ensuring that the fruit ripens without going rotten. This had previously been achieved by the application of fungicide which still meant that upwards of 25 per cent of product was still spoiled. The main growers of pineapples were quite easily identifiable as was the total market potential from import and export statistics.

> IBM failed to forecast the demand for its personal computer accurately so that delivery delays were running at up to six months soon after the product launch. This was in part due to the considerably wider product acceptability throughout all industrial organizations apart from major companies which IBM had initially identified as the potential customers.

GEOGRAPHICAL CONCENTRATION

Though there will be exceptions (for example, the vast majority of Spanish Rioja wine is drunk in the south of England) the majority of consumer products will show a wide geographical spread of demand.

In contrast, industrial markets are often highly concentrated. For example, shipbuilding is limited to few sites; cigarettes are mainly produced in Nottingham and Bristol (with small quantities in other areas).

NUMBER OF POTENTIAL BUYERS

For the majority of consumer goods the potential number of consumers is extremely large. For example, recent government statistics show that 95 per cent of the 18 million households own a refrigerator, 92 per cent a television, 18 per cent a video recorder.

In contrast, industrial companies sell to a far more limited audience.

> A company selling gas chromatography equipment for analysing the content of organic chemical products considered that its market was secondary schools, research establishments and universities/polytechnics. Even with its wide spread of potential buyers the total number of possible contacts was still less than 6,000.

DISTRIBUTION

The large number of consumers and their wide geographical dispersion involve the consumer goods company in large investment in a number of areas:
1. warehousing, inventory and transport facilities;
2. finance and accounts sections to keep track of the large number of outlets or consumers who are the customers;

3.   sales representation to ensure the widest possible distribution of product.

The need for the widest possible distribution also means that consumer goods companies make considerable use of intermediaries such as wholesalers to cover those sectors of the market which it is costly to deal with direct.

Because of the large investment in this area, control of stocks and distribution costs can make a major impact on the profitability of consumer goods companies. This is particularly important where the purchase cycle of the product is short: cigarettes, for example, are bought daily on average, milk and butter only slightly less frequently.

Industrial companies, because of the more specific nature of their market, often do not have to pay as much attention to the issues of distribution. The use of intermediaries will also be more restricted especially where the product is technical in nature and distributors are expected to provide detailed support rather than simply physically stock the product. The high cost of many industrial products and the need to ensure that they arrive undamaged at the final destination has led many industrial companies increasingly to use air freight to transport goods overseas and special delivery services within the country.

NUMBERS INVOLVED IN THE BUYING DECISION

For the majority of consumer goods purchases only one individual will decide which of the competing products will be purchased, although this decision may be influenced by other family preferences. As the unit price of the product purchased increases, so does the number of individuals involved; the full family, for example, may be involved in the decision to purchase a new television set. For most consumer products the criteria used to choose between competitive lines will be broadly similar for all involved in the buying decision. For example, one member of the family might want the new car to be capable of over 100 miles an hour, but will nevertheless be fully aware of other requirements.

In the industrial market many more individuals will be involved in the purchase decision; in a large firm anything up to eight people will have some influence on the buying process, each of whom may have different methods of evaluating the value of the product being offered, and which may often be diametrically opposed to other individual's views. A number of differing influences have been identified as often being present;
1.   The initiator – the person who first thinks of the product requirement.
2.   The influencer – the individual who makes suggestions as to the applicability of the product.
3.   The decider – the individual who has the authority to carry out the purchase.
4.   The buyer – the individual who physically carries out the buying process though he may rely on someone else's authority.
5.   The user of the product.

In a typical factory buying a new chemical for a process one could identify likely individuals who might have an impact on the buying process, their knowledge of the product and the criteria which they would use to judge the product (Table 14.1).

Table 14.1   People involved in the buying process

Individual	Authority	Knowledge	Criteria
Managing director	Final	Very limited	Profit
Production director	Within budget	Substantial	Efficiency/profit
Foreman	Personnel	Limited	Ease of introduction
Shop steward	Informal	Limited	Safety/effect on jobs
Research department	Informal	Extensive	Theoretical
Buyer	Within budget	Limited	Organizational views

Such a diversity of buying influences has an important effect on the way the sales force needs to be trained to sell complex industrial equipment, with the need to explain differing benefits of the product to a number of different individuals within the same organization.

LENGTH OF THE BUYING PROCESS

Within the consumer goods sector the length of the time taken over the buying process is fairly short for the majority of products.

For many industrial products it may take many months to persuade the customer to order a new piece of equipment.

Wiggins Teape, the paper company, finds that it may take up to three months to persuade a designer to use Conqueror paper instead of a competitive product.

Decisions on equipment in government organizations such as the National Health Service may take over a year due to the complex nature of the committee and area structures, with many groups often having some influence on the final decision.

BRAND LOYALTY

There is generally low brand loyalty within the consumer goods market. Research shows that anything up to 50 per cent of consumers will buy different products from one purchase period or cycle to the next, and that over a period of time the consumer will shift or switch between a number of products which constitute a buying portfolio, a fact which has an important bearing on the promotional policy of the company (discussed in Chapter 12).

The implication of this finding for the majority of consumer goods is that considerable investment will need to be made in sales promotion to ensure that brand shares are maintained. Second, it means that the use of introductory offers and low prices during either test markets or new product launches will generally be effective in achieving a fairly rapid level of consumer trial.

All research shows that the industrial purchaser is far more conservative than the consumer goods buyer. Of the three purchasing activities namely:

1.   Straight repurchase – the purchase of the same goods from the same supplier.

2. Modified repurchase – the purchase of different product from the same supplier.
3. New purchase – the purchase of new products from a new supplier.

The first is by far the most common. Indeed many industrial goods buyers will often not consider other competitive products when deciding to repurchase. The implication is that it will be difficult for the industrial goods company to become established with a customer, but once this is achieved the account can be more easily maintained.

> IBM divides its sales force into those who have responsibility for gaining new accounts and those responsible for developing the account once it has been achieved, as the skills required are seen as distinctly different.

DIRECT INVOLVEMENT OF THE SALES FORCE WITH THE END USER

In the consumer goods market the sales force is not directly involved with the end user for the vast majority of products sold through the retail system. This means that the sales force is not involved in explaining the benefits of the product to the consumer, and this role must be performed by other promotional material, including the packaging of the product which has an important role in informing the consumer about the product benefits. The sales force is also not involved in extensive negotiation on price with the intermediary as consumer goods companies lay down clear guidelines on volume and price for their sales forces to follow.

Industrial sales forces are far more concerned with direct contact with the end user, and for small firms they provide the main source of information about products and processes. A recent survey showed that for small firms over 60 per cent of the information they received on products came from contact with sales representatives. For large firms they are still an important source of information, at around 35 per cent; for these firms exhibitions and trade journals are more important. The complex nature of the product in many industrial markets means that the sales representative is often considerably involved in negotiation on price.

INFORMATION REQUIREMENTS FOR PURCHASE DECISION

The normal consumer product is bought without the consumer having received much information on the benefits or otherwise of the product. This is clearly evident for the wide range of grocery items; for consumer durables such as televisions and refrigerators, the information provided will be more detailed but still fairly limited. The most elaborate will be for high value items such as houses and cars.

The limited information required by the consumer has meant that consumer goods companies have to concentrate on emphasizing one or two product benefits in the most effective fashion. Industry sectors such as detergents and beer quite clearly follow this policy with heavy use of television advertising.

Mars Ltd has concentrated on one simple message for its leading confectionery product, the Mars Bar, for the last twenty years: 'A Mars a day helps you work, rest and play'. Similar concentration is shown with its petfood products, Whiskas and Pedigree Chum.

The information requirements of the industrial market are considerably greater than the consumer sector and industrial buyers often need large quantities of data on which to make a decision. Many firms attempt to develop objective methods of evaluating different sales proposals, by ranking and weighting the competitive products' costs and benefits (a process known as vendor ranking).

Product descriptions of Hewlett Packard computers will often run to thirty pages of detailed text.

The development of sophisticated and detailed catalogues which can be given to the buyer as reference material will be an important part of the industrial sales process. The expansion of the Japanese machine tool market share in the United Kingdom was due at least in part to the emphasis placed on providing full technical information.

PROMOTIONAL POLICY

The large numbers of potential purchasers in the majority of consumer markets encourage the widest possible spread of promotional investment consistent with the product and the target market to ensure that no likely customer is missed even if they are not specifically included as being potential customers. Such policies stress the use of mass media, television, press, and radio.

The small number of potential purchasers in the industrial market and their high information requirement underline the need for specific and detailed promotion direct to the interested parties. Emphasis will be placed on direct mail, exhibitions and specialist journals.

BRANDING

The branding of products in both the consumer and industrial markets can be an important factor in product success, in enabling both improved profitability and market share to be achieved. In both market sectors the degree of investment will however remain high.

Kimberly Clark, the American paper multinational, has followed a continuous policy of investing in branding products within the industrial cleaning market in the UK, which has a history of being highly commodity-oriented. This level of investment could probably not be matched by a company with smaller resources.

PRICE SENSITIVITY

Within many consumer markets, price is one of the most important factors in the consumer decision whether or not to purchase. The effects of increasing price in relation to the competition are most marked in commodity markets such as flour or butter. Here a 1 per cent increase in price relative to the competition can lead to a 10 per cent drop in volume, or there is a price elasticity of ten. Petfood in comparison shows an elasticity of around five, sherry and port an elasticity of two and a half to three. The effect on pricing policies that this has is discussed in Chapter 10.

All surveys of the industrial market indicate that price is far less important as an issue in deciding product purchase. Other criteria such as the reliability of the equipment, the reputation of the manufacturer, servicing arrangements and the like carry more weight. For many industrial products it will be a case of providing both the machinery and some of the components necessary for efficient operation. A firm selling industrial cleaning equipment, for example, would sell both the cleaning equipment such as pumps, as well as the chemicals that would be used in the system. Computer firms will sell both hardware and software. This 'systems approach', that is providing the total solution to a particular problem, will make it more difficult for the buying firm to compare one option with another competitive tender.

CREDIT TERMS AND FINANCING

For the majority of consumer products the problems of financing will be minimal; retailers or intermediaries will be given a determined level of credit according to the importance of the account and this will be closely controlled to ensure that the positive cash flow is maximized. With the continuing recession and high level of competition in some market sectors there has been a gradual increase in the tendency of some consumer products companies to offer financing deals – for example, much of the success of Fiat has been ascribed to the low cost finance it has offered in the British car market.

For many industrial product companies the issue of how product sales are financed will be far more important. Vending machine companies, for example, will sell the majority of their products on lease rather than straightforward purchase, which has immediate implications on the cash flow and pricing of the products within the range.

SERVICE AND INSTALLATION REQUIREMENTS

For the majority of consumer products the manufacturers provide very limited technical back-up, as any individual who has tried to get their washing machine rapidly serviced will soon realize.

For the industrial company the degree of technical support will often be crucial in maintaining good customer relations and companies in many fields will need to invest in effective service engineer support.

Diversey, and other industrial cleaning companies, maintain a twenty-four-hour support service at Heathrow Airport to maintain industrial cleaning equipment.

Caterpillar, the market leader in construction equipment throughout the world, attempts to guarantee the delivery of any spare part for Caterpillar equipment, to any part of the world, within twenty-four hours.

Summary

The market that the industrial company faces differs in many respects from that of the consumer goods company. The discipline of the marketing process remains valid, though the emphasis that the organization will need to place on certain parts of its investment policy will differ.

ASSIGNMENTS

1. Your company, highly successful in the marketing of frozen food, has decided to purchase a manufacturer of refrigerated cabinets as a means of diversification. Write a report on the value of such a move and the problems that might exist in the new market.
2. Your company has appointed you as sales development manager for its range of hydraulic equipment in the north of England. Your managing director has asked you to comment on the resources that you need to deal with the task effectively.

YORKIE BAR – A SUCCESSFUL PRODUCT LAUNCH

MARKET BACKGROUND

The market for chocolate confectionery in the United Kingdom has remained static in volume terms at around 340,000 tons since the early 1960s, even though in value the market has grown from £228 million in 1967 to £1,000 million in the 1980s.

Over that period nine major market segments have shown differing levels of growth and decline within the overall static market:
1. solid milk chocolate bars (Cadbury's Dairy Milk);
2. solid milk bars with additions (Cadbury's Fruit and Nut);
3. solid plain chocolate bars;
4. cereal-centre bars (Kit-Kat);
5. other centre bars (Mars);
6. chocolate assortments (Quality Street);
7. chocolate liqueurs (Famous Names);
8. chocolate sweet lines (Smarties);
9. novelties (Easter eggs).

Filled blocks showed a slight decline in market share from 20 per cent in the late 1960s to 17 per cent by the late 1970s, while centre bars had grown from 40 per cent to 46 per cent. Plain chocolate products also continued to decline, as had the market share claimed by imports. The market was characterized by a low level of brand loyalty, with consumers switching between around fifteen different products. It was also quite price-sensitive and the main manufacturers spent heavily on television to maintain their market position.

THE CONSUMER

Consumer profiles are shown in Table 14.2.

Table 14.2   Consumer profiles for chocolate confectionery

| | | % volume | |
Group	Filled bars	Solid bars	Assortments
Age			
up to 15	16	11	5
16–24	21	17	15
25–34	25	24	25
35–49	22	24	26
50+	15	24	28
Sex			
Male	31	37	41
Female	69	63	59
Socio-economic			
ABC1	32	35	47
C2DE	51	54	52
Frequency of purchase (adults only)			
More than twice a week	10	3	—
Twice a week	7	11	—
Once a week	21	17	4
Once a month	39	39	6
Never	23	30	42

THE SUPPLIERS

By the late 1970s Cadbury still led the market with 33 per cent market share, Rowntree Mackintosh with 29 per cent and Mars with 22 per cent. The next largest company, Nestlé, held just over 3 per cent of the market.

Distribution was through CTNs (confectioners, tobacconists, newsagents, of which there are around 48,000 in the United Kingdom), supermarkets and many other outlets such as garage forecourts. Margins were attractively high: CTNs make around 24 per cent on the average chocolate item: supermarkets often around 30 per cent.

THE PRODUCT BACKGROUND

By the end of the 1970s the solid milk chocolate market subsector represented around 11 per cent of the total market. Cadbury had traditionally dominated this market segment with Cadbury's Dairy Milk which maintained a 54 per cent market share. The two other products in the sector were Galaxy (15 per cent) and Aero with 11 per cent.

The steady rise in the raw material costs coupled with the high inflation of the 1970s had meant that manufacturers were tending to reduce the size and thickness of the chocolate bars to maintain the same price position in the market. Rowntree Mackintosh identified a developing market gap for a thick milk chocolate block that would provide a more 'satisfying' taste, making the analogy with thick steaks and thin slices of smoked salmon having the same effect!

The market opportunity was further refined via group discussions to be for a solid thick block of chocolate, more satisfying to eat than existing thinner blocks, presented with nourishing and sustaining connotations (the project name at this stage was Rations), but also as something enjoyable.

THE FINAL MARKETING MIX

Product. A thick mould was chosen which would allow the bar to be divided into six equal portions, and various milk chocolate mixes were tested to arrive at the most satisfactory formulation. Group discussions produced the name 'Yorkie', and the packaging was chosen to reflect the 'solid' nature of the bar.

Price. As one of the criteria for the product was that it should meet the demand for a 'sustaining' food, the pricing was crucial to ensure that it was competitively superior to other products on a weight for weight basis. The prices and weights of the main competitors at the time of launch are shown in Table 14.3.

Table 14.3   Yorkie and its competitors

Product	Weight	Price	Grams/p
Yorkie	62 g	11p	5.6
C.D.M.	48.4 g	9p	5.4
Galaxy	50 g	9p	5.6

One worry of the launch was whether the 10p price point for chocolate confectionery would be important, but as Yorkie was aimed at the sixteen-plus consumer it was considered not to be a crucial element in success or failure.

Promotion. The objectives were to depict Yorkie as a sophisticated adult product associated with the outdoors, which tasted nice and was cheerful and companionable. The commerical theme chosen was action-based with films called 'Tanker', 'Coast to Coast' and 'Snow Plough', which emphasized the outdoor action element. Heavy expenditure at the launch ensured a rapid awareness of the brand image with a national equivalent expenditure of £0.5 million for the launch.

Place. To achieve high distribution, the London TV area was chosen for the initial launch. Full-scale concentration by the national accounts sales force and the use of special commando teams to achieve distribution through the CTNs ensured that within six weeks the product had achieved 90 per cent weighted distribution. An important element in maintaining sales force morale was a newsletter which highlighted successes and failures of the 'Yorkie' campaign.

THE PROGRESS OF YORKIE

Yorkie has become one of the most successful entries into the highly competitive confectionery market and appears to have become established as one of the surviving brands in the chocolate bar market. By the early 1980s it had overtaken Galaxy to become the second brand in the market.

Rowntree Mackintosh have also used the market strength of Yorkie to introduce variants such as Raisin Yorkie to expand shelf presence further.

Comment

The launch of Yorkie illustrates the main marketing mix issues in the consumer goods sector.

THE ICL SYSTEM 25

BACKGROUND

In the early 1960s many industries saw that the benefits of computing would only be realized if sufficient processing capability was made available at the operating unit, rather than using a single mainframe system which required a sophisticated data collection system as well as data transmission. Such systems were particularly appropriate in certain industries, specifically brewing, construction, estate agents, trade unions, solicitors, motor dealers, shipping, accountants, and retailing.

THE AVAILABLE SYSTEMS

Definition of the market into various segments is difficult as products are rapidly changing. There is a steady decrease in hardware costs which means that this year's mainframe computer will be next year's minicomputer and this year's minicomputer will be next year's micro. For example, hard disk storage is becoming increasingly common in the micro market; memory requirements have increased from 64k to 256k or more.

In broad terms the market in the mid-1970s could be divided into:
1. Microcomputers offering limited processing power, the ability to handle two or three other units, and costing up to £7,500.
2. Minicomputers offering greater processing power and the ability to handle

data from a far greater number of terminals, costing from £15,000 to £75,000, depending on the degree of sophistication and the amount of data storage.
3. Mainframes with the largest processing capability and data storage costing over £100,000.

The minicomputer offered the best balance between the cost of computing hardware and the necessary level of data processing power for those companies needing operational separation of data collection and analysis, and were particularly valuable for:
1. Factory data collection – serving to monitor work in progress via a number of terminals.
2. Point of sale – to monitor the progress of stock and cash from separate departmental tills.
3. Contract control – to enable evaluation of differing contracts to be continually updated and reviewed.

THE DEVELOPMENT OF THE ICL SYSTEM 25

The basis for the ICL System 25 lay in the requirements of the Singer Corporation in the United States to be able to invest effectively, overnight, the large sums of money that were held in each of the 2,000 shops throughout the United States. The point of sale terminal and the controller that developed as a result of this defined operational requirement, the System 10, was bought by ICL in 1976 as the Singer Corporation began to suffer financial problems. In 1981 the declining processing power of the product and its inability to interact with many new peripheral devices led ICL to introduce an upgraded version, the System 25. By the early 1980s there were several thousand System 10 and 25 computers installed in various countries with the main area of strength the United Kingdom.

The hardware was therefore a tried and tested system which fitted some elements of the market requirements. Buyer attitudes showed that reliability came fairly high on the list of priorities but there was a range of additional criteria, shown below, with percentage response:
● Technical support: 40 per cent
● Performance/reliability: 22 per cent
● Range of software: 16 per cent
● Expandability/compatibility: 10 per cent
● Price: 10 per cent.

It was noticeable that the industry was primarily concerned with the long-term viability and reliability of the company from which they were buying both hardware and software.

The definition of these major factors allowed ICL to develop a clear view of their necessary marketing mix for the future of the System 25.

PRODUCT

ICL believed that the major product factors to be considered were:

1. to invest heavily in application packages with general or industry-specific features, where necessary developing these in conjunction with the most expert software houses available;
2. to upgrade steadily the processing power of the basic unit;
3. to increase the facilities available, such as high-speed transmission links between units, and bar code reader units for retail outlets.

PRICING

ICL has continued to follow a 'market-place' pricing strategy relating the final price to the market conditions.

DISTRIBUTION/PROMOTION

For many years ICL had concentrated on the sales force as the main method of contacting likely customers, though spending limited sums on exhibitions and the trade press. In the early 1980s it developed a series of demonstration sites, called Computer Point, with the role of:

- identifying the local market
- direct mail to that market
- solution selling
- ease of presentation of working system.

COMPETITION

This came from three areas. First was the steady erosion of the base of the market by the steadily increasing sophistication of the microcomputer. However, these were still limited in specific application software and the ability to handle large numbers of terminals. Second, there were large numbers of competing hardware suppliers such as Honeywell, Burroughs, Univac and IBM. These companies had considerable experience, especially in the manufacture and installation of larger systems. Finally, the software houses themselves were often involved in the distribution of hardware for their specific systems.

ICL was able to maintain its edge over IBM in the UK minicomputer market, as comparable market shares for IBM and ICL by price of installed system indicates (Table 14.4).

Table 14.4   IBM and ICL market share by model range

Range (£000)	IBM (%)	ICL (%)
15–35	2	14
35–75	8	17
75–200	20	17

Overall the market was growing at around 16 per cent per annum. Within the overall market it was estimated that the market share of ICL had remained static at 11 per cent from 1979 to 1983.

Comment

This case illustrates some of the many differences that exist in emphasis between an industrial market and a consumer goods product sector, but how basic marketing principles, applied in a specific fashion, can produce just as successful an end result.

15

INTERNATIONAL MARKETING

TRENDS IN INTERNATIONAL TRADE

International trade has increased fifteenfold in value since 1950. Though a major part of this increase has been caused by rising world price inflation between 1970 and 1980, the underlying trend has been for a steadily increasing percentage of world GNP (gross national product) to be exported (Table 15.1).

Table 15.1   World exports related to GNP

	1950	1960	1970	1980(est.)
Total exports ($ million)	78,300	128,660	313,100	1,180,000
% total GNP	3	4	5.5	6

Much of this trade has expanded between what is termed the 'developed' world, consisting of North America, the EEC (the current eleven members of the European Community), EFTA (the five members of the European Free Trade Association), Australasia (Australia and New Zealand) and Japan. These countries have continued to dominate world trade from the 1950s (Table 15.2).

Table 15.2   Division of world trade (%)

	1950	1960	1970	1980
Developed world	63	67	66	63
OPEC			6	14
Developing countries	27	22	18	27
Centrally planned economies	10	12	10	6

The creation of OPEC (Organization of Petroleum Exporting Countries) in the 1970s did affect the balance of world trade, particularly the growth of exports in what are termed 'developing' countries, LDCs (lesser developed countries) or the Third World. Recently, most rapid growth has been achieved by this sector, especially LDCs in the Far East such as Hong Kong, Taiwan, Singapore, South Korea, Thailand and Malaysia, which has steadily raised the overall percentage of world trade produced by these countries partially at the expense of the major trading blocs, but has also diminished the share of world trade held by centrally planned economies (Comecon, Albania, China, Cuba, Mongolia, North Korea, Vietnam, Laos, Kampuchea).

As might be expected from these figures, over 75 per cent of exports from the developed world are directed towards other countries in this sector. In consequence major trading partners of developed countries will always be other developed countries and this will have important consequences on the level of competition developed countries face in the provision of goods and services in the international environment. Not only will exported items have to compete with an often highly sophisticated home market, they will also have to face pressure from the industries of the other developed economies which will also be attempting to become established.

Countries with high levels of export growth have also shown substantially higher per capita increases in overall GNP than countries with slower export growth, and this would argue that the Pacific Basin countries will be steadily more important in world trade in the 1990s.

One feature of the statistics is that they increasingly understate the level of international involvement. This is because the amount of foreign investment overseas by all the major trading areas is steadily increasing. In 1946 the total level of overseas investment was estimated at around £12,000 million. By 1980 this had increased to £120,000 million of which around 60 per cent originated in the United States. Direct investment in overseas markets obviously reduces direct physical trade flows, though there is an inevitable substantial increase in the level of invisible trade – the movement of revenue from one country to another. As the level of trade investment increases, the accuracy of the trade statistics becomes in consequence less and less reliable in providing a good measure of the amount of international trade.

NATURE OF TRADE

As might be expected the nature of the products exported shows considerable variation between the various trading sectors within the world economies. The developed world shows a far lower reliance on food or other raw materials (iron ore, oil, coal, other minerals) as a percentage of total trade. For example, there are fifty-eight countries in the world dependent on three or fewer crops for 50 per cent or more of export earnings; an additional twenty-two are dependent on minerals for more than 40 per cent of their export earnings. For countries within the developed world the reliance on manufactured goods is much greater, a trend also shown in the LDCs of the Pacific Basin such as Hong Kong (with 90 per cent of earnings from manufacture), South Korea (80 per cent), and Taiwan (60 per cent).

STRUCTURE OF TRADE: TRADE AGREEMENTS

COMMODITY AGREEMENTS

A number of trade agreements exist to promote the interests of commodity producers by attempting to iron out fluctuations in demand and to maintain pricing in what is often a highly volatile international environment. The most well-known, OPEC, had been very successful in maintaining control over oil production and pricing until early 1986, substantially increasing the OPEC countries' share of world trade (see above).

The international tin agreement, set up in 1956, maintained a 'buffer' stock of the metal for many years, with upper and lower price bands. Tin would be bought into stock when the price fell below the minimum price levels. This agreement worked until 1986 when high buffer stocks caused its collapse.

An international coffee agreement was established in 1959 which attempted to set quotas on a country by country basis to maintain prices and smooth out demand. This has continued to operate though the effects of the weather on the producing areas of the main supplier, Brazil, have prevented an entirely consistent approach being adopted.

The international cocoa agreement, signed in 1973, has faced a series of severe problems and has never functioned effectively; similar problems have faced attempts to establish sugar and wheat agreements.

In addition there are a number of formal or informal restrictions placed upon supplier nations to limit their share of the market. The MFA, or multi-fibre agreement, limits the amount of cloth that supplier nations, mainly in the Pacific Basin, can export to Western Europe. Similarly, Japanese car and video manufacturers have been asked to adhere to undertakings to limit similarly the volume of supplies to the EEC.

REGIONAL AGREEMENTS

Within the overall pattern of world trade development, there are inevitably strong regional biases, often reinforced by government to government (bilateral) trading agreements or regional trade associations. An example of the first is the strong trading links between Russia and India on the exchange of machinery and agricultural production.

The EEC, or European Economic Community, is the most important regional trading agreement for the UK economy. Established in 1962 under the Treaty of Rome, it has steadily expanded its membership until, in early 1986, it comprises West Germany, Belgium, the Netherlands, Denmark, Ireland, Spain, Portugal, Greece, Italy, France, Luxembourg, and the United Kingdom. Its aim has been to reduce barriers to trade between the member countries and create a single trading entity, with preference given to members. Provisions in the original Treaty of Rome have also led to the establishment of the common agricultural policy, or CAP, with controls on the levels of production and pricing of a wide range of agricultural commodities (milk, meat, sugar, butter, wine, cereals and olive oil), and co-ordinating bodies for iron, steel and coal production, and long-term plans exist for greater economic and fiscal integration. Preferential terms for certain non-EEC countries have also been established especially for former colonial territories in Africa, the Caribbean, and the Pacific. Agreements also exist with the other European trade area, EFTA.

EFTA, in common with the ASEAN (Association of South East Asian Nations), has a much simpler aim than the EEC – that of reducing customs and tariff barriers between the contributing members. More recently established is the Central American Common Market which also plans the development of a single customs and trading system.

COMECON, the Council for Mutual Economic Aid, is the major bloc in Eastern Europe, with substantial trading preference between partners in that region.

STRUCTURE OF TRADE: INTERNATIONAL INSTITUTIONS

GATT

GATT, the General Agreement on Tariffs and Trade, is a treaty which tries to lay down rules on the level and structure of import duties, non-tariff barriers, and export subsidies. Currently there are eighty-three members. GATT attempts to equalize duties and terms of trade between all member states, though there are a number of exclusions to this general statement of intent – for example, Commonwealth preference whereby Commonwealth goods used to face reduced tariffs was allowed under the GATT rules. Though enforcement of GATT rulings is difficult, it has allowed countries to move more easily towards reciprocal lowering of customs duties and tariff barriers.

UNCTAD

The United Nations Conference on Trade and Development deals with broader issues than those of GATT. Its membership is open to any member of the United Nations. It is especially concerned with issues of international financing and development aid.

OECD

The Organization for Economic Co-Operation and Development comprises the twenty-five member states of Western Europe, North America, Japan, Australasia, Turkey and Yugoslavia. It serves as a forum for international trade development and research.

THE UNITED KINGDOM'S INTERNATIONAL TRADE

Overseas trade has been central to the development of British industry since the early nineteenth century. Total exports in 1984 were £45,000 million, or 25 per cent of the gross domestic product.

As a small island, the United Kingdom is heavily dependent on the import of food and raw materials for manufacturing purposes. Recently the level of imported manufactured goods has been steadily rising, and during 1985 the United Kingdom imported more manufactured goods than it exported. Table 15.3 shows the UK's import/export trade by segment.

Table 15.3   Composition of UK's trade

Item	Exports (%)	Imports (%)
Food	8	15
Basic materials/chemicals	23	35
Fuel	7	4
Manufactures	56	35
Textiles	1	3
Others	3	9

As a member of the EEC, the United Kingdom has developed steadily stronger links with the other members of the Community, and this shows in the trading pattern, by country, which became established in the 1980s (Table 15.4).

Table 15.4   UK major trading partners

Country	Exports (%)	Imports (%)
United States	10	10.5
West Germany	9	11.2
France	7	8
Netherlands	6	6
Belgium	6	5
Ireland	6	4
Italy	2	5
Switzerland	5	5
Sweden	3	3
Canada	2	2
Japan	—	3

These eleven countries take 56 per cent of United Kingdom exports and provide 63 per cent of all imported products. The developing countries in total (other than the oil producing states) provide markets for 14 per cent of British exports, and 11 per cent of imports. The balance of trade has since the 1980s been improved by oil exports; for the previous fifteen years the United Kingdom had tended to run a deficit on visible trade (that is the physical movement of goods) while earning money from invisible trade (tourism, banking and insurance) to offset this shortfall, a sum running at around £6,000 million per annum.

The relaxation of exchange control has made overseas investment by British firms considerably easier and direct foreign investment has risen from an estimated £29,000 million in 1978 to £52,000 million in 1985.

GLOBALIZATION OF MARKETS

Chapter 1 stressed the increasing interdependence of products and markets, which has made an understanding of the international arena far more important for all organizations. The trend towards concentration of industrial activity in few centres or companies, or globalization, will have important and far-reaching effects on all companies and markets which cannot be ignored. The concentration of industrial development is most marked in those sectors of the economy which demand high investment, a high technical content, and have long payback periods due to the complexity of production or the effects of legislation.

Concentration of industrial activity would in consequence be expected, and has in fact occurred in:

1. Large civil aircraft. Boeing of the United States is now the sole manufacturer of large civil aircraft in the United States: Lockheed and McDonnell Douglas have effectively withdrawn to concentrate on the military market.
2. Mainframe computers. IBM and Fujitsu of Japan make up 80 per cent of the world mainframe market.
3. Heavy construction equipment. Komatsu and Caterpillar dominate the world market for heavy construction equipment.
4. Oil. The world oil market continues to be dominated by the 'Seven Sisters': BP, Shell, Texaco, Exxon, Mobil, Amoco, Gulf, with the vast investment in refining and exploration that is required. It is interesting to note that the small independent oil companies spawned by the North Sea discoveries have been rapidly taken over by larger groups.
5. Motor cars. The increasing concentration of the motor trade into six to eight major companies operating internationally has already been discussed; the future of British Leyland needs to be evaluated in this context.

Other industries that are starting to show an increasing concentration include:

6. Drugs and biotechnology. The greatly increased length of time that is required to provide some return on research and development will almost certainly mean that the number of firms active in the market will decline over the next ten to fifteen years. A recent estimate by ICI stated that if it were taking the decision to enter the pharmaceutical market now instead of in 1959, investment costs would have to be of the order of £1,500 million with a repayment period of around twenty-three years.
7. Silicon chip manufacture. The steadily increasing investment needed to produce integrated circuits will lead to a steady reduction in the number of manufacturers in the market.

There are many examples of concentration of international trade outside these particular sectors, in areas where initial investment is often relatively low and payback is fairly rapid, by companies that have managed by astute promotion, control of distribution channels and understanding of the market to continue to dominate internationally. Examples include the cola market (Coca-Cola, Pepsi-Cola), perfume (Chanel, Lanvin, Lenthéric), hamburgers (McDonalds, Burger King), cigarettes (Reynolds, Gallagher), hotels (Sheraton, Hilton).

The growth of the multinational or transnational company has been spectacular since the 1950s and their impact on international trade immense. Indeed, a steadily higher and higher proportion of international trade consists of sales between subsidiaries of multinationals; in many manufacturing sectors this now accounts for over half the total level of country to country trade.

Some of the activities of multinationals, in actively pursuing a policy of maximizing profitability often at the expense of individual countries, have come under closer and closer political scrutiny. For though the multinationals are responsible for an increasing share of world investment, the freedom of action they demand in return often runs contrary to national interests.

THE REASONS FOR OVERSEAS DEVELOPMENT

Companies in these 'superleagues' and others have taken advantage of the opportunities that exist for the organization:

1. Growth. Where a company is restricted in the home market by either market size, market share or legislative restrictions, overseas markets offer many opportunities for growth in volume and profit. Expanded volumes may also provide greater economies of scale allowing the company to compete more effectively in the home market.

2. Taxation advantages. After-tax earnings of multinationals as a group are always consistently 15 to 20 per cent higher than a group of similar companies solely based in the home market. This may argue that the managements of multinationals are more competent than those of other companies; a more likely explanation is that international structuring enables a more effective control of tax liabilities than those companies restricted to a single market.

3. Reduction in risk. Spreading activities across a wide number of countries reduces the risk of being tied to one economy or political system; for a manufacturing company it may also reduce the risks inherent in a single production site (see Chapter 11).

Lonrho, the multinational trading company, was in the early 1960s primarily active in Africa. Realizing the economic problems developing in the continent it followed an active acquisition policy in the United Kingdom diversifying into hotels (the Metropole group), newspapers (the *Observer*) and vehicle distribution (VW). The reduction in exposure to the African market has meant that profitability has steadily grown.

Dalgety was once primarily engaged in agricultural product distribution in Australia and New Zealand. Acquisition of interests in the United Kingdom and elsewhere such as Spillers Foods has done much to stabilize what was traditionally a very cyclical business.

4. Access to finance. Development overseas generally allows the company access to a wider funding environment which may mean that it is able to lower borrowing costs for its entire operation.
5. Competitive advantages. Wide exposure of the company to differing competitive market structures will have two benefits:
   (a) It makes the company aware of likely competitive pressures on its core markets earlier than would otherwise be the case. The company with a subsidiary operating in Japan will be forced to monitor this market closely and have practical experience of product and promotion strategies of all the main companies, whereas the company based solely in northern Europe will only be aware of these factors slowly and at second hand.
   (b) It allows the company a worldwide ability to produce and test new products which may be derived from any corner of an international network. IDV, with its network of distilleries worldwide, such as those in the UK, USA, South Africa, Mauritius, Kenya, and Sri Lanka, has an active policy of interchange of new product developments between the various countries from which many of its successful product introductions have been derived.

The international environment will however pose a number of problems which the company will need to evaluate and overcome.

Demand variation. There have been a number of attempts to define demand patterns in relation to socio-economic factors, all of which are subject to certain qualifications.
1. Family incomes. Certain authors see a useful method of division on the level of family disposable income, dividing the world into:
   (a) universal low incomes, characteristic of subsistence economies with an income of less than $350 per annum;
   (b) majority of low incomes, seen in some centrally planned economies with average incomes below $880 per annum;
   (c) mostly low but some very high incomes with average incomes of below $880 per annum;
   (d) low, medium, and high incomes, characterized by countries with an emergent middle class with incomes greater than $1,250 per annum;
   (e) mostly medium incomes, characterized either by countries achieving a high level of income redistribution by taxation (e.g. Scandinavia) or managing to create high levels of governmental employment (Middle Eastern countries).
2. Stage of industrialization. A similar plan derives inter-country divisions from the level of industrialization in the society, namely:
   (a) subsistence agriculture with little urbanization;
   (b) pre-industrial society with slow urbanization and heavy reliance on overseas manufactured goods;
   (c) underdeveloped countries with low capital and high labour-intensive manufacture such as footwear, building materials and canned goods for the home market;

(d) industrialized countries where the large majority of the population is involved in manufacturing activities;

(e) post-industrial society where only a minority of the population is involved in manufacturing and the majority will be involved in the service sector.

3. Development of the middle class. Some authors consider that the evolution of the middle class is central to the growth of consumer demand and see a division into:

(a) primitive societies;

(b) revolutionary society;

(c) countries in transition;

(d) affluent countries;

(e) classless societies.

4. Degree of central government involvement. The nature of central government involvement is also considered to have an important influence on the level of demand ranging from the rigid centralized systems of Eastern Europe, mixed levels of state intervention as shown in Western Europe, and the broadly non-interventionist policies of the United States.

Cultural differences. Cultural variations may have important effects on the way in which the firm can operate within the international environment. The differences in colour perception have already been commented upon (see Chapter 8): religion may forbid the consumption of a particular product in a particular market; conservatism in a market may resist the rapid spread of new purchasing patterns.

The average Frenchman uses twice as many beauty products as does a woman.

The average Belgian drinks double the quantity of pure alcohol per year consumed by the average Swiss.

The average Australian spends far less on indoor games/toys than the average European even allowing for the differences in climate.

The number of books bought per capita in New Zealand is far higher than in the United Kingdom.

Legal and financial constraints. Many countries will impose a varying number of restrictions upon expatriate companies which they do not face in the home market. These can range from demands on the nature of product quality and contents (for example packaging may have to specify ingredients in greater detail or some ingredients will need to be changed), to the ability of the firm to send money out of the country or to own property within the country, and the right of the firm to employ the type of individual that it wishes to.

Malaysia has passed a series of labour laws relating to employment of nationals, the 'bumiputra' or 'son of the soil' legislation. This lays down the proportion of Malays that must be employed at all levels within the firm.

Control problems. Wide geographical separation of operating units means that control of what are often diverse operations becomes a more complex and demanding task. These problems will often be exacerbated by local customs or laws reducing the number of expatriates that can be employed in the overseas subsidiary.

The Midland Bank experienced considerable problems with its expansion into America via the Croker Bank in California; the difficulties of managing a bank in an overseas market with high exposure in the agricultural loan sector eventually led to its sale to the Wells Fargo company at a considerable loss.

Rigid control from the centre will, however, mean that the local subsidiary is unable to react effectively and speedily to changes in the local environment. In consequence many international firms go through cycles of centralization followed by periods of decentralization, as top management attempts to find the best compromise between local flexibility and lack of clear direction from the centre.

Pricing and costing problems. A company operating overseas will often face considerable problems in pricing its goods in its overseas markets. The involvement of other intermediaries in the distribution process, changing import duties, local price control regulations, exchange rates, the need to decide on the price level at which goods will be exchanged between subsidiaries, and where profit is to be generated, will all influence the pricing and costing decisions.

STRATEGIC ISSUES IN INTERNATIONAL DEVELOPMENT

The firm developing overseas will need to consider three main issues:
1. Production factors.
2. Product factors.
3. Distribution factors.

PRODUCTION

Table 15.5   Factors in the central/local production decision

Factor	Local	Centralized
Product	Simple	Complex
R & D levels	Low	High
Unit price	Low	High
Quality control considerations	Low	High
Labour cost	Low	High
Labour skills	High	Low
Transport cost	High	Low
Transport availability	Low	High
Tariff barriers	High	Low
Customers	Local	Multinational
Capital availability	High	Low
Capital cost	Low	High
Political stability	High	Low
Economic stability	High	Low
Market potential	High	Low

There will be a series of pressures for and against centralization of production or local manufacture, which any multinational company will need to consider before the development of overseas manufacture plants (Table 15.5).

PRODUCT

The firm will need to evaluate each overseas market in the same way that it analyses its home market to decide what product strategies should be followed in the market. Broadly, it is faced with a number of options concerning how it should or should not modify product and promotional themes developed in the home market.

The options include:

1. Straight extension. This involves the manufacturer distributing overseas the identical product to the home market using the same promotional material. Examples of this approach can be found in many manufacturers of machine tools.
2. Communication adaptation. The firm maintains the identical product to the home trade but creates new promotional material for the specific market or groups of markets. This is the common form of strategy developed by car manufacturers: a standard product but promotional material specifically developed for individual markets.
3. Product adaptation. Specific markets may demand changes in packaging design, different perfumes, or differing formulations due to local conditions, while the promotional techniques used remain the same.

   Lux, produced by Unilever, sells in over eighty countries worldwide with an estimated total annual tonnage of 190,000. Though the long-running promotional message remains 'The world's most beautiful women use Lux', the product differs considerably from market to market in respect of colour, hardness of soap, and type of packaging material used.

   Nestlé, though successful in developing an instant coffee market in Japan, has failed to make any impact on the chocolate market, which in Japan consists mainly of products made from flavouring and vegetable fats.

4. Product and promotional adaptation. The demands of the market require the product and the promotional material to be substantially different. Compare, for example, Surf washing powder sold in West Africa and Surf on sale in Europe. One is formulated for hand washing and heavy soiling and has a high level of active ingredients, while the other is formulated for use in certain washing machines and for a lighter level of soiling. The promotional material developed reflects this difference in usage.
5. Diversification. In order to maximize market opportunities the company may need to produce entirely new products and promotional material.

The risk and reward potential for product change overseas mirrors that of the home market; straight extension of product and promotion is the lowest risk path, and diversification the highest.

DISTRIBUTION SYSTEMS

The way in which the company distributes overseas will be partly determined by strategic considerations and partly by market factors. The firm will need to consider:

1. Long-term market potential. What will the firm need to invest in the market to realize its long-term potential? Is it prepared to run operations in a specific market at a short-term loss for long-term gain? At what volume levels will it be prepared to establish local representation?
2. Control criteria. How important is it to the firm that the product is sold to specific customers at specific prices and maintained at a particular level?
3. Geographical constraints. How difficult will it be physically to service the market? Because of the vast distances involved in servicing the markets, the US and Australia often demand that manufacturers consider the use of wholesalers in the distribution chain.
4. Legal constraints. Does local legislation make it essential that local firms are involved in the distribution process? Once established, can agreements be terminated with ease – what implications does that have for the long-term development of the companies' products?
5. Tariff barriers. What barriers exist to prevent the firm operating freely in the market?

As with product development for overseas markets there are a number of ways the firm can distribute each of which has a level of risk and reward. The level of investment varies according to whether the firm exports, establishes joint ventures or local subsidiaries, and the level of reward measured against such levels of investment.

Export

Wholesalers. Wholesalers exist for a number of overseas markets who buy in the home market and then ship overseas for their overseas operations or those of associates. The advantages for the manufacturer in using these channels is that payment takes place without risk. The disadvantages, however, are that the supplier has no control over where the product is sold, its pricing, or any long-term planning for the product's future development.

Buying houses. Certain major store chains maintain overseas offices which buy product for the store group. Though the supplier is certain of payment and the markets in which the product will appear, the firm is still unable to control pricing or long-term developments. The buying power of the store groups may also mean that the product is sold at a profit lower than that which might be achieved through other distribution methods.

Confirming houses. These are companies that act as buying agents for a variety of overseas store groups and distribution companies combining orders for onward shipment. The supplier is still faced with a degree of uncertainty concerning long-term demand.

Specialist export firms. Specialist import and export firms can help the small firm to become established in overseas markets, but the export firm will often have its own priorities within a particular market which may conflict with that of the suppliers.

Agents/distributors. In order to overcome the lack of control inherent in many of the other arrangements, the supplier will often establish agency arrangements in the overseas territories. These can be of two broad types: the agent, who has sole selling rights within a particular market but does not normally maintain stocks of the imported product, and who gains a commission on each delivery; and the distributor, who maintains stocks of all products and provides a higher level of service. Entering into agency agreements has advantages and disadvantages for the supplying company. It involves a legal commitment which is often difficult to break; it also implies the need for the supplier to develop long-term plans for the country in conjunction with the distributor or agent. In return the supplier is able to define more accurately the pricing, distribution and promotional planning for the product in the overseas market.

Joint ventures

The supplier company can join with foreign companies in the local market to set up production and distribution structures. This can either be achieved by:
1. Licensing, whereby the supplier grants the right to the local company to produce a particular product in return for a royalty or licence fee. Though this is fairly straightforward it may mean that the return from the market is limited and at the end of the licence arrangement the local company has gained sufficient expertise to become a formidable competitor in the market.
2. Franchising. The development of franchising has been particularly important in the growth of many service-based companies overseas (see Chapter 16).
3. Joint ownership. Becoming established in many markets may demand the involvement of a local partner. The advantages are that the overseas company is able to gain rapid access to the local market and market information. The main disadvantages are that the joint venture may break down due to disagreements between the two parties and, second, that as neither company is totally responsible for the progress of the joint company, it will be seen as of secondary importance to both companies.

Local subsidiaries

Investment in the establishment of local subsidiaries will create a potentially high level of risk if the economy or political stability becomes eroded in the overseas territory; it does, however, allow the firm to become solidly established in the local market.

Summary

International trade is a vital part of the United Kingdom's business activity, and an understanding of the issues of international marketing will be important for most medium or large-sized companies. The disciplines of the marketing process apply to all overseas markets tempered with an understanding of local variations and specific problems.

ASSIGNMENTS

1. You are working for a small company producing fine art materials (high quality paper, inks, etc.) and are asked by the managing director to provide a report on how the company should approach the development of export business and the issues that would need to be considered.
2. From published material develop a profile of the international structure of one chosen industry.
3. You are asked by your local chamber of commerce to produce a discussion paper on the merits of setting up a central co-operative overseas marketing department. Prepare your speech.

MILTON-LLOYD AND 'TATTI'

BACKGROUND

Milton-Lloyd was a small British company that had become established in the 1970s as the distributors of a small perfume company's products in the Middle East. From 1977 it began to manufacture and export its own products, and won a Queen's Award for Export Achievement in 1981.

THE MARKET

The Middle East markets (Table 15.6) contain wide variations of population, GNP, and varying levels of Westernization and sophistication.

Table 15.6 The Middle East markets

Country	Population (000)s	GNP per capita (£)	Imports (£ million)	Perfume market (£ million)
Bahrain	400	2,730	1,345	1.7
Egypt	41,000	230	3,402	6.2
Iraq	13,432	1,205	2,104	3.8
Jordan	3,172	590	1,000	1.7
Kuwait	1,311	8,635	2,646	8.8
Lebanon	3,200	800	1,000	4.7
Libya	2,983	4,105	5,240	4.8
Oman	919	1,985	676	0.8
Qatar	270	8,295	549	1.5
Saudi Arabia	7,500	3,685	13,571	30.0
Syria	9,655	535	1,400	1.8
UAE	850	6,090	4,290	6.8

In 1980 market sales were dominated by France with 73 per cent of total perfume sales, and the USA second with 18 per cent.

Though the markets are widely disparate they can be divided into three main groups:

1. 'Free' market economies with a developed commercial sector and few restrictions on importation and the remittance of money: Bahrain, Kuwait, Oman, Saudi Arabia, UAE.
2. 'Mixed' economies with a developing commercial sector but with considerable control over the movement of foreign exchange: Egypt, Iraq, and Jordan.
3. 'State' run economies with rigid centralization: Libya, Syria.

In addition to variations in markets, the Middle East also shows considerable diversity in culture, law and the way in which trade in perfumes has developed. In most cases there are a number of underlying themes that a perfumery exporter would need to consider:

1. Target group. Throughout the Middle East both men and women are consumers of perfume products; the separation between male cologne products and women's perfumes is not as significant a factor as in Western Europe.
2. Consumption levels. Women in many Arab societies spend a lot of time together in the home, and trial and gifts of perfume between members of the family is fairly common. In addition, perfume is traditionally passed around at the end of meals. Both these factors mean that perfume consumption is significantly higher than in Western Europe, and perfume tends to be purchased in larger unit quantities than is normal in those countries.
3. Religious law. The Koran prohibits the consumption of alcohol; in consequence any perfume product sold in the Middle East must have a methanol rather than ethanol base.
4. Commercial law. Almost all Middle Eastern countries make it impossible for Western firms to sell in their markets without some form of local participation. Agency agreements once signed are extremely difficult to terminate.
5. Climatic conditions. For much of the year the Middle East is extremely hot and humid. This affects the style of perfume purchased; heavy, clinging fragrances are preferred to products with a light bouquet.
6. Advertising constraints. In many countries there is limited access to advertising.
7. Perception of perfume. Perfume is seen in the majority of Middle Eastern markets as a sophisticated traditional product and a status symbol; the appeal of perfumes such as 'Charlie' or 'Tramp' which have been so successful in the United States, positioned as they are to take advantage of the youthful working woman, do not have a ready-made market in the Middle East.
8. Pricing. As a large amount of perfume is bought as a gift, pricing is not an especially crucial factor in the purchase of fragrances; the relatively low duties paid on perfume in the majority of Middle Eastern countries with open markets and high per capita incomes further reduce the importance of price.

THE DEVELOPMENT OF 'TATTI'

The name. The name was chosen to associate the perfume with the more traditional products in the upper market, mainly from France. It was essential that the name should be neutral when translated into Arabic, but have modern connotations.

Packaging. This was designed to emphasise further the premium positioning by using a gold background with silver oblique stripes and the brand name, in flowing cursive script, also at an angle. It was important that the pack should be able to stand out against its competitors.

The bottle. A standard 50 g bottle was chosen in contrast to the normal 30 g on sale in Europe. Frosted glass and a premium, gold foil covered cap maintained the impact of the carton design.

The perfume. A strong fragrance was chosen and was dissolved at a higher concentration than European perfumes; 10 per cent perfume content compared with 5.6 per cent.

Pricing. The product was priced at the same level as Jovan and Max Factor, but below Lancome and Chanel. The high pricing enabled the company to invest heavily in point of sale activities which were the most cost-effective promotional method in the majority of markets.

Distribution. By using local distributors and offering superior trade discounts the company was able to achieve good distribution. The retailers were offered a 30 per cent margin plus two bottles free with every fourteen, raising the retail margin to 45 per cent – considerably higher than that offered by the competition. The distributors also received a higher than average profit margin on the product. The price structure was:

- Price ex London: 100
- Landed cost (freight, duty): 118
- Cost to wholesalers: 153 (distributors' margin 23 per cent)
- Cost to retailers: 168
- Cost to consumer: 240.

The use of prepacked point of sale material also encouraged wider purchase and more immediate store impact.

The success of Tatti can be seen in the growth of the company's export sales (Table 15.7).

Table 15.7   Export sales of Tatti

Year	Sales (£000)
1978	800
1979	1,365
1980	2,275

The most important markets in descending order of importance in 1981 were:
Libya
Saudi Arabia
UAE
Kuwait
Qatar
Oman
Bahrain

This showed that it had managed to become established in a wide range of Middle Eastern markets with a new competitive product.

Comment

Segmentation and product design in the international environment produced a successful product for a small company in a competitive market sector.

16

THE MARKETING OF SERVICES

Services and the marketing of services have become increasingly important in the second half of the twentieth century. Since the 1950s, throughout the main industrialized nations there has been a steady growth of the service sector as an employer and as an important constituent of the economy. Some authors have identified the point at which the manufacturing sector employs less than half the work-force as the start of a 'post-industrial' society where services have become the prime driving force of the economy. Table 16.1 shows the percentage of employment provided by three main sectors in the United States by year. Note that manufacturing includes both construction and mining.

Table 16.1   The growth of the service sector in USA

Sector	1870 (%)	1920 (%)	1940 (%)	1980 (%)
Agriculture	57	27	18	3
Manufacturing	25	34	33	28
Services	18	39	49	69

A similar picture emerges for the British economy. At the turn of the century mining and shipbuilding were both employing over 400,000 workers; by the late 1980s total employment in the two sectors will probably be around 200,000.

The trend towards greater service employment continues as recent figures for the British economy indicate. Table 16.2 shows the percentage of employment within the British economy. It omits the number of self-employed, up from 8 to 11 per cent of the working population, that are almost all involved in some aspect of the service economy. These figures include the large percentage of the working population employed by the public sector including the nationalized industries (energy, mining, transport) as well as directly employed civil servants.

Table 16.2   Employment by sector in Great Britain

Sector	1978 (%)	1985 (%)
Agriculture	1	1
Energy	3	3
Mining	5	3
Engineering	14	11
Other manufacture	11	9
Construction	5	4
Catering/retailing	16	18
Transport	6	5
Finance	6	8
Other services	24	26

It can be seen clearly that a steadily decreasing percentage of the population will be employed in traditional manufacturing industry and that service sector companies will become increasingly important to the economy.

The importance of the service sector as an employer is underlined by the fact that the National Health Service, with an estimated one million employees, is now the biggest single employer in Western Europe: far outstripping large multinational companies – Unilever employs only 300,000 worldwide, and General Motors 800,000.

There are many factors that have fuelled this growth of services, including:
1. Increasing affluence. Growing prosperity has meant that families or individuals have more money than is necessary for the bare essentials and have discretionary income to spend on gardening, gambling, housing or other services. It has also meant that financial institutions have developed to handle the additional money that is available: building societies, banks, unit trust companies, and finance houses. Increasing affluence has also meant that the number of charities and the amount raised by them has become steadily greater.
2. Changing family structures. The higher number of women at work and the smaller household sizes have led to increases in nurseries, take-away meals, laundry services.
3. Changing expectations. Rising expectations have led to an increased demand for holidays and all forms of entertainment.
4. Increasing leisure. Longer holidays and decreased working hours have substantially increased the demand for travel, education, sport and leisure.
5. An ageing population. There has been a steady increase in the need for the provision of health and maintenance and repair services.
6. Greater number and complexity of products. This has meant an increasing requirement for specialists to handle repair, advice and maintenance.
7. Increasing complexity of legal framework and governmental involvement in the functioning of society. The numbers in government employment have dramatically increased since the Second World War due to the wide-ranging involvement of government in day-to-day activities.

8. Unemployment levels. The high and continuing levels of unemployment have meant a steady growth in the numbers of self-employed, most of whom work in the service sector.
9. Increasing sophistication of communication and information requirements.
Sectors that have grown as a result of these influences include:
1. Government services such as social security, health, local borough services, housing, water and electricity.
2. Charities and pressure groups such as Oxfam, Save the Children, Friends of the Earth, ASH, and CAMRA.
3. Recreational services such as restaurants, sports, hotels, and gambling.
4. Communication services such as newspapers, television, telephone, and radio.
5. Distributive services such as retailing and wholesaling.
6. Professional services such as accountancy and hairdressing.
7. Financial services such as banking and insurance.

NON-PROFIT MARKETING – A SPECIAL ISSUE IN THE MARKETING OF SERVICES

The growth of pressure groups and charities has led many authors to define the specific requirement of non-profit marketing within these organizations. It can be considered that these organizations are trying to understand the market best so as to reach their objectives in the most efficient way possible, and could apply the marketing process without major difficulty.

Marketing principles can be applied in such organizations provided the organization is able clearly to define its objectives and the target market which it is attempting to influence.

> ASH, Action on Smoking and Health, has a number of objectives. First, it campaigns against cigarette advertising, for more non-smoking areas in public places, and for more restrictions on the distribution of cigarettes. This will involve direct contact with the public and, on a different level, with politicians. Second, it is continually attempting to raise more revenue to carry out its objectives.

Further, non-profit organizations will often have to take a very long-term view of their actions. Whereas a profit-led organization can continually monitor its investment programme to ascertain its effectiveness, a non-profit body is less able to do so.

FRANCHISING – A GROWTH AREA IN SERVICES

A recent phenomenon has been the growth of franchising in a wide range of activities. The concept of franchising involves a central organization developing and promoting a service which is then leased or sold to individuals on an area basis. The franchisee receives training and often product from the company and is expected to meet national standards, and pays a fee based on turnover to the franchiser. The advantage for the owner of the business is that franchises are far less likely to fail than other types of operation; the disadvantage being the limited degree of freedom and high levels of payment that may be involved. The United States has shown a considerable growth in the franchising concept and it is reported that one in three of new businesses is a franchise. Well-known companies in the UK with a large number of franchises include:

Dyno-Rod (drain clearance): 88
TNT (distribution): 400
Singer (sewing machine sales and service): 205
Prontaprint (printing design and execution): 289
Kentucky Fried Chicken (fast food): 380
Wimpy: 400
Holland & Barratt (health food retailing): 37
Benetton (fashion retailing): 150
Body Shop (beauty products): 55

THE PROBLEMS OF APPLYING MARKETING CONCEPTS TO SERVICE ORGANIZATIONS

The problem of the intangibility of the service – it is difficult to separate out the importance of the various factors that make up the service, namely: the product sold; the price at which it is sold; the way it is distributed; the way it is promoted; the people involved; the way in which the service is carried out; and often the physical environment in which the service is performed.

The problem of the heterogeneity of the service – because of the large number of factors that make up the service it will be difficult to ensure that the level of service always remains the same.

The problem of the perishability of the service – because the service involves a physical action either by the staff or the consumer it cannot be stored or stockpiled.

The problem of the ownership of the service – because the consumer will only have limited and occasional access to the service there will be a lack of control by the customer over the nature of the service.

The problem of the inseparability of the service – the production of the service and its consumption will be instantaneous.

In consequence the service company is faced with a number of promotional and operational problems that require specific attention.

Demand fluctuations are often very difficult to manage

The service company will need to forecast demand accurately to ensure that adequate resources are available.

One McDonald's outlet in Japan holds the world burger record at over 36,000 in a twenty-four-hour period during a religious festival. Good planning had ensured that adequate staff were on hand to serve the lines of customers. Even so, the money collected had to be dumped in bags for delivery to the bank the following day as the tills could not handle the volume of business.

The service company will need to consider ways of producing standard items which can improve the efficiency of the organization to cope with the unusual.

Benetton manufactures a substantial quantity of its woollen garments in a neutral grey which can then be dyed to meet rapidly changing colour demands of fashion.

Banks are continually trying to reduce the involvement of bank tellers by providing cash for customers and taking deposits by the use of appropriate technology.

The use of product bar codes by supermarkets has two advantages. It reduces the costs of pricing every item and it (theoretically) speeds up payment at the till.

Hilton Hotels has recently introduced an overnight checkout system by which the customer's bill is prepared during the night and paid by credit card left with the cashier. This reduces the congestion at the cashier's desk in the morning and may lead to reduced staffing requirements in the long term.

The service company will have to consider how to increase the use of facilities during periods of low demand.

Many computer bureaux offer reduced rates for 'off-line' rather than 'on-line' processing, which can be carried out at night when there is a substantial reduction in overall demand.

The difficulty of maintaining the standard quality of the service

Firms will need to ensure that staff are continually trained and evaluated to maintain consistency.

British Airways has concentrated on the development of staff resources by in-company training to improve the quality of the service that it offers.

Firms will need to lay down clear quality control guidelines to ensure that standardization is maintained.

DHL, the air courier business with a worldwide office network, lays down strict rules about the speed at which parcels must be despatched and the acceptable time for any particular activity against which individual offices and employees can be judged.

It is difficult for the firm to persuade new customers to sample the service

The Post Office runs a variety of schemes to try and persuade companies to develop direct mail campaigns, by providing free trial periods.

It is difficult to have any distinctive edge over the competition as the service it offers will not be patentable and can be easily copied

Firms will require to invest heavily in branding their activities to gain competitive advantage, and emphasize special features not present in the competition.

One of the largest increases in advertising expenditure over the last ten years has been shown by the main retailing chains, especially Tesco and Sainsbury's.

The lack of the consumer's personal involvement with the company's service can mean a potential low level of customer loyalty

Pan American Airlines runs a Five Continents Club for favoured customers which ensures them of special service and informs them via a newsletter of special offers and events, trying to involve the customer more closely with the airline.

McDonalds emphasizes its community role and, via 'Ronald McDonald', the friendliness of the organization.

The environment in which the service takes place will often be crucial – many services are not transportable

In consequence, service companies will often have considerable difficulties in expanding, requiring both suitable personnel and suitable premises as they cannot normally operate through third parties.

Marks and Spencer, the most successful British retailer in the post-war period, has experienced considerable difficulties in profitable expansion overseas. Though it has been established in Canada for many years it is only the subsidiary discount stores that are profitable; the traditional Marks and Spencer stores have not been particularly successful. Similarly, expansion into Europe with five stores in France and one in Belgium, though profitable, is not yet as successful as the United Kingdom operation.

Credit card companies have solved the problem of internationalization by combining into transnational groupings – Barclaycard has become a member of the Visa network, Access a member of the Master Card organization.

The limited time in which the service company can be in contact with the consumer

The company will have to work as efficiently as possible during the time that it has available.

Townsend Thorensen, the ferry company, has invested considerable sums of money in speeding up the flow of traffic on and off the ferries as this is crucial to the profitable maintenance of a ferry service.

Hypermarket designers try to ensure that there are more than enough tills to cope with periods of maximum demand, to ensure that the throughput of the store is maximized whenever possible.

Technology will be important in increasing the length of time that the consumer can remain in contact with the service.

Many hotels now provide room bars so that expensive hotel staff do not have to be employed in keeping the hotel bar open for residents after hours.

It is difficult for the consumer to judge quality/price relationship in advance of purchase

The firm will have to emphasize the benefits of the service.

M & G largely pioneered the unit trust movement in the UK by concentrating on the long-term financial benefits.

In contrast to many consumer companies, service organizations will often have to stress the tangibility of the item offered whereas consumer companies will often attempt to increase the intangibility or 'image' component of their products.

In common with consumer and industrial companies, service organizations will be faced with the same problems of price, the degree of involvement of the sales force, length of the buying process and other factors (discussed in Chapter 14). As service companies cover a wide range of activities the importance of these factors will vary according to the nature of the service itself. For example, petrol stations and grocery stores must be highly competitive on price, whereas for market consultancy projects price is not necessarily the major consideration.

Companies that offer highly tangible services such as fast food, petrol and groceries show many of the characteristics of the consumer sector: those that are intangible exhibit some of the characteristics of the industrial market.

Summary

The marketing mix for service organizations is more complex than that for consumer and industrial products, raising a series of different problems which need to be overcome to develop an effective competitive position.

ASSIGNMENTS

1. You have joined a firm of estate agents which has been recently taken over by a national insurance company. You are asked to prepare a report on how the marketing approach could improve the level of profitability and what issues would need to be considered.

2. As a marketing consultant you are asked to advise a small chain of travel agents about how the application of marketing principles could improve their performance. Produce a document that you would use.

BUILDING SOCIETIES AND BANKS

Over the last fifteen years the competitive position of banks, building societies and the National Savings Bank in the personal sector has substantially changed, with the building societies gaining an increasing share of the personal saving sector (Table 16.3).

Table 16.3   Personal savings by sector (%)

Year	Banking sector	Building society	National Savings Bank
1969	39	27	34
1972	35	33	31
1974	40	38	21
1977	32	48	20
1983	32	47	20

This effectiveness of the building society movement in attracting money is reflected in the rise in the number of total accounts, up from 8.3 million in 1971 to 20.3 million in 1980, with an average balance on share accounts of £1,600.

The growth in deposits achieved by the building societies is matched by a similar achievement in the personal loans sector. Building societies currently have 67 per cent of this market, the banks 10 per cent, with the remainder equally divided between local authorities, finance houses, insurance companies, and to a limited extent retailers.

Reasons for the success of the building societies are seen as their extensive branch network and convenient location; a relaxed atmosphere; convenient and easily understandable deposit and withdrawal arrangements; convenient opening hours including Saturday morning. Above all the security offered by the building societies and the high rate of interest compared with the banks made them a far more attractive method of saving than the banks. With the steady growth of the branch network, building societies have also entered market sectors that were previously the preserve of the clearing banks. Increasingly they provide automatic cash dispensers, and cheque books. Proposed government legislation will allow them to enter further into the financial services market, permitting them to offer unsecured loans, trade in foreign currency and expand in the provision of pensions and business finance.

Building societies are not the only competition that the clearing banks face. The National Savings Bank, Trustee Savings Bank and some of the foreign banks such as the American Citibank compete in the personal savings market. Merchant banks and unit trust groups have also made some progress in increasing their consumer savings market share.

This growing competition is seen by the clearing banks as posing a long-term rather than a short-term threat. More important in the short term is the steadily increasing cost of maintaining the branch network and staff levels to service the customer base. With a branch network of 11,000 offices between the big four banks (Barclays, National Westminster, Lloyds and Midland) such issues are especially important. These problems have lead them to reappraise their marketing strategy. For a major clearing bank these are now defined as:

1. Short term:
   (a) to increase or decrease deposits of certain types;
   (b) to increase or decrease loans of certain types;
   (c) direct customers to certain services.
2. Longer term:
   (a) to increase bank market share;
   (b) to spread customer types to minimize risk;
   (c) to increase the range of services to compete more effectively;
   (d) to improve return on capital employed by improving the efficiency of the banking process.

Currently the clearing banks see themselves operating in five market sectors:

1. providing money transfer;
2. providing cash and deposit facilities;
3. providing loans;
4. providing financial advice;
5. providing asset security.

In order to achieve these objectives and to compete with other financial institutions the banks have attempted to follow an appropriate strategy for each market sector.

Money transfer. This sector is identified by the banks as one of the most important for the majority of employers and a substantial minority of employees. They emphasize the ease of transfer from organization to individual account, and from there the payment of bills. The potential growth in this area is shown in the analysis of current account holders in the United Kingdom for 1983 (Table 16.4).

Table 16.4   Profiles of current account holders 1983

Group	Current account (%)
All male	67
All female	60
Age	
15–19	26
20–24	64
25–34	75
35–44	73
45–54	68
55–64	64
over 65	60
Social class	
AB	86
C1	75
C2	60
D	47
E	40

Three main sectors of the population have therefore been identified by the clearing banks for particular attention: women, students and school leavers, and weekly paid workers.

Women have historically had fewer accounts than men because fewer work; there is a tendency for many to leave financial affairs in the hands of the husband and also, according to a survey, a feeling that banks are often 'frightening'. The increasing number of women in work and the fact that more and more decisions are taken jointly by married couples are seen by the banks as implying that this 'unbanked' sector will largely disappear by the mid-1980s and requires little additional action.

Students and school leavers offer the clearing banks major market expansion opportunities – on average 900,000 students leave school every year. Banks have continued to expand campaigns aimed at students by:

(a) educating students with regard to the services the banks offer;
(b) developing introductory offers to encourage students to open bank accounts – travel vouchers, discount vouchers, cash cards, low-cost loans, are all examples;
(c) maintaining a 'flexible' approach to overdrafts.

The success of such policies can be seen in the evidence that 90 per cent of students in higher education have a bank account at the end of the first year at college. Similar schemes have been developed for teenagers and children, but with less significant results.

The main emphasis for banking development in the case of weekly paid workers is the involvement of the employer, whose costs can be cut considerably by a movement towards bank transfer.

Cash and deposit facilities. Banks have invested large sums both to improve banks' physical environment so that they can compete more effectively with building societies, and in the rapid expansion of electronic banking allowing customers to withdraw, deposit money, and carry out routine tasks such as ordering cheque books and statements without the intervention of the cashiers. Faced with a continued erosion of the personal savings market, banks have also substantially increased their interest rates to improve cash inflow from investors.

Providing loans. Banks have entered the mortgage market increasingly over the last five years aiming at the top of the market, to provide loans of over £15,000. Via the credit card companies in which they share interests they are also actively expanding the personal finance loans that they provide to their customers.

Providing financial advice. With the change in the structure of the Stock Exchange, banks are starting to consider their savings role far more critically. Already present in the unit trust market, they are starting to experiment with American-style 'one-stop' financial centres. In addition they are expanding into other areas such as estate agents with the 'Black Horse' network owned by Lloyds Bank as an example.

Asset security. Banks continue to offer the most effective service in this area with an expanding market in safe deposit boxes and night safes.

Comment

As the financial services sector becomes more competitive, the banks will face increasing problems in marketing their expensive facilities.

PART 5

ORGANIZATIONS

17

ORGANIZATIONS AND MARKETING

The theory of marketing often ignores the cardinal fact that plans can only be made to work through people, especially the people within the organization. Many studies point to the way in which people operate within the organization as crucial to the success of any company, and any project that involves change will need to consider the human aspect very closely.

Marketing management will need an understanding of the mechanics of defining job functions and job descriptions, how to analyse potential recruits, and how to motivate staff most effectively. It will also need some understanding of the problems that exist within organizations, and why similar plans will succeed in one company and fail dismally in another.

Senior management may develop detailed strategic plans for the organization; it may bring in marketing personnel to develop these plans, but quite often the addition of 'marketing' to the organization fails to have the effect of producing the necessary strategic thinking or implementation.

Surveys of successful firms commonly suggest that four main factors are important:
1. adequate control over finances;
2. decentralized decision-making;
3. attention to customers and products;
4. motivation of employees.

Other elements of success suggested by other authors include keeping close to the original expertise of the firm, or 'sticking to the knitting', and having clear corporate goals. There will obviously be a number of reasons why an organization is unable to meet these criteria, but the main areas of concern for the organization intent on pursuing a policy of change and development are set out below.

ORGANIZATIONAL BARRIERS

Many companies exist with rigid lines of authority and defined areas of responsibility. A large company might, for example, have the following structure:

1. The sales department which is responsible for achieving budgeted level of sales.
2. The finance department that is responsible for the invoicing, credit and financial control.
3. The export department responsible for overseas sales development.
4. The research department responsible for the conception of new ideas and the development of prototypes.
5. The production department responsible for the production and distribution of the finished product.
6. The personnel department responsible for the grading of staff and their recruitment.
7. The marketing department responsible for profit on a product line and group basis, and possibly:
8. A legal and patent department.
9. A corporate planning department responsible for the long-term planning for the organization.

Such structures encourage a number of trends within any organization.

N.I.H. (Not Invented Here). Rigidly structured departments will resist outside suggestions for improvement. For example, the research department may receive ideas from the sales force for product improvement, but because the responsibility for new product development rests with the research department it will downgrade the value of the suggestion.

Slowness of response. Decisions will often need to be passed up the chain of command and then down another, as senior managers will often wish to retain authority.

Interdepartmental hostility. Each department will attempt to maximize its share of company resources and will see other departments as potential competitors. Valuable time and effort will be concentrated on the problem of dealing with other departments, rather than more serious company problems.

Interdepartmental conflict will often lead to the necessity to compromise over a number of key issues (Table 17.1).

Duplication of effort. Many departments will contain individuals doing essentially the same job as others in different departments. For example, the Civil Service maintains not only a department the Central Office of Information, but also individual information departments in each of the main ministries.

Preoccupation with status rather than responsibility. Rigid organizational barriers encourage individuals to concentrate more on building up power bases.

Table 17.1   Main areas of conflict between marketing and other company departments

Department	Their criteria	Marketing criteria
Finance	Strict credit	Credit policy to expand sales
	Pricing to recover overheads	To maximize volume
	Rapid cost recovery	Long-term recovery
	Fixed budgets	Volume-related expenditure
	Few customers	As many as possible
Sales	High sales promotion	Emphasis on media investment
	Few new products	Many new products
Export	Modified packaging	Standard packaging
	Modified promotional material	Standard promotional material
Production	Few variants	Many variants
	Economic production runs	Minimize out-of-stocks
	Low stockholdings	High stockholdings
	Functional product values	Design/appeal criteria
R & D	Pure research	Customer-related research
	Emphasis on features	Emphasis on benefits
	Long-term research	Short-term benefit
Information	Few reports	Diverse reports

These problems have led several major companies to consider ways by which internal new business ideas (often termed 'intrapreneurism') can best be encouraged. This will often mean that the firm will set up a new company to deal with the development of the novel concept, realizing that progress of the project will be practically impossible within the current organizational structure. The Saturn project of General Motors is an example of such a company separated from the main organization to develop new manufacturing processes to compete more effectively with the Japanese volume car producers; IBM produced the personal computer (the IBM PC) by the same process.

COMMUNICATION BARRIERS

Many companies believe that the barest minimum of information should be provided for managers and employees. Information regarded as needing security will often include:

1. The profitability of particular products – this information will often be unavailable to line managers responsible for their day-to-day administration.
2. The profitability of the operating unit.
3. Long-term plans for individuals and units within the organization. This is often called the 'mushroom' principle – that the work-force should be kept in the dark as long as possible.
4. Pay and conditions of everyone within the company.

Information flow is vital for the success of any enterprise. First, effective information flow makes employees feel far more involved in the success or otherwise of the business enterprise, and acts as an important method of motivating people to improve achievement. Second, it reduces the suspicion that exists in any group of people that events may be occurring which will significantly affect their position and authority, thereby improving morale throughout the entire organization. Third, it significantly speeds up the time taken for individuals to become effective within the organization – the so-called 'learning curve' – as employees will be able to gain rapidly all the information required to perform their jobs effectively, information which in a secretive organization will only be acquired informally and over a long period of time. Finally, it considerably expands the capacity of the organization to meet changing conditions, as individuals will be aware of the general problems the organization faces and will carry out their individual tasks with that understanding in mind.

The group approach to problem solving seen in Japanese management is successful in minimizing these communication problems by crossing the disciplinary barriers and increasing the involvement of all managers of a certain level in the decision-making process.

SINGLE CORPORATE ATTITUDE TO PROBLEM SOLVING

Outside some consumer goods companies, most companies are dominated by single corporate philosophies, either technical, financial or sales. Often these attitudes lead to success over a number of years and, therefore, become enshrined within the organization as the single appropriate method to solve all the problems that are encountered. Executives with such backgrounds have, according to one author, 'an almost trained incapacity' to appreciate long-term strategic problems, and fail to understand specific requirements of different market sectors. There are several noticeable examples of this philosophy leading to major problems: the collapse of Rolls-Royce followed a complete concentration on the engineering aspects of the jet engine; the Rolls-Razor empire of John Bloom failed through concentration on sales at practically any price. Within companies with such single-minded concentration on one particular solution, the attempt to introduce marketing concepts will inevitably lead to failure; change will be resisted at all costs. Earlier chapters have stressed the necessity for the organization to cope with change, and an organization that develops a successful formula must be prepared to revise or even dismantle the structures that it has created, as otherwise change will destroy the firm.

LIMITED HORIZONS

Many individuals within marketing departments and other areas of the business will, by training and work experience, be narrow in their thinking, with a tendency to concentrate on the promotional area of the marketing mix; this becomes seen as central to the function of the marketing department. Thus, the marketing department becomes engrossed in the logistics of defining sales promotions, evaluating advertising campaigns, supervising the printing of leaflets, instead of concentrating on other important areas.

The impact that they will have on the organization will consequently be limited and the marketing department will be increasingly seen as a specialist department offering fairly limited expertise.

This problem is compounded within many organizations by confusion about what marketing involves; and how rapidly it becomes, for example, confused with 'advertising' or 'sales', or in a service company with the concept of 'customer service' above all else – management may for example consider that sending all staff on a customer-orientation course is the solution to all marketing problems. The firm may also concentrate far too extensively on the market and the consumer, ignoring the vital element of the competition and what *it* is trying to achieve. Even the most sophisticated marketing companies may face such problems. Procter and Gamble, in its development of the disposable nappy market with Pampers, reached almost total brand dominance in the United States in the late 1970s with 75 per cent of the market. Kimberley Clark introduced a competitive product in 1979, Huggies, which provided a closer fit. Procter and Gamble, ignoring the competition, saw market share drop towards 50 per cent, until in 1985 it decided to re-equip totally its ten factories at a cost of $500 million.

Finally, the planning process central to marketing will conflict with shorter-term financial horizons essentially concerned with control of company revenue over the current year. Strategy becomes, in these environments, dominated by financial measures such as return on investment, forgetting the issue of how the investment may improve the long-term competitive position.

It has been argued by some authors that the investment environment within the United Kingdom and the United States encourages the concentration on short-term profitability rather than longer-term strategic planning. Companies performing badly in the short term are increasingly vulnerable to takeover bids; maintaining profitability remains an important way of reducing this threat. It is suggested that the Japanese financial environment which has a far lower rate of company takeover activity is much more fertile ground for long-term planning.

RESEARCH RATHER THAN ACTION

The ability of market research to predict is fairly limited particularly in the area of new goods and services. Furthermore, research is often used as a substitute for decision-making rather than as something that contributes to the final action. Ensuring that the market research will actually provide objective answers is a final major problem, as inevitably many research programmes will be aimed towards producing the desired result rather than unbiased data on which to take decisions.

Summary

Planning, especially marketing planning, as it involves the co-operation of all departments within an organization, cannot be effectively implemented if the individuals resist change. Any marketing planning process must as a result take the human factor into account.

ASSIGNMENTS

1. You are working for a large organization with many departments which has just experienced a major product launch failure due to interdepartmental problems. Write a report on the issues that might be involved and how the company should attempt to overcome a future repetition of the same problem.

2. As a marketing consultant you are asked to advise on the restructuring of a major organization with 200 operating units into three main divisions: consumer, industrial, and service. Write a letter to the chairman of the group outlining your approach and the important organizational issues that would need to be considered.

RADIUS COMPUTERS

THE BACKGROUND

In early February 1986, the managing director of Radius Computers UK was about to call a meeting to discuss the company's predicament following potentially disastrous sales figures in the home computers market over Christmas. It had become a matter of urgency, since the Radius board were even now having to consider the necessity of making a further approach to the company's creditors to increase the level of borrowing. The MD had already received a series of memos from senior managers about sales over Christmas 1985.

COMPANY PROGRESS

Radius had achieved early success in the UK home computer market, and still held around 55 per cent market share. This had been achieved by entering the market relatively early with a range of cheap, easy to use models at a time when its closest competitors' products were over 30 per cent more expensive. With the fierce price competition initiated by Radius the market had been quickly saturated with cheap, 48k home computers, but the company had managed to maintain its competitive edge on price.

Given the conditions in the market it had become essential for the company to reassess its position but there had been fundamental differences about the line the company should take. Some of the options put forward by the nine-man board of directors included:

1. Radius had made its name at the cheap end of the home computer market and should seek to consolidate its position there. Its computers were well liked but often unreliable. The emphasis should be placed on improving quality and consolidation of market position: this need not affect profitability since the cost of replacing faulty goods was already quite substantial.

2. Heavy investment in research and development had been largely responsible for the company's rapid penetration of the cheap home computer market. The fact that sales of cheap home computers were beginning to plateau indicated that consumers were becoming computer-literate and wanted more powerful models. The emphasis should be placed on research and development to achieve future profitability for Radius.

3. With the forthcoming saturation of the home market Radius should seek to expand overseas – not in the USA where a number of British home computer companies had burned their fingers but in Europe where home computers had not yet become established.

4. The current decline in the market was probably a short-term feature and the company should invest in persuading consumers of the benefits of home computing, and help the retailers to expand the range of products that they stock.

5. Overcapacity in the market was a result of too many manufacturers in the early stages of an expanding market. Radius with its emphasis on low priced products giving value for money would rapdily force other companies out of business. Keen pricing would be crucial to the success of this policy.

As a result of these views the company has continued to pursue a number of policies:

1. to maintain its presence in the cheap home computer market but without making a noticeable impact on improving the reliability of its products;

2. to price and promote aggressively;

3. it had spent heavily in an attempt to move up-market, offering a new range of more powerful computers at an attractive price which were, however, incompatible with each other as well and with the cheaper models: although more reliable; in this area Radius was still at a disadvantage to its competitors' more expensive products.

4. the company had also begun to explore export markets and had invested in the development of a dealer network in France, Belgium, Germany and Holland.

Substantial borrowing had been essential to finance these operations.

Unfortunately for Radius the fierce competition that had characterized the cheaper end of the home computer trade moved up-market as other companies resolved to pursue similar courses of action and major retailing chains began to reduce the range of products they stocked. By mid-1985 Radius had planned to launch an all-inclusive range comprising a 128k computer, with disk drive and printer at a price 30 per cent lower than its main rival, while continuing to sell large quantities of its bread-and-butter lines, the 32k and 48k packs. Though initial sales were disappointing due to supply and quality problems, the aim had been to achieve a high volume of sales over the Christmas period even though this might involve the company in reducing its margins on the 128k all-inclusive pack, and increasing the level of promotional support.

However, sales had been disappointing and the managing director was reviewing the memoranda he had received on the subject.

MEMO

To: The MD
From: Bernard Breeze, Director of Marketing
c.c. Directors of Production, Sales and Export, Finance
Subject: Xmas sales

I draw to your attention the disappointing preliminary figures for sales over the Christmas period. These are set out in the attached table (Table 17.2) and show last year's figures for purposes of comparison.

Table 17.2   Radius sales figures 1984/85

Model		Volume			Value (£000)	
	1985	Plan 1985	1984	1985	Plan 1985	1984
32k	210,000	350,000	350,000	9,450	15,005	13,500
48k	350,000	500,000	450,000	34,650	62,000	55,000
128k	15,000	40,000	—	3,000	8,000	—
128k pack	30,000	70,000	—	9,000	21,000	—
Totals	505,000	960,000	800,000	56,100	106,005	68,500

I consider that most of the problems we have encountered have resulted from the failure of other departments to meet the needs of the organization adequately.

I would draw your attention to problems in various departments.

Research and production

We have continually been bedevilled by problems of quality control in the production department. Not only did those problems seriously delay the launch of the 128 and mean that the marketing department had to take corrective action, they continue to bring the company a bad press from the computer magazines. The issue of software development has also not yet been satisfactorily controlled. The expansion of home computing very much depends on the provision of adequate software: promises in this area have yet to be fulfilled and we are still selling a range which is lacking some of the essential support it should be receiving.

It would appear that the director of production is of the opinion that I am better able than he is to explain to the finance director the reasons for the record levels of unsold stock. That was the clear implication of their memos. It is now three years since the decision was taken on the advice of the production director, with the support of research and development, to increase our production capacity at a substantial cost. Last year the new machinery was installed despite the warning issued by my department in the middle of 1984 (my memo to the board of 30 June 1984) that the decision to go ahead was probably premature because the home computer market seemed to be going through a period of instability. This advice was ignored because of the production needs of the 128k and at the same time increased the demands on my department to achieve a good return on investment through increased sales. As you know, our efforts were rewarded with substantial Christmas orders obtained in the face of fierce competition from five national retailing outlets for the 32k and 48k. For reasons which are still unclear to me production had geared itself up to producing large numbers of the 128k, and by the time a turn about was achieved we were a month behind our delivery dates and four of the five orders were cancelled. The production director is as able to explain these facts to finance as I am.

Finance

The failure of the finance department to act in a number of areas has also had a deleterious effect on the company's performance. Because of the late arrival of the 128 it was necessary to run special promotions with two of the major chains. Because this had not been budgeted for, the finance director in your absence refused to allow the expenditure. In consequence major sales that would have been achieved were lost.

With the 32 and 48k range we have also had major problems on credit terms. The amount of credit major chains are allowed has always, in my many years' experience in the electrical trade, been flexible around Christmas. The rigid insistence on company rules meant that two of the major discount chains that had indicated their willingness to take large quantities of stock reduced their orders to one quarter of what had been anticipated.

Sales and export

The sales department has reduced the effectiveness of the company drive to higher profitability in a number of ways.

First, the amount of effort that has been diverted into the export field has had very deleterious effects on performance at home. One of the most important national account managers, David Channon (responsible for the establishment of Radius in the ROM and Cable computer shops), has been solely occupied with training distributors' sales forces in Belgium and France (with no effect that I can ascertain). Sales in these outlets have plummeted because he has been sidetracked.

Second, the insistence of the sales department on continual heavy discounting has created confusion in the mind of the consumer. He is no longer aware of what he should be paying for one of our products except for the clear idea that if he leaves it a couple of months, it will be considerably cheaper. Though we are known for value for money products this process must not be continued too far.

The major forecasting error that the export department made (an actual sale of 35,000 units compared with a forecast of 120,000) has caused many of the problems that we have encountered with the production department not having the time to fulfil firm orders for United Kingdom customers. Our competitors who appear not to have such big expectations of the overseas market are only too happy to step in when we fail to deliver, and several school contracts I know have been lost as a result.

Finally, the demands of the export department on the technical information department mean that there are innumerable delays in other areas; the delay in the brochures for the 128 can be laid at this door.

MEMO

To: The MD
From: Simon Simple, Director of Production
c.c. Directors Marketing, Finance, Sales and Export
Subject: Company problems
Following a meeting of the production department that I held after receiving your memo, we feel that a significant reorganization of how the company works must be instituted to ensure that these events do not reoccur.

Marketing

Obviously the fundamental problem for the marketing department is the inability to predict accurately the level of sales of the entire range, which leads us into the impossible position of being incapable of planning production with any certainty.

The production department planned its work in 1985 in accordance with the marketing department's projections as it has always done in the past and will doubtless continue to do in the future. These had anticipated no real growth in demand for the 32k and 48k – but we would increase production slightly for export – which would be counterbalanced by demand for the 128k. What happens is that we end up with demand for the 32 and 48 and not for the 128 and production has to scrap all its work schedules and make all the practical adjustments to the real world.

This underlines the lack of commitment to the 128 shown by this division, with its failure to produce technical brochures on time and the low level of support that the brand was given.

I find it quite absurd, given the amount of R & D money spent in perfecting the Radius 128k, that the advertising support given in its launch year should be so much smaller both in absolute terms and as a percentage of overall development costs than the advertising support given to its less powerful Radius predecessors in their launch years. It is hardly surprising, therefore, that since nobody knows that it's on the market nobody buys the thing.

The marketing department is also continually suggesting that quality problems are instrumental in reducing the level of sales of the computers in the range. My department has become accustomed to hearing colleagues imply that we are given to developing and supplying them with less than perfect goods to sell. Were these revolutionary machines of ours so imperfect I doubt whether they would have become so firmly established in the market. More people still buy our 32 and 48k, in the teeth of nonsense about reliability, than those of any other manufacturer. If, however, we do not promote them at every conceivable opportunity then no one will buy them. That is the clear lesson of the failure of the 128k to achieve the desired levels of sale. Last year, promotional support for our products was cut right back by the marketing department for the first time in Radius's history. It concluded that there was no evidence that the heavy spending was a good investment. I trust that the director of marketing is now satisfied that he has the evidence in the form of a record drop in sales and warehouses bulging with unsold stock.

Sales and export

We experience major problems in the export area. What our colleagues do not appear to understand is that, first, the technical specifications for each of the European countries are different and this involves considerable time and money to surmount. Second, the host of 'minor modifications' which we are continually being requested to perform creates enormous backlogs in the research and evaluation section.

Cancellation of special orders has also become fairly commonplace, followed by another 'urgent' order appearing out of nowhere, causing havoc in what is supposed to be a production process geared for high volumes.

Finance

The finance department also appears to have reduced the efficiency of the department in a number of ways. During the year the new invoicing system has caused nothing but problems with the suppliers. Second, the amount of time managers have had to spend investigating and quantifying quality control problems has got completely out of hand.

MEMO

To: The MD
From: Hugo MacIntyre, Director of Sales and Export
c.c. Directors of Marketing, Production, Finance
Subject: Sales in 1985
In response to your memo, I would of course agree that overseas and home sales have been disappointing. Overseas, I feel that it is too early in the export thrust to say definitely that our achievements in selling cheap, UK manufactured computers will not be viable in the long term, though a volume shortfall of 95,000 units is a worrying feature. In my opinion certain definite problem areas have surfaced in the past year which the company can itself control.

Production

I have spent a considerable amount of time over the past year in singularly futile discussion on quality control with the directors of production and research and development. The quality and reliability of our computers is a perennial question even in the home market and they appear to be totally unable, or perhaps I should say unwilling, to understand its relevance to export. I cannot therefore see any steps being taken to correct the problem.

It becomes much more difficult and expensive for us to try to sell faulty goods overseas and in a number of instances it has already cost us orders. Furthermore, in many European markets we can foresee that we shall become vulnerable on price – if our products are not up to scratch on quality we will be sunk before long.

Production appears to be incapable of helping us to develop vital overseas business by being sufficiently flexible to produce special product, and technical support appears to be very slow in forthcoming.

Finance

The unfavourable credit terms currently being offered by the finance department to agents interested in selling Radius computers have seriously hampered our efforts to enter certain markets. Unless these terms are revised and brought into line with those offered by other hardware companies those markets will remain closed to us.

The finance department also appears not to understand how important deep discounting is to move large quantities of stock with the major retailing chains; preventing these deals from going through is tantamount to withdrawing from the market and clearly shows in our poor sales performance.

Marketing

The marketing department does not appear to appreciate the special problems of selling in a competitive industry on either side of the Channel. Educative advertising does not move the boxes – what the consumer wants is a good deal on price or added value in the software area. This is what we should be concentrating on.

Where we do need the leaflets and instruction manuals is overseas and here we have further problems. The publicity material adapted from the UK market by the marketing department is not only unsuitable but the translations are appalling. It is hard enough to understand the computer manuals when they are in English, and if the company is to have a less nationalistic outlook more attention should be given to this.

MEMO

To: the MD
From: Alfred Fry, Director of Finance
c.c. Directors of Marketing, Production, Sales and Export
Subject: Company financial problems
In response to your memorandum on the company's problems, I consider that procedures need to be significantly improved in a number of areas to reduce the feckless behaviour of certain departments.

Marketing

Budgetary control must improve. Advertising and promotion should not be allowed to proceed unless the plan has previously been authorized. Promotional budgets continue to run 30 per cent over plan.

Forecasting systems are lamentable. The forecast demand against the actual sales is continually at variance and must be corrected.

Sales and export

The costing of each sale must be more accurate; some orders continue to be supplied at a loss.

Both the marketing and sales departments must understand the issues involved in credit control and why close control in this area is vital for company survival.

Production

The production department must understand that production targets and purchases significantly affect cash flow; that quality control problems are leading to a high level of product returns that are putting an increasing strain on company resources; that production targets on delivery dates must be realized.

COMMENT

How should the company approach the various organizational problems?

INDEX